DAVID EGAN

COAL SOCIETY

A History of the South Wales Mining Valleys 1840-1980

GOMER PRESS
1987

WELSH HISTORY TEACHING MATERIALS (14-16)

A project funded by the Welsh Office Education
Department and based at University College, Swansea

Director: Dr. Gareth Elwyn Jones
Research Officer: David Egan

Steering Committee:

O. E. Jones, HMI (Chairman)
Alun Morgan, HMI

Ian Green
Mrs. Mary-Lynne Perren
Miss Elaine Thomas
Mrs. Peggy George

Secretary: Brian Duddridge
Secretarial Assistant: Mrs. A. M. White

Printed by Gomer Press, Llandysul, Dyfed
First Impression - May 1987

ISBN 0 86383 239 3

CONTENTS

ACKNOWLEDGEMENTS

I should like to acknowledge the help and assistance of the following people who in various ways have contributed to the writing of this book: the members of the *Welsh History Teaching Materials (14-16) Project* Committee; J. F. Lane, Headmaster, Mountain Ash Comprehensive School; David Maddox, Adviser for History, Mid-Glamorgan County Council; C. N. Jones, History Department, Mountain Ash Comprehensive School; Dr. Keith Strange, Treorchy Comprehensive School; Dr. Hywel Francis, South Wales Miners Library, University College Swansea; Professor David Smith, Department of the History of Wales, University College Cardiff; L. J. Williams, Department of Economics, University College of Wales, Aberystwyth; Dr. A. V. John, Thames Polytechnic; Dr. Siân Rhiannon Williams , B.B.C. Wales; Brian Davies, Big Pit Mining Museum, Blaenavon; Bill Jones, Welsh Industrial and Maritime Museum; Huw Williams and the Rev. Len Deas. My greatest debts are to my wife, Susan, and my children, Kate and Owen, and it is to them that I wish to dedicate this book.

David Egan

MAPS

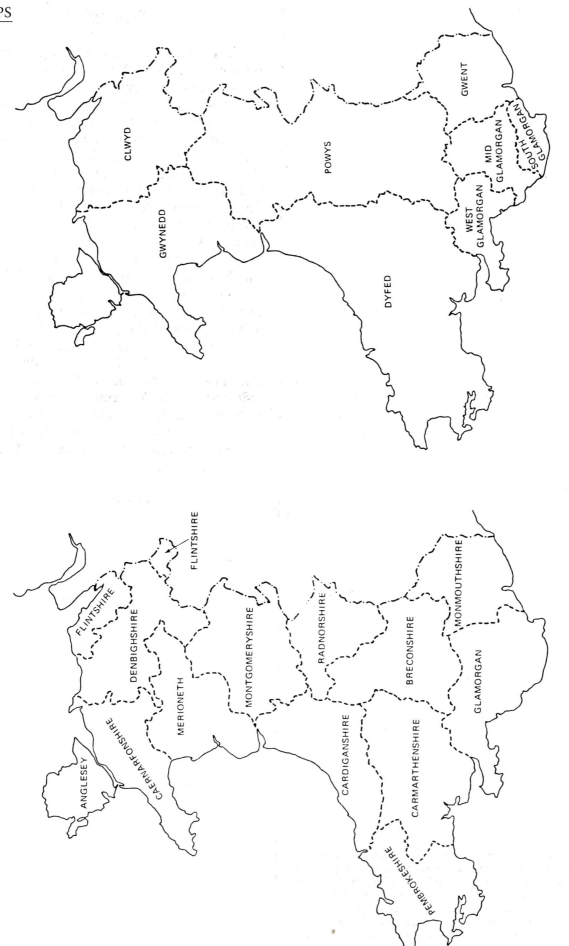

1. The Counties of Wales: Old and New

The Counties of Wales since 1974

The Counties of Wales, 1536—1974

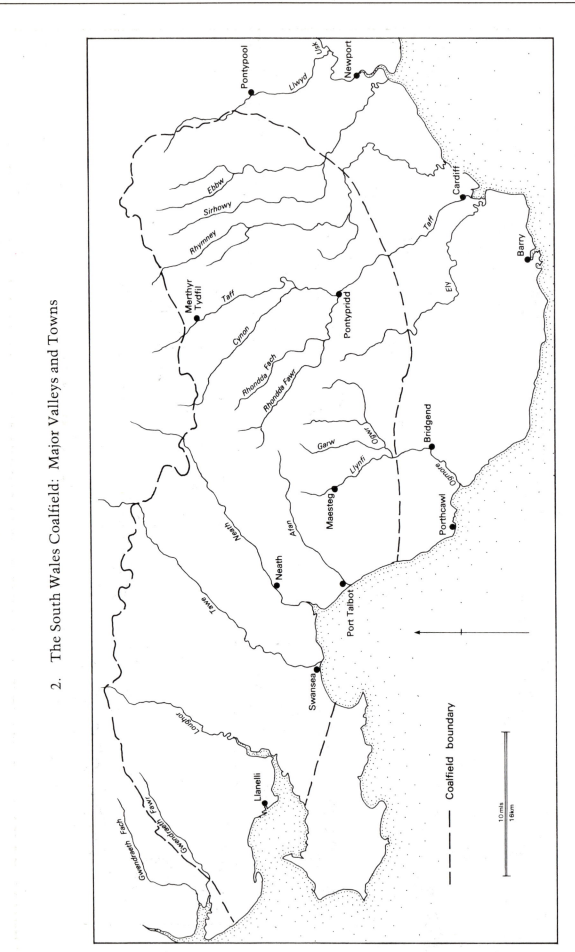

2.   The South Wales Coalfield: *Major Valleys and Towns*

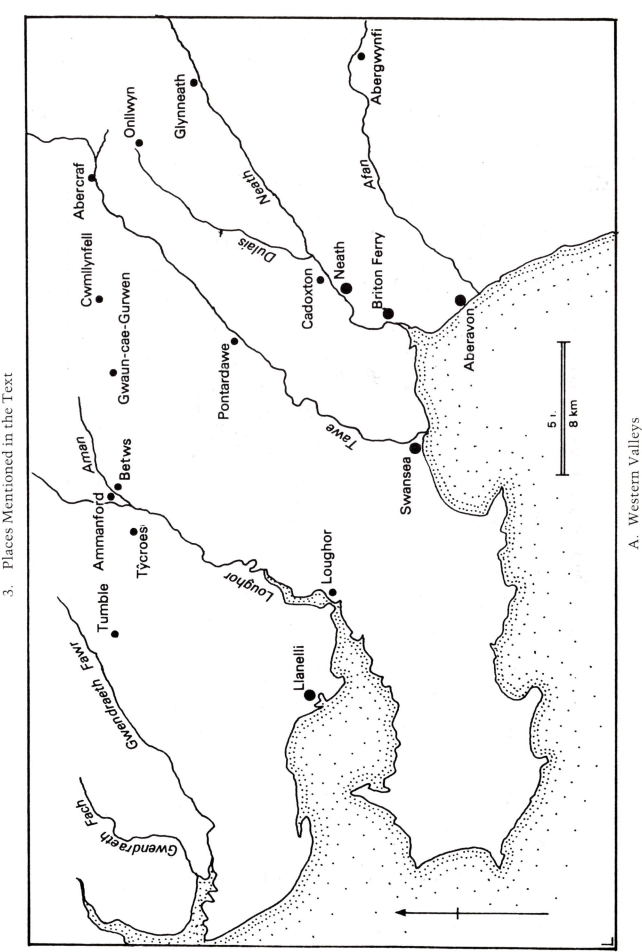

3. Places Mentioned in the Text

A. Western Valleys

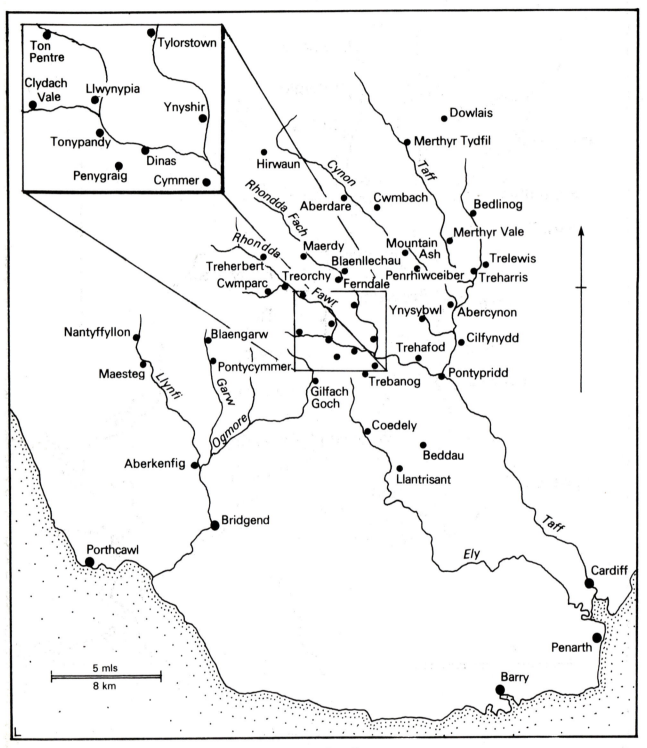

B. Central Valleys

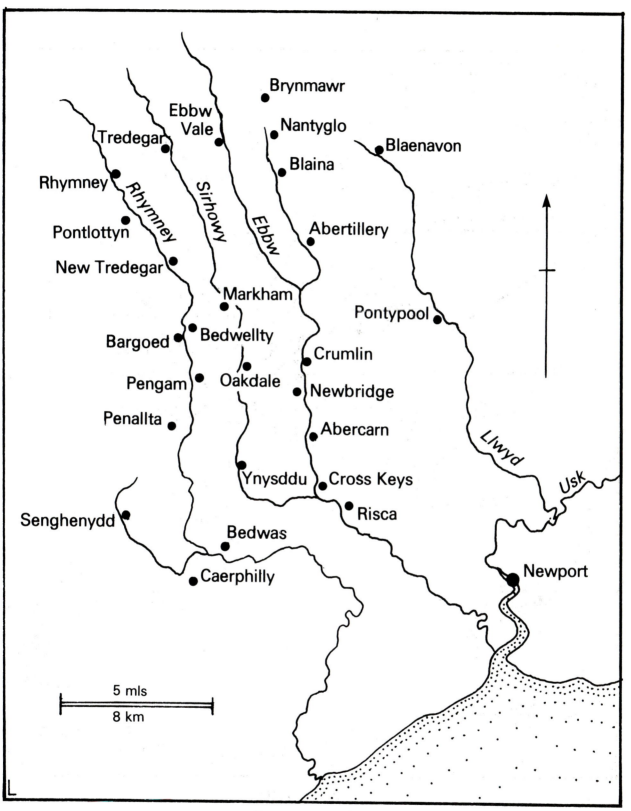

C. Eastern Valleys

Time Line

1248—Earliest reference to the use of coal in Wales (at Neath)

1695—Humphrey Mackworth begins development of the coal industry in the Neath area where coal used to smelt copper ore.

1760—Growth of iron industry in South Wales leads to increase in coalmining. Most demand for South Wales coal for next hundred years to smelt iron ore.

1786—Formation by Thomas Charles of Sunday School Movement in Wales. Provide main form of Education in South Wales coalfield for next hundred years.

1800—Gradual development of sale-coal industry in South Wales.

1831—First organised trade-unions among the miners of South Wales.

1837—Abernant Colliery in Cynon Valley opened. Marks beginning of importance of the area in sale-coal industry for next 20 years.

1839—Opening of West Bute Dock, Cardiff. Marks beginning of expansion of South Wales ports.

1841—Opening of Taff Vale Railway from Merthyr Tydfil to Cardiff. Marks beginning of railway network in South Wales valleys.

1842—Mines Act passed by Parliament. No women or boys (under 10) to be employed underground in future.

1851—Admiralty Report declares South Wales steam coal to be most suitable for use of Royal Navy. Marks start of rapid expansion of South Wales steam coal industry.

—Census of Religious Worship reveals growth of Nonconformity in Wales.

1855—First train of Rhondda steam coal sent from Treherbert to Cardiff. Marks beginning of rise of Rhondda as major coalmining valley in South Wales.

—Limited Liability Companies begin to replace individuals in ownership of coal industry.

—Revival of National Eisteddfod marks growing popularity of Eisteddfod movement.

1867—Parliamentary Reform Act leads to working-class householders in town having right to vote.

1868—Radical Nonconformist Liberals win many Parliamentary seats in Wales. Marks beginning of Liberal domination of Welsh politics.

1870—Education Act establishes School Boards. Primary education becomes available to most children.

—Longwall replaces Pillar and Stall as main mining technique.

—Spread of choirs, bands and organised sport in South Wales valleys.

1871—Amalgamated Association of Miners establishes strongest trade union yet among South Wales miners.

1873—South Wales Coalowners Association formed.

1875—Sliding Scale Committee set up to decide wage levels of South Wales miners.

1880—Gradual development of anthracite coalfield.

—Spread of Miners' Halls and Institutes.

1881—Welsh Sunday Closing Act—public houses closed on Sundays.

1885—William Abraham (Mabon), miners leader, elected to Parliament for new Rhondda seat.

1889—Welsh Intermediate Education Act sees spread of secondary school education in Wales.

1898—Following defeat of miners in six months lock-out, South Wales Miners Federation formed.

1900—Keir Hardie elected to Parliament for Merthyr Tydfil. First 'Labour' M.P. from Wales.

—Spread of Coal Combines in South Wales Coalfield.

1904-05—Religious Revival sweeps Wales.

1905—Wales defeats New Zealand 'All Blacks' in rugby international at Cardiff.

1908—South Wales Miners Federation affiliates to the Labour Party.

1909—Spread of 'Independent Working Class Education Movement' in South Wales.

1910-11—Cambrian Combine Dispute and riots at Tonypandy.

1912—National Miners Strike wins minimum wage.

1913—Peak production of South Wales coalfield.

—439 men killed at Universal Colliery, Senghenydd.

1915—South Wales miners' strike wins new wages agreement.

1916—South Wales coalfield taken over by the Government.

1918—Labour Party replaces Liberals in most coalfield seats in General Election.

1919—Royal Commission on Coal Industry recommends nationalisation of the industry.

1921—Coal industry handed back to coalowners. Followed by miners defeat in lock-out and reduced wages.

1925—Royal Commission on the Coal Industry.

1926—General Strike and Miners' Lock-out ends in defeat for miners, reduced wages and longer hours.

1927—First hunger march against unemployment leaves South Wales.

1930—Height of mass unemployment in South Wales and emigration from the area.

1934—Struggle between S.W.M.F. and Company Unionism at height.

1944—National Union of Mineworkers formed.

1947—Coal industry nationalised and National Coal Board set up.

1955—Widespread pit closures begin in South Wales.

1972—First national miners' strikes since 1926.

1984-5—Miners strike against pit closures.

Historical Evidence

In this book we shall study the history of the South Wales mining valleys. The author will tell part of the story. The sources will tell the rest of the story. These sources are mainly documentary, although there are also many visual sources.

Documents

Documents are those written records of any period in history which survive. Everything which is written down or, more recently, typed, is a document and may be of some use to the historian. Any notes which you might write to each other are historical documents. They might, sometime in the future, be of use to a historian—if they survive. It is highly unlikely, of course, that they will survive. More important documents than those, affecting the lives of hundreds of people—or millions of people, have not survived. These papers have been eaten by rats, destroyed in floods, burned or torn up or just decayed. Out of what has survived we try to find out what has happened in the past.

Other sources

We do not only have documents, or written sources, to help us build up a picture of the South Wales mining valleys. Buildings of the time which still stand tell us a great deal about wealth, living conditions, life-style, and religious habits for example. Any clothes, or furniture, miners' equipment, trade-union banners or even pots and pans help to build up the picture. Anything which survives from the period is of some value.

Evidence

The documents, buildings, artefacts (the name given to man-made and woman-made articles) together make up our *evidence*. This is all that remains of the past. We cannot know anything about the past if there is no evidence. It is only from what survives that we can build up a picture of the past. This is what makes *primary* evidence so important and why it is important to understand the difference between *primary* and *secondary* evidence.

Primary evidence

People studying history divide their sources of information into primary sources and secondary sources. The topic of our study is the history of the South Wales mining valleys. Therefore all those documents, buildings, or artefacts which actually came into existence during the period we are studying are *primary* sources of evidence. That does not mean that they are all of equal value. Some primary evidence is very important indeed. For example colliery records can give us essential information about how coal was mined and what wages were actually paid to miners, although in fact very few such records have survived. The records of miners' trade unions can provide important information on what working conditions in collieries were like and the demands which miners put forward to improve these conditions. Acts of Parliament tell us what laws were passed to regulate the mining industry. Not all records give us quite such detailed and 'official' information as this. Newspapers, for example, which are often used as a primary source by historians, sometimes give us only the view of the journalist who writes a report or the editor of the newspaper. Some people write autobiographies which tell us the story of their lives from their point of view. This kind of evidence we call *personal* or *media* evidence. The information provided by such evidence may not be as reliable as, say, an Act of Parliament. It is still very important indeed because it will at least tell us something about the person who wrote it even if it does not tell us a great deal about the topic. Sometimes it can provide us with information which, although less reliable than 'official' evidence, gives us a much clearer understanding of how people led their lives, even if it is only one person's view. These sources, therefore, if they come into existence during the period which we are studying, are also primary sources.

Secondary evidence

This is not the first book to be written by an historian on the history of the South Wales mining valleys. There are many other books which have been written in our own times on different aspects of the history of the area. Such historians have built up their picture, often using primary sources. When they write down their ideas in books these books become sources of information themselves. The books which students of history write, are called *secondary* sources. In other words secondary sources are those accounts of the history of the

South Wales mining valleys which have come into existence *since* the events which are part of that history have taken place.

In all the Sections and Chapters of this book, the parts of the story which the author has written are secondary sources. The rest of the story is told by other people. Most of the extracts are primary sources; some of them are secondary sources.

Many people who go on to study history as adults have the idea that primary sources are true and secondary sources are merely opinions. This is not so. Let us suppose that you write a diary of everything which has happened to you today and that it survives for a hundred years. Let us suppose, too, that in a hundred years time a historian is trying to reconstruct life in your school. Is the class register likely to be accurate? Yes, probably, within narrow limits. But the historian may want to get an idea of what people thought of their schools in the twentieth century, so he or she will use your diary. It is a primary source for the period, like the register. But now the historian has got to be very careful. He is dealing with a literary source. How truthful a picture do you think your diary would give, and how complete will the information be? It is just the same for us looking at our period. There are many useful primary sources but we have got to be very careful with them. Can you think of any reasons why people writing at the time might have deliberately set out to deceive others around them and the people who were likely to read about events later?

1.—Introduction

In 1805 Henry Gastineau, an artist, visited the Rhondda Valley. The kind of scene he saw there is shown below in his painting of Berw y Rhondda (near modern day Trehafod at the mouth of the two Rhondda rivers).

Source 1

Source: T. H. Sheperd, after H. Gastineau; 'Berw Y Rhondda'. National Museum of Wales.

Forty-two years later another traveller visited the Rhondda. His name was Charles Cliffe and he found that most of the area had hardly changed since the time of Gastineau's visit. Here is part of what Cliffe wrote about the Rhondda in a book published in 1847:

Source 2

The valley stretched for a distance of eight or ten miles between two nearly parallel lines of hills, broken by a succession of cliffs of singular beauty . . . The emerald greeness of the meadows in the valley below was most refreshing . . . The air is aromatic (sweet smelling) with the wild flowers and mountain plants. A Sabbath stillness reigns . . . it is the gem of Glamorganshire.

Source: C. Cliffe. *The Book of South Wales*, 1847.

Sixty years later Arthur Morris, an historian, visited the Rhondda valleys. This is how he described the area in a book published in 1908:

Source 3

The river Rhondda is a dark, turgid, and contaminated gutter, into which is poured the refuse of the host of collieries which skirt the thirteen miles of its course. The hills—have been stripped of all their woodland beauty, and there they stand, rugged and bare, with immense rubbish heaps covering their surface . . . The whole length of the valley has become transformed . . . the din of steam engines, the whirr of machinery, the grating sound of coal screens, and the hammering of the smithies proceed increasingly night and day, year in and year out. An unheard of wealth of industry and

Source 4

This photograph of Ferndale in the Rhondda Fach Valley, taken at about the same time as Morris' visit, shows you the kind of scene he describes in Source 3.
Source: C. Batstone. *Old Rhondda in Photographs*, 1974:

a great population have simultaneously sprung up together during the past sixty years . . . The industrial townships of this valley appear to be inseparably connected in one continuous series of streets of workmens cottages to Pontypridd.

Source: A. Morris, *Glamorgan*, 1908.

In one lifetime the Rhondda was transformed from a sleepy rural area with a population of 1,998 people in 1851, into one of the fastest-growing centres of population in the world, which by 1911 had a population of 152,781 people. This remarkable change in the Rhondda had to some extent or another, happened in all the other valleys of West Carmarthenshire, Glamorgan and much of Monmouthshire. In the Gwendraeth, the Amman, the Tawe, the Nedd, the Dulais, the Afan, the Llynfi, the Ogwr, the Garw, the Ely, the Rhondda, the Cynon, the Taff, the Rhymni, the Sirhowy, the Ebbw, the Llwyd and a host of smaller valley settlements, a new society developed in the second-half of the 19th century. The development of these valley communities changed Wales as a whole and the nation's history. Even today, when they are passing through something of a crisis, the valleys as an entity are a special and unique part of what makes up Wales and its history for the last century.

The factor which caused these great changes in South Wales and brought this 'new society' into being was the existence of rich and plentiful supplies of coal in the valleys. By the end of the 19th century South Wales was one of the most important coal producing and exporting areas in the world. Along with the much smaller coalfield of North-East Wales (which is not considered in this book but was an area which underwent many of the same experiences as the South Wales coalfield), the coal industry at its peak provided employment for one out of every ten persons in Wales and many more people were dependent, in one way or another, upon the industry for their livelihood.

The period of the great expansion of the coal industry in South Wales was approximately from 1840 to 1920. Of course during this period and especially in the previous century there were other important industries in South Wales. Before about 1840 most people depended on *farming* for their livelihood, but there were many other industries in Wales such as woollen cloth, lead, copper, iron and slate as well as coal. In the 18th century two of these industries developed in a major way. In South-West Wales (particularly at Swansea, Neath, Aberafan and Llanelli) the most important centre of the copper industry in Britain grew up. Along the heads of the South Wales valleys (especially centred on Merthyr Tydfil) the iron industry flourished with some of the largest ironworks in the world being founded. In these areas (along with the iron, copper, lead and slate producing areas of North-East and North-West Wales) the first large-scale industralization of Wales took place. People poured in from the Welsh countryside to work in these expanding industries and to form the first industrial towns in Wales.

Even during the period 1840 to 1920 when the coal industry did dominate the way of life of people in South Wales, there were still other industries and occupations which were important. Large numbers of men worked in industries such as steel, tinplate, engineering and transport (railways and docks). Women also worked in these industries and even more so as domestic servants, shop assistants and office workers.

Most historians would agree that *the* major development in the history of South Wales during the last century and a half has been the rise of the coal industry, the experience of the people who worked in it and depended upon it and the growth of the valley communities they created. It is this experience which we shall concentrate upon in this book.

2.—The Industry
The Geography and Geology of the South Wales Coalfield

This section deals with the geography and geology of the coalfield and the importance these factors had upon the development of the industry. Sources 5, 6 and 7 give the basic information:

Source 5

Source: J. H. Morris and L. J. Williams. *The South Wales Coal Industry 1841-1875, 1958.*

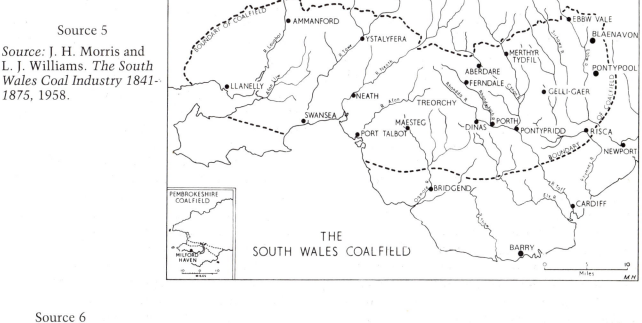

Source 6

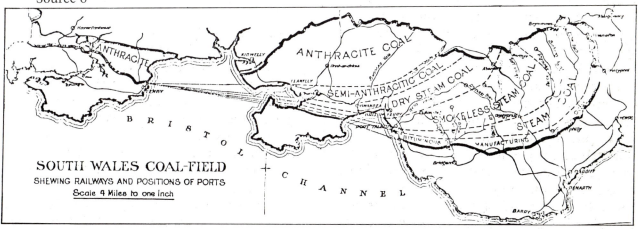

Source: F. J. North. *Coal and the Coalfields in Wales, 1926.*

Source 7

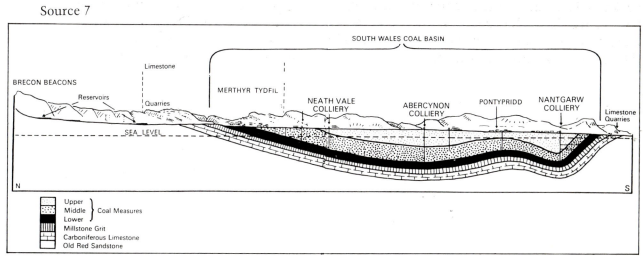

Source: H. J. Savory. *A Geography of Wales, 1968.*

The basic geography of the coalfield is shown in Source 5. The South Wales coalfield is the largest continuous coalfield in Britain. It covers nearly 1,000 square miles and extends from Pontypool in Gwent westwards as far as St. Bride's Bay on the west coast of Pembrokeshire. The width of the coalfield at its widest point is eighteen miles and it occupies much of the counties of West Glamorgan, Mid Glamorgan and Gwent, and parts of western Dyfed and southern Powys. The surface of the coalfield is carved into a series of deep and narrow valleys where most of the coalmining has been carried on and where the mining communities have grown up.

Sources 6 and 7 deal with the geology of the coalfield which has had an important bearing on the history of the coal industry in South Wales. Coal is a mineral formed from the dead bodies of plants (a little like fern trees) which existed over 300,000,000 years ago. These plants became swamps which after centuries of changes in the earth formation of our planet were squeezed into solid masses below the surface. The plants became layers of coal and they were sandwiched under the earth's crust between layers of rock and shale which had been formed from mud. The width of these layers of coal varied from a fraction of an inch to several feet and the depth of them in the ground also varied. The coals which were deepest in the ground were the eldest and had the highest carbon content, which meant they were the slowest to catch alight but gave off the most heat. The coals nearest to the surface had exactly the opposite qualities and those in the middle ranges had varying qualities. In South Wales there was a much greater variety of types of coal than in other British coalfields. Source 6 shows the areas of the coalfield where particular types of coal could especially be found. It also shows the three main types of coal which existed in South Wales which were:

1. *Anthracite:* the deepest in the ground and with the highest carbon content. Therefore these coals were not suitable for burning in an open grate or in steam boilers, but they were popular for use in central heating furnaces and in stoves for heating greenhouses and hothouses.

2. *Steam Coals:* South Wales was particularly rich in these coals which were found in the deep and middle ranges of the coalfield. The best steam coals burned with little smoke and gave a bright hot fire. They were particularly popular for use in the steam boilers of ships and railway engines.

3. *Bituminous Coals:* fairly close to the surface, these were used for many different purposes including burning in open grates, manufacturing gas and smelting metals.

Source 7 is a section across the South Wales coalfield from Merthyr to Cardiff, along the Taff valley, showing modern day collieries and underground coal measures. It illustrates how the South Wales coalfield is really like a basin: on the edges of the coalfield (the rims of the basin) the coal comes near to the surface; at the centre of the basin the coal is at its deepest.

These geological factors were to have an important effect on the development of the coal industry in South Wales. To summarize, the main points of importance are:

1. There are many different types of coal in the South Wales coalfield. Demand for these coals occurred at different times and so the regions of the coalfield where these coals were to be found developed separately.

2. Because the coalfield is shaped like a basin the earliest coalmining was carried out near the edges of the coalfield where the coal came nearest to the surface and the later stage of the industry's development was when the deepest coal was worked.

3. Because the South Wales coalfield was an area of mountains and valleys, the coal measures were uneven and disturbed underground. Therefore the cost of mining was always high in South Wales. Many men were needed to mine the coal and maintain the mines and much more timber was needed to prop up underground roofs.

The History of the Industry to 1840

There has been a long history of coalmining in South Wales. There is evidence that the Romans knew of the existence of coal during the time that they occupied Wales. However, it was not greatly used by them or anyone else until the 13th century. Thereafter, although the development of a separate coal industry did not really begin until the 19th century, coal was increasingly being mined in South Wales up to that time. There were four main stages in this early development:

1. The slow growth in the use of coal for fires in the home and by some industries from the 13th to the 17th centuries.
2. The use of coal by the copper industry in the 17th and 18th centuries.
3. The use of coal by the iron Industry in the second half of the 18th and 19th centuries.
4. The early growth of a 'sale-coal' industry in the late 18th and early 19th centuries.

Development up to the 17th century

The earliest reference we have to coal being used in South Wales is at Neath in 1248. By 1551 an average of 20,000 tons a year was being mined in the whole of Wales and this increased tenfold to 200,000 tons by 1681. Most of this mining was done on the edges of the coalfield where the coal came near to the surface and it was local landowners who developed the industry. The main areas where this mining was done were Neath, Aberavon (where monks in the local abbeys were involved), Pembrokeshire and especially Gower. Here are some extracts from the accounts of the Lordship of Gower for a colliery at Kilvey in 1400:

> Source 8
> The accountant answers for £155.13.6 for 179 lasts (last = 16 tons) 2½ wayes (way = 4 tons)

of sea-coal from the pits there this year . . . money paid to 3 hewers, for hewing 161 lasts of coal . . . for each last 9d. . . . and to 30 porters carrying the said lasts from the pits to the exits, each last 2½d. . . . carrying the said lasts to the waterside . . . and carrying from the land to the ships . . . And in making and mending barrows . . . Making new picks and refitting old ones . . . And in candles . . .

Source: J. U. Nef. *The Rise of the British Coal Industry,* 1932.

From what we can imagine from this source the techniques of mining were to change very little for the next 500 years. Notice also that the coal is being taken to ships. Indeed a good percentage of the coal mined was exported. After 1560 Welsh coal was taken mainly to Cornwall and Ireland, but some went to Europe and even as far as the American colonies. By this time the anthracite coal of Pembrokeshire was in great demand. Here is a map of the Pembrokeshire coalfield at this time showing the main collieries and the main ports from which coal was sent. It is followed by a description of the methods and dangers of mining in Pembrokeshire taken from the royal records in 1561.

Source 9

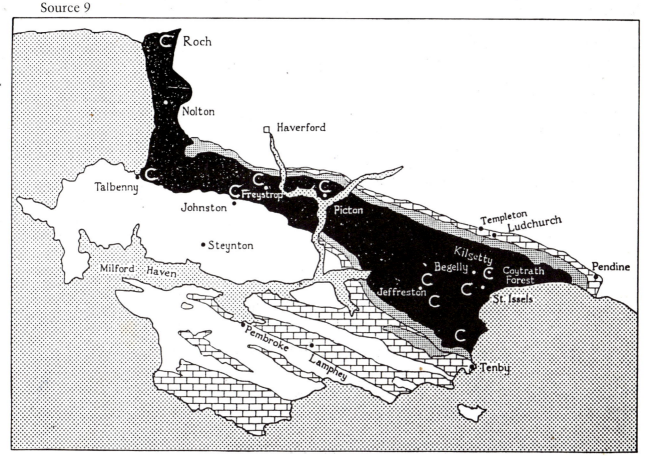

Source: W. Rees, *Industry Before the Industrial Revolution,* 1968.

Source 10

They work from six o'clock to six o'clock and rest an hour at noon and eat bread . . . and drink . . . The dangers in digging these coals is the falling of the earth or else the sudden irruption of standing water in old works . . . sudden damps that happen . . .

Source: Memoranda on The Queen's Remembrancer's Roll, *1561.*

What is meant here by 'sudden damps'? Coal was now used more in people's fires in the home, as timber was becoming scarce. It was also used increasingly by blacksmiths, lime-burners (to produce powdered lime as a ferti-lizer) and in a growing number of industries to smelt or refine things such as salt, sugar, soap and hops. So the industry was growing although it was still very small (in 1681, by comparison, in the North-East of England 1,225,000 tons of coal were mined) and not all that important to the local economy (in 1603 coal was the eighth most important export from Pembrokeshire—just behind oysters!).

The Copper Industry

By the end of the 16th century another of the industries using coal was the copper industry and for the next 150 years the growing needs of this industry created a further expansion in coalmining in South Wales. It took a great amount of coal to smelt copper and so it was more economical to bring copper from Cornwall and North Wales to be smelted in South Wales than the other way around. By the early 17th century, Neath was the main centre for copper-smelting in Britain and with its copper works and coal mines it grew into Wales' first indust-rial town. The close relationship between the two industries can be seen here in this painting of 1805 (Source 11) which shows a colliery near Neath Abbey with, in the background, the smoke of the copperworks.

The local collieries were very much a part of the copper industry rather than separate con-cerns and from 1695 onwards both were developed by their owner Sir Humphrey Mack-

Source 11

Source: National Museum of Wales.

worth. Here is an account written in 1705 of Mackworth's role in developing the local coal mines:

Source 12

Sir Humphrey Mackworth, in the year 1695, began to adventure great sums of money in finding and recovering the coal . . . These coal works do employ great numbers of men, women and children . . . The nature of these works are such, that seven men, three cutters and four waggoners work in each wall of coal . . . The waggoners have great skill to keep the wagons upon the rails through the turnings and windings underground . . . The waggon-ways go on wooden rails from the face of each wall of coal, twelve hundred yards under-ground, down to the waterside about three quarters of a mile from the mouth of the coalpit.
Source: The Case of Sir Humphrey Mackworth and the Mine Adventurers, 1705.

What part of this Source helps us to understand the scene in Source 11? By the early 18th century Swansea replaced Neath as the main centre of the copper industry because it had a better port through which copper ore could be brought in and coal exported. By 1845 Swansea produced 55% of the world's copper and the demand for coal from the copperworks led to the opening of many new mines in the Swansea area.

The Iron Industry

The growth of the copper industry turned Swansea into Wales' second largest town. The largest by the beginning of the nineteenth century was Merthyr Tydfil and its growth brings us to the next stage of the development of the coal industry—its part in the spectacular growth of the iron industry in South Wales. The use of iron in South Wales has as long a history as that of coal. However, until the middle of the 18th century the industry was small and scattered throughout Wales. The reason for this was that the smelting of iron-ore had to be done by using timber. As a result timber became increasingly scarce and its price increased. This in turn led to an increase in the price of iron and held back its use. To be sure of having enough timber, iron furnaces needed to be scattered so that they did not have to compete with other works. However, after experiments in the early 18th century (by the Darby Family at Coal-brookdale in Shropshire) it was found that coal (turned into coke) could successfully be used to smelt iron. What this led to in South Wales can be worked out from this map showing the number of iron furnaces which developed in South Wales after 1760 and the account taken from a tourist's guide to Monmouthshire in 1801, which follows.

Source 13

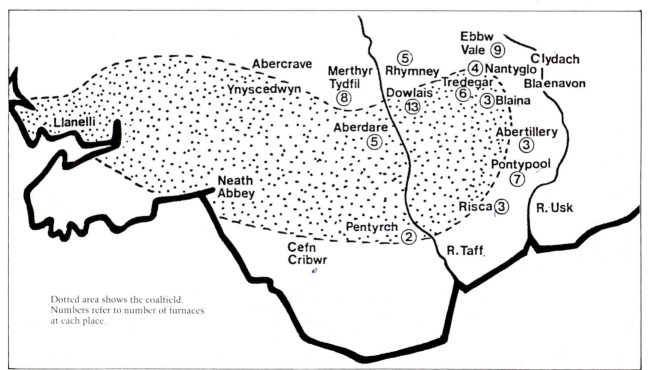

Source: B. Davies, *The Iron Industry in Wales 1750-1850*, 1983.

Source 14

About forty years ago the ironworks discovered the making of iron with pit-coal instead of charcoal (timber) . . . Hence a district which contained such extensive mines of ore and coal, quantities of limestone and numerous streams of water, could not fail . . .

Source: W. Coxe, *A Historical Tour Through Monmouthshire*, 1801.

Right along the edges of the South Wales Coalfield then (and particularly on the northern edge, or the Heads of the Valleys as we call it today) a whole new industry and society grew up after 1760 and flourished for the next century. By 1850 40% of Britain's total output of iron was produced in these works and although much of it was exported, Welsh iron helped to build Britain's 'industrial revolution' of the 18th and 19th centuries. Merthyr Tydfil (along with its near neighbour Dowlais) was the main centre of this thriving industry. Not only did it become the capital city of Wales in everything but name it also became the 'iron capital' of Britain. Source 15 is an account of iron smelting at the Dowlais Ironworks in 1850 as reported in the newspaper the *Morning Chronicle*, which shows the use of coal and the other raw materials mentioned earlier in Source 14. Source 16 is a painting from 1820 of one of the largest works outside Merthyr, the Blaenavon ironworks:

Source 15

The daily consumption of coal at these works is estimated at 1,000 tons . . . Fourteen blast furnaces . . . refineries . . . mills and forges . . . Here the process of smelting begins. Through four large doors . . . men and women . . . throw into the furnaces the materials with which the iron is made: Welsh iron ore . . . raw coal and limestone . . . The ores yield the iron, the coal the necessary combustion (heat) and the limestone . . . a flux by which the metal is separated from the earthy parts of the ore . . .

Source: The Morning Chronicle, 1850.

The growth of the iron industry led to a major increase in the demand for coal. The Iron-masters opened mines along the edges of the coalfield and the production of coal just for the ironworks was about 2 million tons a year by 1840. Again it is important to note that the coal mines were not separate concerns—they were linked closely to the ironworks and owned by the Ironmasters. The importance of the colliery side of their businesses can be seen by the numbers of coalminers employed within the total workforce. Source 17 gives figures for the Dowlais Ironworks in 1841. The coal miners are the numbers 'at the collieries'. In what works were those people employed 'at the mines and patches' engaged?

Source 16

Blaenavon Ironworks.
Source: National Library of Wales.

Source 17

Nature of Employment	Estimated No. of Adults		Children and Young Persons		Total	
	M	F	M	F	M	F
At the blast furnaces	938	40	20	6	958	46
At the forges and mills	1097	30	210	28	1307	58
At the collieries	924	50	236	20	1160	70
At the mines and patches	1012	80	233	157	1245	237
At the farms	111	—	—	—	111	—
	4082	200	699	211	4781	411
					411	
					5192	

Source: Report of the Royal Commission on the Employment of Children, 1842.

The Early Sale—Coal Industry

In 1840 2 million tons of coal were mined in South Wales for the ironworks. About another 1 million were produced for the copper industry, other industries and for use in fires in the home. Another 1½ million were by now being shipped out of South Wales and in this figure we can see the growth of what was called the 'sale-coal' trade which is the final period of the expansion of the coal industry up to 1840. 'Sale coal' means that whilst most of the coal mined in South Wales up to 1840 went to the iron and copper works, some of it was always sold for other uses in and outside South Wales. The Ironmasters and the owners of copper works were always prepared to sell any surplus coal they did not need, but in addition some of this 'sale coal' was mined and sold from small mines that did not actually belong to these men. In this we can see the beginnings of what was to become known as the 'independent sale-coal trade'. There were many other industries which needed coal and there was a growing use of coal-fires in the home. Some of this market was in Wales itself but a great deal of the 'sale-coal' was exported to Ireland, France and other parts of Britain. Source 18 is evidence from a Government Inquiry in 1810 showing the amount of coal shipped from the port of Newport in 1808 and 1809 and the places it was sent to.

Some of this coal came from mines owned by Thomas Powell who was a timber-merchant at Newport Docks. He saw that there was a demand for South Wales coal and opened a number of small mines in Monmouthshire and shipped the coal through Newport. In the Rhondda, Walter Coffin, a businessman from Bridgend, opened small mines in the Dinas area

Source 18

AN ACCOUNT of the Quantity of all COALS and CULM exported from the Port of Newport, in Monmouthshire, to be carried Coastwise, in the several Years 1808 and 1809; distinguishing the Places to which they were intended to be carried.

From whence.	NAMES of the PLACES to which sent.	1808.		1809.	
		COALS. Tons.	CULM. Tons.	COALS. Tons.	CULM. Tons.
NEWPORT	Chepstow	6,259		6,949	
	Gloucester	13,162		16,169	
	Bristol	45,484		55,556	
	Bridgewater	35,989		41,713	
	Minehead	1,316		1,580	
	Ilfracombe	729		753	
	Bideford	312		2,011	
	Barnstaple	1,753		3,047	
	Padstow	4,727		3,929	
	St. Ives	3,093		1,117	
	Scilly	156		104	
	Penzance	262		152	
	Falmouth	294		381	
	Truro	792		827	
	Fowey	481		154	
	Plymouth	4,508	Nil.	1,377	Nil.
	Dartmouth	4,342		4,014	
	Exeter	4,131		2,157	
	Lyme	—		66	
	Bridport	—		100	
	Southampton	—		59	
	Portsmouth	229		—	
	Cardiff	—		28	
	Milford	913		574	
	Tenby	119		—	
	Haverfordwest	55		30	
	Pembroke	78		—	
	Cardigan	18		80	
	Aberystwith	743		726	
	Barmouth	—		42	
	Pwllheli	171		26	
	Carnarvon	61		30	
	Beaumaris	80		—	
	TOTAL	130,298		145,631	

Custom-House, London, 2d April 1810.

William Irving.
Inspector General of Imports and Exports.

Source: Report of Select Committee on the Petition of South Wales Colliery Owners, 1810.

from 1809 and began to send his coal down to the ports. At this time, however, it was still the West Wales ports of Swansea and Llanelli which exported most of the sale-coal. This was because the great problem faced by these early coalowners was transporting their coal to the ports. Source 19 shows coal being taken from Merthyr Tydfil to Cardiff in 1790. This helps us to understand why the Customs Report for the port of Cardiff in 1782, which follows, could be so gloomy about prospects for the coal trade.

Swansea and Llanelli had one great advantage over Cardiff and Newport in this respect. The painting, Source 21, of coal being shipped at Landore, Swansea, in 1792 should provide the clue.

The building of canals and tramroads in the 1790s was a help to the coalowners of East

Source 19

Source: National Museum of Wales.

Source 20

We have no coal exported from this port, nor ever shall, as it would be too expensive to bring it down here from the internal part of the country.
Source: E. L. Chappell. *History of the Port of Cardiff*, 1939.

Source 21

Source: Royal Institution of South Wales.

Wales and both Walter Coffin in the Rhondda (joined by George Insole who opened mines at Cymmer in 1844) and Thomas Powell in Monmouthshire increased their activities. However, until the coming of the railways in the 1840s West Wales continued to have this great advantage in the sale-coal trade.

By the 1840s although there was a growing 'sale-coal' trade the greatest use of South Wales coal was still in local industries and the amount of coal mined for sale by independent coal-owners was still small compared, for example, to the Northumberland and Durham coalfield.

Up to 1840 it was the bituminous and anthra-cite coal of South Wales which was being mined. The high quality steam-coal of South Wales had hardly been touched, and, as the future was to show, this was the coalfield's greatest resource. The growing use of the steam-engine in transport would supply the demand that was needed for this type of coal. There was, however, another problem to solve before steam-coal could be mined and most experts in the early 19th century thought this would prove impossible. Facts about the geology of the coalfield given earlier provide the clues to solving this problem.

The History of the Industry 1840-1920

The Scale of Expansion

The steady rise of coal production in South Wales meant that by 1840 about 4½ million tons a year were mined in the coalfield. Reliable figures for this period are difficult to come by, but that level of production probably doubled in the 1850s. The figures in Source 22 show the staggering rise of coal production in South Wales thereafter and how important a part South Wales played in the overall growth of the coal industry in the United Kingdom.

Source 22

Year	Output of the South Wales Coalfield	Output of the United Kingdom	Proportion of South Wales output to Output of UK
1865	12,656,336	98,150,587	12.9 per cent
1875	14,173,143	133,306,485	10.6 per cent
1885	24,347,856	159,351,418	15.3 per cent
1895	33,040,114	189,661,362	17.4 per cent
1905	43,204,071	236,111,150	18.3 per cent
1914	56,830,072	287,411,869	19.7 per cent

Source: The South Wales Coal Annual, 1915.

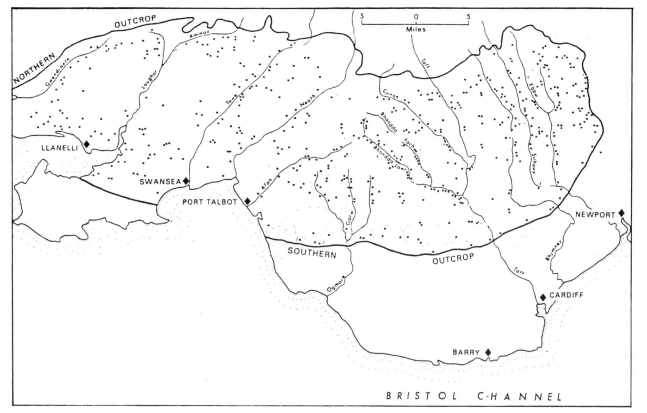

Source 23

Source: K. O. Morgan, Rebirth of a Nation: Wales 1880-1980, 1981.

The Cardiff Customs report of 1782 (Source 20) was to prove one of the great false predictions of history, for by 1914 Cardiff was the greatest coal exporting port in the world with exports of nearly 16 million tons a year. In the process it had grown into the largest town in Wales and the bustling centre of a world empire in coal that was to make South Wales and its coal internationally famous. South Wales was the last of the British coalfields to develop in a major way, but between 1840 and 1914 it was the fastest developer, undergoing a 155-fold increase in production during the 19th century! The number of coalminers increased about twenty-fold to 231, 545 by 1914 and as Source 23 shows, by 1915 collieries dotted the whole coalfield.

Altogether this was one of the most dramatic developments in the history of Wales and it totally transformed the valleys of the South Wales coalfield and the way of life that was led there. Up to 1840 coal was mined near to the edges of the coalfield, but this widescale development of the industry after 1840 took place because of the new and increasing demand for high quality South Wales steam coal. This was to be found at the centre of the coalfield—within the valleys themselves.

The Merthyr and Cynon Valleys

The mining of coal *within* the valleys was the great feature of the period 1840 to 1920, but this development did not all happen at once, rather it took place at different times in different places. It was at Waun Wyllt, near Merthyr, in 1824 that a husband and wife, Robert and Lucy Thomas, became the first to mine the 4' seam of steam coal. Through the Cardiff merchant George Insole their coal was shipped to London where it was used by steamboats on the Thames and aroused considerable interest because it was fairly free from smoke but raised a high quantity of steam power. In the Cynon Valley, the Ironmasters the Waynes also began to mine steam coal on their properties and soon Thomas Powell, the Newport merchant and owner of sale-coal mines in Monmouthshire, also began to open mines in the Aberdare area. David Davis of Blaengwawr joined them in the now rapid development of the steam-coal seams of the Cynon Valley. The sources below show development in the Cynon between 1840 and 1874, when it was the leading area in the development of the industry. The map showing

the main collieries in the valley by 1874 is followed by a scene on the colliery surface at Powell's Middle Dyffryn Colliery and by a notice issued by David Davis advertising the qualities of his coal:

Source 24

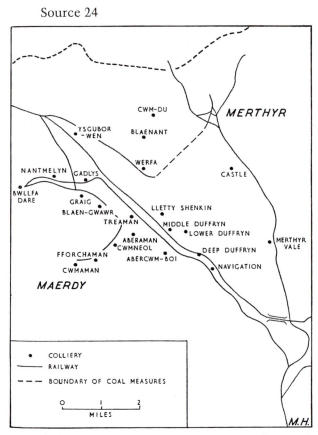

Source: J. Morris and L. J. Williams. *The South Wales Coal Industry 1841-1875*, 1958.

Source 25

Source: Illustrated London News, 1855.

The other major pioneer in the Cynon was John Nixon, one of a large number of mining men from the already developed coalfields of the North-East of England who saw the great potential in South Wales. In 1860 coal was reached after seven years of sinking at his

Source 26

Blaengwawr Steam Coal Wharf,
Bute Ship Canal, Cardiff
1st. April, 1848.

Having for some time past opened Collieries in the Neighbourhood of Merthyr which are now in full operation, I am in a position largely to increase my supply. The quality of my Blaengwawr Coal has met with the approval of Her Majesty's Government, and is placed on the list of Coals supplied by Contract for the use of Her Majesty's Steam Vessels. I beg respectfully to solicit your attention to the Copies of letters on the other side received from the Store Keeper General of the Admiralty, London, and other parties who have tried my Coal as proof of its superior quality and adaptation for Steam purposes generally, more especially for Steam Navigation, and I most confidently solicit your favors.

I am,

Yours very respectfully,

David Davis.

___

Qualities of Coals required for Steam Vessels.

The most appropriate kind of Coal for the service of Steam Vessels ought to possess the following properties viz: The power to generate intense heat, accompanied with flame. Great economy in consumption. A high specific gravity and combustion should take place without noise. All these qualities are found in the Blaengwawr Steam Coal, and is highly esteemed for the use of Steam Boat Boilers of all kinds, but particularly for the tubular Boilers for which it is especially adapted. The specific gravity of this fuel is very considerable, the same weight of Coal occupies much less space than any other, and this joined to its durability renders it very valuable for Steam Vessels taking long voyages.

DIRECTIONS

Keep the fire about four inches thick; a thorough draft of air then passes through the Coal, and as it burns it swells & bursts, giving the most intense heat. When the ash accumulates it should be cleared by a hooked instrument under the Bars.

The Blaengwawr Steam Coal is Shipped

by whom Orders are received, and also by
Mr W. F. Stanton, 9, Love Lane, East Cheap, London.

Source: W. W. Price Collection, Aberdare Public Library.

Navigation Colliery at Mountain Ash. This event led to great celebrations and in a speech given to mark the occasion, reported by the *Merthyr Guardian*, Nixon explained his part in the development of the Cynon Valley:

Source 27

"I believe I am right when I say that we have here from 4000 to 5000 acres of coal to be worked. I look to Mountain Ash surviving Aberdare in prosperity . . . I will tell you the cause of my coming down here . . . In the year 1840, I went to London from the North of England, and I happened to go on board one of those boats now called the penny boats . . . I saw the stoker throw continuously coal into the furnace, and when I looked at the funnel I saw no smoke. This was a wonder to me, as in the North I had been used to see smoke . . . I asked him to allow me to look at the coal and said 'I will give you a shilling; and if you will let me feed the fire I will give you another' . . . I threw some coal on the fire . . . but there was no smoke . . . I then asked him where he got the coal, and he replied from Meartheere in Wales. He could not say Merthyr . . . I at once made it my business to come down here . . . At that time there was no railway to Aberdare, and the coal had to be conveyed down by the Canal. I went to Mr. Powell, and told him that if he wanted a market for his coal at Duffryn, I was willing to . . . introduce his coal into France . . . The year 1840 was a great epoch in this district, as that was the year when the first cargo of coal was shipped foreign from Cardiff. That cargo was taken to Nantes, and given away to the consumer . . . That same year we entered into a contract to supply them with 3,000 tons."

Source: Merthyr Guardian, 12 May, 1860.

The Rhondda Valleys

By the 1860s the Cynon Valley was beginning to be overtaken by the Rhondda as the main centre of the 'coal boom'. In the 1850s bituminous coalmines were opened there in growing numbers but it was the winning of the steam coal on the land of the Marquis of Bute at Cwmsaerbren, Treherbert, after 1850 which showed that the deep steam coal measures of the Rhondda could be reached. It also brought the new Taff Vale Railway to the head of the Rhondda Fawr—but it was not until the 1870s that businessmen with sufficient nerve and money appeared to make a concerted attack on these rich seams. Source 28—details of collieries opened in the Rhondda Fawr from 1850 to 1914—shows how the pace quickened and how steam-coal took over. In what period are most of the steam-coal mines sunk?

Source 28

Date	Steam Coal Seams	Bituminous Seams	Original Owner	Location
1860		Glyncoli Level	C. James	Treorchy
1862		Bwllfa Level	Richardson & Carr	Ton Pentre
1862		Brithweunydd Level	Daniel Thomas	Trealaw
1863		Llwynypia Colliery	Glamorgan Coal Co.	Llwynypia
1863		Blaenclydach Coll.	Bush & Co.	Blaenclydach
1864	Pentre Colliery		Curteis, Green- hill & Ware	Pentre
1864	Bodringallt Colliery		Warner, Simp- son & Co.	Ystrad
1864	Llwynypia Colliery		Glamorgan Coal Co.	Llwynypia
1864		Cwmclydach Coll.	D. & E. Thomas	Cwm-Clydach
1864		Pen-y-graig Colliery	Penygraig Coal Co.	Pen-y-graig
1865	Tydraw Colliery		Thos. Joseph	Blaen-y-cwm
1865	Tynewydd Colliery		Ebenezer Lewis	Nr. Treherbert
1865	Abergorchy Colliery		G. Insole & Son	Treorchy
1865	Parc Colliery		D. Davies & Partners	Cwm-parc
1865	Maendy Colliery		D. Davies & Partners	Ton Pentre
1866		Adare Colliery	Daniel Thomas	Pen-y-graig
1869		Ynyswen Level	Morgan Jones	Treorchy
1869		Dinas Colliery	Daniel Thomas	Dinas
1869	Blaenrhondda Colliery		Cardiff & Merthyr Steam Coal Co.	Blaenrhondda
1870		Gelli Colliery	E. Thomas & G. Griffiths	Gelli
1870	Dare Colliery		D. Davies & Co. Ltd.	Cwm-parc
1872		Trealaw Colliery		Trealaw
1872		Glynmoch Coll.		Treorchy
1872	Fernhill Colliery		Ebenezer Lewis	Blaenrhondda
1872	Clydach Vale Colliery No. 1		S. Thomas & J. Riches Co.	Clydach Vale
1872	Llwynypia Nos. 4 and 5		Glamorgan Coal Co.	Llwynypia
1874	Clydach Vale Colliery No. 2		Thomas, Riches & Co.	Clydach Vale
1876	Tynybedw Colliery		E. Thomas & G. Griffiths	Pentre
1877	Eastern Colliery		D. Davies & Co. Ltd.	Ton Pentre
1877	Gelli Colliery		E. Thomas & G. Griffiths	Gelli
1877	Lady Margaret		Marquis of Bute	Treherbert
1877	Cymmer Colliery		G. Insole & Son	Porth
1879	Pandy Colliery		Naval Coll. Co.	Tonypandy
1880	Ely Colliery		New Naval Coll. Co.	Pen-y-graig
1881	Dinas Colliery		Dinas Steam Coal Co.	Dinas
1881	Bertie, Trefor, Hafod Colls.		William Thomas Lewis	Hafod
1891	Clydach Vale Colliery No. 3		Cambrian Coll. Co.	Clydach Vale
1892	Nantgwyn Colliery		Naval Coll. Co.	Pen-y-graig
1910	Anthony Colliery		Naval Coll. Co.	Tonypandy

Source: E. D. Lewis, The Rhondda Valleys, 1959.

Such developments turned the Rhondda Valleys into perhaps the most thoroughly-mined and famous coal-producing area in the world. By 1914 there were 53 large collieries in the two valleys, 21 of which employed 1,000 or more miners underground. In the Rhondda Fach it was David Davis of Aberdare who was the main coalowner, sinking pits at Ferndale and Tylorstown. In the Rhondda Fawr a number of soon to be famous coal-owners were involved in the growth of the industry. Most of them were Welshmen but there were some 'incomers' such as the Scottish mining engineer Archibald Hood, who opened the Glamorgan Colliery at Llwynypia, shown here.

Source 29

Source: A. P. Barnett and D. Wilson-Lloyd (Eds.), *The South Wales Coalfield*, 1921.

Source 30

PLAN OF THE UNDERTAKING OF THE OCEAN COAL CO. LTD 1893.

Source: I. Thomas. Top Sawyer: *A Biography of David Davies of Llandinam*, 1938.

Source 31

DEVELOPMENT OF OCEAN COLLIERIES, 1870–90

Colliery	Date when coal was first worked	1870	1880	1890
		No. of men employed		
Maendy .	May 1866	528	810	1220
Parc .	Aug. 1866	678	832	748
Dare .	April 1870	310	354	388
Western .	Jan. 1876	—	723	745
Eastern .	July 1877	—	460	1018
Garw .	July 1885	—	—	573
Lady Windsor .	Dec. 1886	—	—	891
Total no. of men employed . . .		1516	3179	5583
Total output . *tons*		341,271	1,152,951	1,726,480

Source: I. Thomas. Top Sawyer: *A Biography of David Davies of Llandinam*, 1938.

Of the Welshmen perhaps the most famous and powerful was David Davies of Llandinam, Montgomeryshire, who had made his name as a builder of railways before entering the coal industry in the Upper Rhondda Fawr, where he had 4 large collieries sunk between 1865 and 1877. Like many of the Coalowners who established themselves first in the Rhondda and Cynon, he then led the movement into as yet untouched valleys. His Ocean Coal Company eventually opened pits at the head of the Ogwr and Garw valleys as well as the Lady Windsor Colliery at Ynysybwl. Sources 30 and 31 show the growth of the Ocean Company up to 1893.

The Monmouthshire Valleys

Although the Rhondda, Cynon and Taff Valleys were at the forefront of this tremendous expansion of the industry, all the valleys of central and eastern Glamorgan and of Monmouthshire were exploited to various degrees. Here are details of some of the major colliery developments in Monmouthshire showing also how the iron companies have joined in the expanding coal trade:

Source 32

The initial letters appended to the name of the Colliery indicate the kind of Coal produced, viz.—(C) Coking; (G) Gas; (H) Household; (M) Manufacturing; (S) Steam.

Name of Owner.	Commercial Manager and Shipping and Commercial Office.	Name of Colliery.	Railway.	Railway Station.	Colliery Manager.	No. of persons employed at the Colliery.
Powell's Tillery Steam Coal Co., Ltd.	Acting Commercial Manager: A. K. Jones, 31, Mount Stuart Square, Cardiff ..	Powell's Nav. (C, M & S)	G.W.R. ..	Talywain ..	A. Frowen ..	550
Do.	Do.	Tillery, Gray, and Vivian (C, H, M & S)	G.W.R. ..	Abertillery ..	Tom Evans ..	2,600
Price & Smith	Gwerthonor Quarry, Gilfach, near Bargoed	Rhoswen (H)	L. & N.W.R.	Bedwellty ..	—	12
*Rhymney Iron Co., Ltd.	F. B. Saunders, Merthyr House, Cardiff	Pengam (C, M & S)	B. & M.R. ..	Pengam ..	Edward Merriott	553
Richards, James & Co ..	D. O. Davies, Dowlais Chambers, Cardiff	Argoed (H, C & G)	L. & N.W.R.	Argoed ..	Hugh Caldwell	50
Salt, Thos. F.	Gwentland House, Oak Street, Abertillery	Arrel & Rhiw Colbren (H,S)	G.W.R. ..	Abertillery ..	Wm. James ..	30
Stone, J. & W.	Wm. Greyson, North Blaina Collieries, Blaina, Mon. (Head Office: 7 India Buildings, Liverpool).	North Blaina (C, M & S)	G.W.R. .. L.&N.W.R.	Blaina ..	T. R. Williams	496
Do.	Do.	North Blaina Slope ..	L. & N.W.R.	Brynmawr ..	Thos. Williams	207
Tir Pentwys Black Vein Steam Coal Co., Ltd.	B. Nicholas, Man. Director. Registered Offices: Osborne Road, Pontypool. W. S. Fletcher, Secretary—86, Dock St., Newport, Mon. and Exchange B'dings, Cardiff	Tir Pentwys (C & S)	G.W.R. ..	Pontypool ..	T. P. G. James	1,422

Source: The South Wales Coal Annual, 1915.

One of the major Monmouthshire concerns was the Powell Duffryn Company which also owned pits in the Rhymney and Cynon valleys. It was one of the companies which pioneered the greater use of coal by specialist treatment of it on the colliery premises. Here from a brochure issued by the Company is a description of this work at its Bargoed Colliery and it is followed by photographs of the coke ovens (Source 34) and the washery (Source 35) built at this Colliery:

Source 33

The small coal is brought by belt conveyors from the steam and bituminous pits at Bargoed to the Washery, where it is first separated into five sizes, the three larger of which are sold as nuts, beans and peas, and find a ready market,

both in this country and on the Continent. The two finer sizes are sent by aerial Ropeway to concrete bunkers at the coke ovens, having a capacity of 1,200 tons.
Source: Powell Duffryn Steam Coal Company 1864-1914, 1914.

Source 34

Source: Powell Duffryn Steam Coal Company 1864-1914, 1914.

Source: Powell Duffryn Steam Coal Company 1864-1914, 1914.

The Anthracite Coalfield

Problems in creating a demand for certain types of coal were not so easily overcome in West Glamorgan and Carmarthenshire and here the coal industry did not expand in the same way as it did elsewhere during this period. The local anthracite and semi-anthracite coal had particular qualities which led to problems in using anthracite in ironmaking, steam-engines and household grates. It was not until the 1880s that these problems were overcome and then anthracite found a growing use in stoves for home central heating, in hothouses and green-houses. As figures in Source 36 show, there-after there was a slow but steady growth in production and certainly the West Wales coal-field had a rare resource in its anthracite coal.

Compare these figures with Source 22, however, and you will see that up to 1920, at least, the anthracite industry was a fairly small part of the whole industry in South Wales:

Source 36

Year	Anthracite Output in South Wales	Anthracite Output in United Kingdom	Percentage of South Wales to Total
1900	2,203,468	2,5235,150	87.3
1905	2,789,178	3,112,054	89.6
1910	4,032,212	4,379,490	92.1
1914	4,370,239	4,718,993	92.6

Source: The South Wales Coal Annual, 1915.

Markets and Uses for South Wales Coal

Once it was shown in the 1850s and 60s that the deep steam coal of South Wales could be mined, the problem was no longer the winning of the coal but the winning of markets. Like all new products it had to be 'sold' to a possible market. This was why, as was mentioned earlier, George Insole took Robert and Lucy Thomas' coal to London in the 1830s. It was also why, when John Nixon took coal from the Cynon Valley to France, (as he mentions in Source 27) he actually gave it away and why David Davis published Source 26. What does he say there about the qualities of South Wales steam coal which he thinks are its best selling points? Who does he say backs up his opinion of his coal and why would this be important? Finding the answer to these questions will help towards discovering what the major market for South Wales steam coal became and why this helped the industry to grow so dramatically. A further clue comes from the names of many South Wales coal companies which have words such as 'Ocean', 'Naval' and 'Navigation' in their names? The crucial turning point was the various trials carried out by the Admiralty from the 1840s onwards to find the best coal for the use of the British Navy. Although the battle between South Wales and the North-East of England was to continue until 1875, the 3rd Report on these trials in 1851 just about clinched the result in favour of South Wales. Here is an extract from this report:

Source 37

THIRD REPORT.

TO THE RIGHT HONOURABLE LORD SEYMOUR.

MY LORD,

*Museum of Practical Geology,
2nd April, 1851.*

We have now the honour to present our Third and last Report on the value of different varieties of British Coals for the purposes of the Naval Service.

Table, shewing the average value of Coals from different localities.

Locality	Evaporating power or number of lbs of Water evaporated from 212° by One lb of Coal	Rate of evaporation or number of lbs of the ovaporated per hour	Weight of lbs of onecubic foot of Coal used as fuel	Space occupied by One Ton in Cubic Feet	Results obtained in experiments on Cohesive power of Coal	Per Centage amount of Sulphur obtained in Coal.
Average of 37 samples from Wales	9.05	468.2	53.1	42.71	60.9	1.42
do. 17 do. Newcastle	8.37	411.1	49.8	45.3	67.5	0.94
do. 28 do. Lancashire	7.94	447.6	49.7	45.15	73.5	1.42
do. 5 do. Scotland	7.70	431.4	50.0	49.99	73.4	1.45
do. 8 do. Derbyshire	7.58	432.7	47.2	47.45	80.9	1.01

Source: Report on the Coals Suited for the Steam Navy. Parliamentary Papers, 1851.

What was good enough for the British Navy was good enough for other navies in the world and for merchant ships as well. South Wales steam coal had been given the stamp of approval and the major expansion of the industry took place to meet the demands of steam-coaling stations all over the world. The importance of the export trade and the places

South Wales coal was sent to can be seen in the figures for 1914 from the South Wales Coal Annual (Source 38). Look back at Source 22 and work out what proportion of total output from the coalfield was exported. Source 39 (page 22) is a typical advertisement by a Coal Company on the qualities of its coal.

Source 38

*COAL EXPORTS, 1914.

SUMMARY OF TOTALS.

Geographical Division.	Cardiff.	Newport.	Port Talbot.	Neath.	Swansea.	Llanelly.	Total 1913
	Tons.	Tons.	Tons.	Tons.	Tons.	Tons.	Tons.
Arctic, Baltic and North Sea	286,695	6,508	2,807	..	188,570	22,363	1,041,797
Coasting Limits, Hamburg to Brest	966,091	151,594	69,234	..	751,289	92,322	3,929,718
North French Limits ..	771,584	165,679	415,855	..	391,053	2,598	2,891,101
North Spanish and Portuguese Limits	629,893	254,060	36,869	..	26,902	4,260	1,599,775
Near Mediterranean Limits ..	2,575,861	573,402	36,435	..	333,802	387	8,237,551
Upper Mediterranean Limits ..	1,908,316	44,141	9,018	..	11,729	..	2,120,704
North African, etc., Limits ..	553,277	201,851	15,468	..	48,598	..	1,508,540
West African Limits ..	575,700	4,077	20,187	..	6,836	24	1,336,775
East African Limits ..	145,187	19,187	5,284	..	1,408	..	304,673
Red Sea, Persian Gulf, Indian, etc., Limits	317,971	27,295	..	..	9,613	..	592,642
Far East Limits	43,212	..	..	..	1,003	..	109,026
Australasian and Pacific Island Limits	7,989	..	..	..	..	..	7,003
North and South America, Pacific Ports Limits ..	69,244	6,993	110,909	..	1,893	..	459,394
North and South America, Atlantic Ports Limits ..	2,194,634	450,757	2,636	..	12,034	796	5,512,517
Total Exports to foreign Countries	11,045,654	1,905,544	724,702	..	1,784,730	122,971	29,651,216

Source: The South Wales Coal Annual, 1915.

Although production for export dominated the South Wales coal industry and most of this was for use in steamships, as the following fixtures, taken from the records of the South Wales Coalowners Association, show, there were other uses and markets as well.

Source 40 *(See opposite column)*

It should also be remembered that many Colliery Companies earned extra profits and gave additional employment through what were known as 'subsidiary industries'. Many collieries had brickworks using clay from the underground workings to make bricks for their own use and for sale. Another example was wagon-making. At the Ferndale wagon shop of D. Davis and Co. wagons were made for their own use and that of other companies (Source 41).

Source 40

DISPOSITION OF THE TOTAL OUTPUT.

From Collieries in Monmouthshire and South Wales for the year ending 31st December, 1891—30,263,000 Tons.

Exported at Bristol Channel Ports, either as Coke, Coal, or Patent Fuel	18,540,000
Sent to Liverpool, London, and Southampton, for Shipment or Bunkers	1,925,000
Used at Iron Works, Tin Works, Steel Bar and Smelting Works	4,086,000
Consumed at Collieries	1,513,000
Converted into Coke	1,067,000
Locomotive Coal Supplied to the Railway Companies ...	950,000
Supplied to Workmen	580,000
Supplied for House Coal and Manufacture of Gas at Cardiff, Newport, and Swansea	390,000
Balance Supplied and Consumed for various purposes ...	1,212,000
	30,263,000

Source: South Wales Coalowners Association Records, National Library of Wales.

Source 39

Ocean (Merthyr) Steam Coal

Proprietors:

The Ocean Coal Company, Ltd., Cardiff

Output over 10,000 tons per day

This Coal is unrivalled for Steam Navigation and Railway Purposes. It is well known in all the Markets of the world for ECONOMY IN CONSUMPTION, ITS PURITY AND DURABILITY. It is largely and in many cases exclusively used by THE PRINCIPAL STEAM NAVIGATION COMPANIES at home and abroad.

Ocean (Merthyr) Steam Coal

was solely used by the Cunard Company Steamers "MAURETANIA" and "LUSITANIA" in creating a record for the most rapid Atlantic Passages. The OCEAN COMPANY supply the requirements of the ENGLISH ADMIRALTY for trial trips, for the use of the ROYAL YACHTS and other special purposes, and in addition the ITALIAN ROYAL NAVY and the SPANISH NAVY, as well as RAILWAY COMPANIES at home and abroad. THE OCEAN COAL COMPANY, LIMITED, have the largest un-worked area of the celebrated Four Feet Seam of Coal in South Wales.

Source: The South Wales Coal Annual, 1915.

Transport

Improvements in methods of transport were absolutely crucial to the development of the coal industry after 1840, for the mining areas were inland and isolated by poor transport facilities from the ports. The market for South Wales steam coal was to be mainly for export and so improved transport and dock facilities were essential. The building of canals between 1720 and 1840 did improve transport for industry in South Wales and they were particularly useful for carrying heavy loads like coal. The Glamorgan Canal from Merthyr to Cardiff, for example with its branch to Aberdare opened in 1804, was to help the early development of the sale-coal industry in the Cynon Valley as can be seen in Source 25.

It was, however, the coming of the railways which really opened up the steam coalfield after 1840 and made the great coal and export boom possible. The Taff Vale Railway from Merthyr to Cardiff was begun in 1841 and branch lines into the Cynon and Rhondda Valleys soon followed. By 1852 this line was linked to the Great Western Railway which joined South Wales to the Midlands and London, and as it snaked westwards across South Wales, branch lines were opened into the valleys of Monmouthshire, West Glamorgan and Carmarthenshire. Gradually each of the mining valleys were linked to the ports, and mining developments then became possible.

Source 41

Source: A. P. Barnett and D. Wilson-Lloyd (Eds.), *The South Wales Coalfield,* 1921.

Not only were the railways essential to the coal export trade, they also allowed easier travel by many miners to work and provided the only major alternative for the employment of men in the mining valleys outside the coal industry. In the difficult terrain of the valleys many great engineering feats were required to build the railways. Here is one of them, the Crumlin Viaduct, shown in 1857 (notice how rural the area still is at this time). It is followed by a photograph of coal wagons at the railway sidings near Ferndale Colliery and another showing the build up of wagons at Cardiff Docks which gives a striking impression of the size of the export trade and the importance of the railways to it.

Source 42

Source: The London Illustrated News, 1857.

Source 43

Source: A. P. Barnett and D. Wilson-Lloyd (Eds.), *The South Wales Coalfield,* 1921.

Source 44

Source: National Museum of Wales.

Docks *also grew dramatically*

The docks ~~which these wagons were waiting to~~ ~~enter had also grown dramatically.~~ In 1839 the building of the West Bute Dock at Cardiff marked the first development of the ports of South-East Wales (Cardiff, Barry, Penarth and Newport) which from 1850 onwards enabled them to overtake the early lead of Port Talbot, Llanelli and Swansea in coal export. Source 45 shows ships being loaded with coal from 'staiths' or coal-drops at Cardiff Docks in 1860 and it is followed by an advertisement of 1914 showing the facilities available and the trade of the port, which had grown into one of the busiest in the world.

Source 45

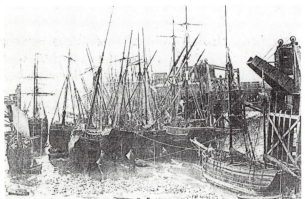

Source: Cardiff City Library.

Source 46

CARDIFF RAILWAY COMPANY.

BUTE DOCKS, CARDIFF.

Chairman: THE MARQUIS OF BUTE.
General Manager: C. S. DENNISS.

AREA, ETC.

The **Bute Docks** are 163 acres in extent, and vessels loading up to 12,000 tons regularly trade here.

The **Queen Alexandra Dock** has a water area of 52 acres. It is 2,550 feet in length, 800 to 1,000 feet in breadth, and 50 feet in depth from the coping, and is capable of accommodating the **Largest Vessels Afloat.** The Sea Lock is **850 feet in length** between the gates, and **90 feet in breadth,** with a depth of water over the sill of **42 feet** at ordinary spring tides, and **32 feet** at ordinary neap tides. This dock is connected with the Roath Dock, 33 acres in extent, by an intercommunication passage on the same water level; thus giving **85 acres** of modern walled dock accommodation. Vessels loading or unloading in either of the Bute Docks (excepting West) can enter or leave *via* Queen Alexandra Sea Lock.

WHARF SPACE AND YARDS.

Large provision is made for stacking Timber, Deals, Iron Ore, etc., Timber Ponds, **28 acres** in extent, with **Competitive Railway Communication to all parts.**

FACILITIES FOR SHIP REPAIRS, ETC.

There are **12 Private Graving and Floating Docks,** ranging up to **800 feet** in length, with **Separate Proprietaries,** and one Public Graving Dock **600 feet** in length. There are also several Marine Engineering Firms, thus giving Shipowners an opportunity of obtaining tenders for repairs of every description.

RAILWAY ACCOMMODATION.

Cardiff is the **Natural Port** for **Birmingham** and the **Midland District,** as the **London and North Western, Midland,** and **Great Western Railway Companies** have direct communication from the Ship's Side.

DOCK CHARGES.

These are much below the average of our **Great Ports.** Vessels can generally procure an outward cargo to any **Port in the World,** thus giving the **Bute Docks** an advantage for **Imports,** as vessels do not require to change ports.

TRADE.

The **Bute Docks** were opened in the year 1839, and the IMPORTS and EXPORTS in 1914 were as follows:—Imports, **1,881,394 tons;** Exports, **11,173,025 tons;** Total, **13,054,419 tons.**

Source: The South Wales Coal Annual, 1915.

The table in Source 47 taken from the South Wales Coal Annual of 1915, shows the rise of Cardiff, Newport and the fortunes of other South Wales ports during the great coal boom of the 19th century. Notice the rise of Barry Docks from 1889. They were built by David Davies of Llandinam and other Rhondda Coalowners to avoid what they considered to be the high charges made by Cardiff Docks. A new railway line linked the docks to the mines of the Upper Rhondda and soon Barry rivalled Cardiff as the greatest coal exporting port in the world. Source 48 is an aerial view of Barry Docks during their heyday.

Source 47

EXPORT OF COAL AND COKE AT SOUTH WALES PORTS						
Year	Cardiff	Penarth	Barry	Newport	Port Talbot	Swansea	Llanelli
1885	6,678,133	2,795,025	—	2,684,111	—	1,239,338	—
1895	7,542,220	2,507,913	5,051,822	3,359,829	—	1,721,079	—
1905	7,294,020	3,740,061	8,651,511	4,186,430	1,072,676	2,653,447	376,565
1914	10,278,963	3,992,405	10,875,510	5,465,713	1,711,808	3,749,449	288,762

Source: The South Wales Coal Annual, 1915.

Source 48

Source:
Aerofilms Limited.

It was not only the docks of the South Wales coastal towns which benefitted from the rise of the South Wales coal industry. Cardiff a tiny village of 1,870 in 1801 grew into Wales' premier town with a population of 164,333 a century later. Newport and Swansea were not far behind and all became bustling commercial centres. They were perhaps the major 'by-products' of the emergency of 'Coal Society', yet, although only a few miles away from the mining valleys, they developed as very different types of community.

Coalmining Techniques

The rise of the South Wales coal industry in the nineteenth century would not have been possible without improvements in the techniques of mining coal. In particular we need to look at changes in the way coal seams were reached, the methods that were used to actually mine the coal, the haulage and winding of coal from the coalface to the pit top and the ventilation and drainage of mines.

Reaching the Coal

Source 49

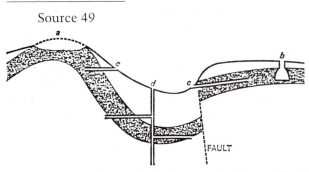

Types of coal-mining activities. Coal measures are shaded: a. Open-cast excavation; b. bell pit; c. drift mines; d. deep mines with shaft and galleries.
Source: D. Morgan Rees, *The Industrial Archaeology of Wales.*

The most straightforward method of reaching coal is opencast mining, which, when the coal seams come close to the surface, simply involves removing the top soil until the coal is exposed. This method is of course still used today, but up until the 19th century it was just about the only method of reaching coal used in South Wales, where it was known as 'outcropping' or working the coal 'patches'. This is why most early coalmining was done on the edges of the South Wales coal basin where the coal came close to the surface. The great advantage of this method was that it was cheap—all future advances to deeper and deeper seams would need increasing amounts of money to be spent before the coal was even reached. By the 19th century, however, the growing demand for coal from the iron industry meant that deeper seams had to be reached. This was done partly through what were known as 'bell pits'. Source 49 includes one illustration of these and Source 50 shows absolutely clearly what was involved and how these pits got their name.

Much more common at this time, however, was the driving of *drift mines*—a passage into a hillside to reach the coal seam. Source 49 also

Source 50

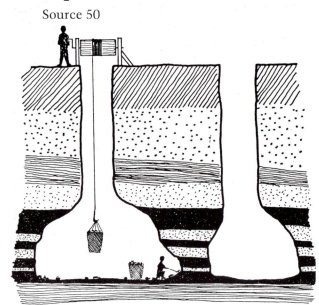

Source: D. Morgan Rees, *The Industrial Archaeology of Wales.*

shows this type of mining. These drifts were known either as *levels* or *slants* depending on the angle that they had to be driven at to reach the coal seams. These methods have also survived to the present day and slant mines have always been common in the anthracite coalfield of West Wales. Here is a photograph of an entrance to a slant mine at Cwm Mawr Colliery, Tumble in the 1950s.

Source 51

Source: National Museum of Wales.

By the 1840s most of the coal mined in South Wales was worked from levels and the evidence of this can be seen today on the hillsides along the Heads of the South Wales valleys. The great advantage of bell-pits and levels for the Ironmasters was that they could be abandoned once any problems such as flooding, gas, or roof-falls developed and new ones could be fairly cheaply opened to replace them. It took the demand for deep steam coal after 1840, therefore, to create a reason for methods of reaching coal to be developed. It was in fact the much greater time and expense involved in sinking deep shafts to reach steam coal which held back the development of the coal industry for so long. Details of the expenses involved in sinking John Nixon's Merthyr Vale Colliery between 1869 and 1875, give an idea of what was involved (Source 52). They are followed by two photographs: one is of sinkers at the Universal Colliery, Senghenydd in the 1880s and the second of the sinking of Markham Colliery in 1911 (Source 54, page 29). Why are the sinkers dressed as they are?

Source 52	
Labour	£79,245
Superintendence	9,708
Engine House	7,385
Machinery	11,167
Ropes	1,682
Rubbings, Castings etc.	33,746
Bricks	5,369
Timber, Nails etc.	13,267
Powder & stores	27,156
Sidings	4,922
Ironmongery & materials	1,671
Underground Rails & Sleepers	1,233
Horses and Keep	1,369
Cottages	22,028
Roads, streets & drains	2,364
Railway branch	12,942
Farm	2,757
Quarry	3,336
Rent, Rates & Taxes	2,589
Total	243,936

Source: South Wales Coalowners Association Records: National Library of Wales.

Source 53

Source: H. C. Jones, *Old Caerphilly and District in Photographs,* 1979.

Mining Coal

Once sinking was completed, passages (known as headings) would be driven from the bottom of the shaft to the coalface. Other passageways (known as roadways) would be driven so that coal and miners could travel back from the face to the shaft bottom and areas for stables, trams and machinery would also be laid out. The two sources below attempt to show what the layout would be like underground in these deep mines. The first is part of a plan of workings at the Merthyr Vale Colliery up to the end of 1877; the second is a diagram of a more modern colliery (Sources 55 and 56).

Source 55

Source: South Wales Coalowners' Association
Records; National Library of Wales.

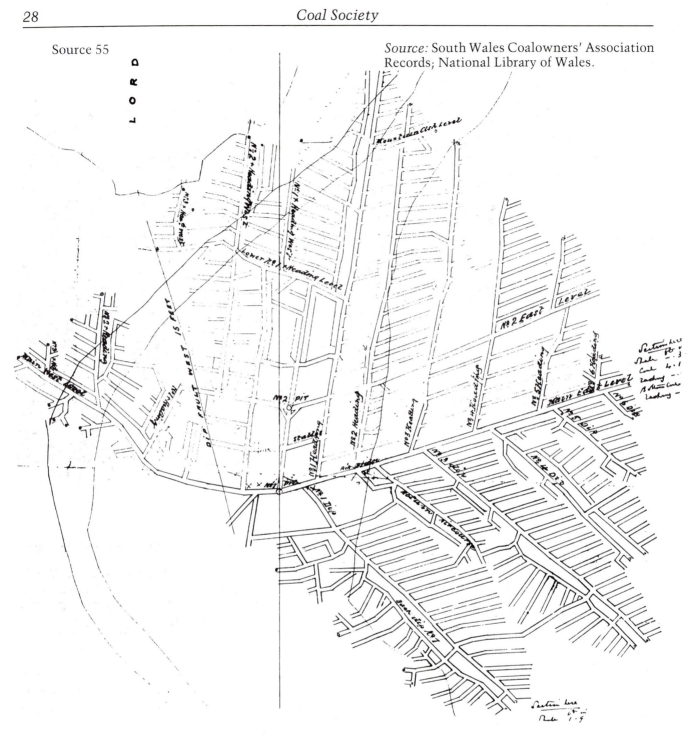

Source 56 *(See page 29)*

These two sources also show the different
methods of actually mining the coal which
developed in deep mines. In the first source it is
the *'pillar and stall'* method which is being
used. This account by a newspaper reporter in
1850 of mining at Abercarn Colliery describes
what this involved:

Source 57

Parallel with the roadway run what are called
the 'stalls', which are chambers whence the
workmen raise the coal . . . About every ten
yards pillars are left, thirty feet square . . . they
are afterwards either removed . . . or not, as the

necessities of the owner require . . . To these
stalls the trams are taken; they are then filled
with coal . . . marked with the miners' initials
and hauled away by horses, in order to be raised
above ground.

Source: The Morning Chronicle, 1850.

This method was to remain the most usual
one of mining coal in South Wales up to the
1860s. Why were the pillars left? Source 56
shows the method called 'longwall' which
replaced 'pillar and stall' in most South Wales
mines in the 1870s. This meant the whole coal
face being worked at once, with colliers moving
the face forwards as they mined the coal.
Timber pit props were used to do the job once

Source 54

National Museum of Wales.

Source 56

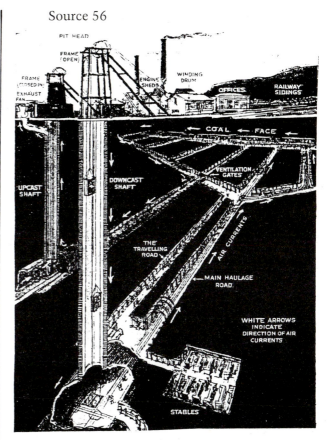

Source: M. H. Haddock, *In and Under Britain,* 1948.

done by pillars. Why would the Coalowners have been keen to replace 'pillar and stall' with the 'longwall'?

Whether by 'pillar and stall' or by 'longwall' the basic task of getting (or hewing) the coal was the job of the miner known as the *collier.* Although many kinds of machines were introduced into mines up to 1914, this work was nearly all done by the labour of the collier using mandril, shovel, curling-box and sometimes gunpowder. Source 58, taken from the South Wales Coal Annual in 1914, shows how few coal cutting machines were used in South Wales even compared to other coalfields. Compare the amount of coal obtained by machines to the overall production figures for 1914 given in Source 22, to see just how much coal was mined by hand. In the source which follows, E. H. Hann of the Powell Dyffryn Company explains to a Royal Commission in 1919 why so few machines had been introduced into South Wales mines:

Source 59

This slow progress is due chiefly to three things, firstly, most of the coal seams contain slips or breaks every foot or two, and thus loosen the coal, a feature peculiar to South

Source 58

COAL CUTTING MACHINES IN MINES.

NUMBER OF MACHINES, MOTIVE POWER EMPLOYED AND QUANTITY OF COAL OBTAINED BY THEIR USE, IN THE VARIOUS INSPECTION DISTRICTS DURING THE YEAR 1912

	1912		
DISTRICT.	Number of Machines	WORKED BY		COAL OBTAINED
		Electricity	Compressed Air.	
				Tons.
Durham	149	59	90	923,716
Liverpool & North Wales	148	24	124	1,270,645
Manchester & Ireland	159	9	150	542,027
Midlands & S'th'rn	147	58	89	1,124,561
Newcastle	255	51	204	1,745,595
Scotland	771	593	178	7,742,470
South Wales ..	111	50	64	592,529
Yorks. & N. Mid ..	601	290	311	6,184,421
Total 1912 ..	2,144	1,134	1,310	20,025,964
Total 1911 ..	2,146	998	1,148	18,666,677

Source: The South Wales Coal Annual, 1913.

Wales. Secondly, the weight or crush is far greater at equal depths in South Wales than in any of the other fields, thus rendering far more face timber necessary, and increasing the difficulty of safely maintaining the necessary space for the machine, likewise other troubles in the faces. Thirdly, the fact that small faults or dislocations are so much more numerous than in other districts, and so frequently prevent the development of or interrupt the progress of a face. A less frequent trouble is the presence of water which, however, is sometimes absolutely fatal to the attempt to use the machines.

Source: Report of the Royal Commission on the Coal Industry, 1919.

The photograph below shows miners working at a mine in Ton Pentre, Rhondda, and it is followed by a description of a collier's work by a Blaenavon miner.

Source 60

Source: K. Hopkins (Ed.), *Rhondda Past and Future*, 1975.

Source 61

Coal cutting in those days was a very skilled operation . . . if you had a pretty active roof. . . the coal would crush and it would be easy to mine, and your chief worry would be control of the roof. But other times you would have to hole or undercut it. You would lie on your side and hack away and hole it under as much as a yard. And then there were various methods of getting it down, sometimes you would have to sprag it . . . and then you would withdraw these sprags . . . You would hear groans and cracklings and it would fall. Otherwise you would have to drill a hole and put gunpowder in or use clamps and wedge . . . and that would exert the pressure on the coal and eventually bring it down.

Source: W. H. Taylor, Blaenavon. South Wales Miners Library Taped Interview.

Haulage and Winding

Once the coal had been mined it then had to be loaded into trams to be taken by the *haulier* to the pit bottom ready to be wound to the surface. In the early development of coalmining haulage would sometimes be done by human muscle power (look at Source 123 in Section IV), although as Source 12 shows the use of underground waggonways (or tramroads) also began very early. In the deep mines of the period after 1840 horses were used increasingly (look at Source 116 in Section IV for a photograph of a haulier with his horse), but as horses were expensive to buy and to keep, from 1860 onwards mechanical means of haulage were also being introduced. On the main roadways the haulier would link together a number of trams into what was known as a 'journey' and these would be hauled in to the pit bottom by wire ropes powered by an engine worked off compressed air. Similar advances were made in *winding* the coal up the pit. In the early shallow mines a windlass (to be seen in Source 50) or what was known as a 'horse-gin' or 'whimsey' (which used animal power on the surface) would be used. Source 11 shows a horse-gin being used and a detailed drawing of one taken from a mining textbook of 1887 appears in Source 62 *(See page 31).*

Eventually this was replaced by the water-balance, a method of winding which was only used in South Wales. Here is a photograph of a water balance at Cwmbyrgwm Pit and it is followed by an engineer's account of one in use at a Bargoed pit in 1862 (Source 64).

Source 63

Source: National Museum of Wales.

Source 64

The tram containing about 20cwt. of coal is placed on the top of an empty water bucket at the shaft bottom; and the empty tram on the

Source 62

Source: R. Hunt, *British Mining*, 1887.

bucket at the top; this bucket upon being filled with water descends, raising the full tram of coal and the empty bucket from the bottom. A valve is placed at the bottom of each bucket and immediately on its arrival at the shaft bottom, the valve is lifted and the water let off.

Source: Transactions of the Manchester Geological Society, 1862.

It was not until the 1870s and the spread of really deep mines that the water-balance was replaced by metal cages wound up and down shafts on steel ropes powered by steam-engines. It was then that the wood or metal headgear which was to become the typical symbol of a mine, became common. Just as common on a colliery surface were the engine-houses with their huge steam-engines which until the 20th century and the spread of electricity, became the main source of power on colliery sites.

Ventilation and Drainage

Steam-engines were also to be crucial in better drainage of mines. Water was always a great problem in mining. Underground streams and sometimes massive lakes were often disturbed by mining operations. The dangers of flooding were always present and some mines were permanently 'wet' with miners working up to their waists in water. In early mines (levels and slants) whenever possible drainage channels known as 'adits' were driven to carry off water naturally. In deeper mines until steam pumps

were developed, huge buckets were used to wind water up the pit. The steam pump was an important step forward but water continued to be a major problem in mining. So did the problem of gases which could either suffocate miners (carbon dioxide or 'choke damp') or, more seriously, explode when in contact with a naked flame (methane or 'fire-damp'). Disasters caused by gas as well as the many other dangers faced by miners are dealt with in Section IV of this book. Although Sir Humphrey Davy's famous safety-lamp did help to deal with the problems of gases in South Wales where the deep steam coal mines were known as being fiery and dangerous, better ventilation of mine workings was more important. Source 56 (look back at it again) shows that there was a second shaft in this colliery. How did this help with ventilation? The following account by a newspaper reporter in 1850 of the ventilation used at a Monmouthshire colliery helps to explain the system:

Source 65

The general system in use is extremely simple. Air becomes lighter as it is heated, and therefore ascends—the space which is occupied, being, in turn, filled with cold air which descends. As the workings proceed, two pits become necessary—one called the 'up-cast', for the ascending of the upward and impure current of air—the other the 'downcast' shaft for the downward supply of pure-air.

Source: The Morning Chronicle, 1850.

It was not until 1862, however, that second shafts were made compulsory by law and in many of the early deep mines young children were still employed to sit all day in the dark to open and close 'ventilation doors' to check the spread of foul air. One of the first artificial means used to improve underground ventilation was the use of a furnace at the bottom of the upcast shaft to increase the flow of impure air out of the mine. Here is a photograph of such a furnace at the Bwllfa Colliery, Aberdare in the early 1900s:

Source 66

Source: National Museum of Wales.

By the 1880s ventilating fans and pumps were being used in South Wales mines but until the introduction of electric fans in the twentieth century, the coalfield continued to have a bad reputation for its gassy and dangerous mines in which explosions, large and small, were frequent.

There can be no doubt then that the great demand for South Wales steam-coal from 1840 onwards did lead to major improvements in mining technique. These along with Acts of Parliament and the introduction of Mines Inspectors also helped to improve safety conditions below ground. However, the major factor in increasing the production of coal was the labour of the coalminers and they continued to face difficult and dangerous working conditions as we will see in Section IV of this book.

Further work on the evidence

1. Look carefully at Source 8 and then try to answer these questions:
   a. What type of historical evidence do you think this is for the history of the coal industry in Wales in the 15th century?
   b. What do you think is meant by the term 'sea-coal'? Why is it important to understand what such terms mean when you are using historical evidence?
   c. What do you think candles were being used for?
2. Look carefully at Source 26 and then try to answer these questions:
   a. Why is this a piece of primary historical evidence for a study of the development of the coal industry in South Wales?
   b. Why do you think David Davis created this piece of evidence?
   c. Describe in your own words the qualities which David Davis says his coal possesses, that will make it popular for use with steamships?
   d. Do you think David Davis is in a good position to supply the information given in this evidence? Why do you think he might be biased?
   e. What other piece of evidence in the previous section of the book backs up the claims that David Davis makes?
3. Look carefully at Sources 21, 25 and 43 and then try to answer these questions:
   a. What methods of transporting coal are shown in each of these sources?
   b. Why were the methods shown in Sources 25 and 43 important for the development of the coal industry in South Wales?
   c. Of the three sources which do you think is the most reliable piece of evidence? Why do you think this?

3.—The Coalowners
Landlords and Coalowners

Landlords and Leases

The first point to make about the Coalowners is that the vast majority of them did not actually *own* coal at all. They owned the equipment and the buildings of their collieries, but the actual land above and below ground, and the coal seams, belonged to *Landlords*. In Wales in the 1870s, 60% of the land was owned by great landowning families. The nobility and gentry of Wales who owned all this land added up to 571 people. For centuries these landlords had added to their wealth by renting out most of their land to farmers. When they discovered, however, that under their land there were valuable minerals such as coal, iron ore, copper and lead, they realised that here was another way of adding to their wealth. As we saw in the previous section of this book some Landlords worked these minerals themselves, but usually they preferred to lease these minerals and the land on which they were found, to men and companies who would develop them—these were the people who we refer to as the Coalowners. Source 67 is part of a lease whereby Crawshay Bailey (the landlord) leased out his mineral lands in the Upper Rhondda in 1866 to David Davis and his partners.

Source 67 *(See opposite column)*

Mineral Rights

Under the terms of such leases Landlords would receive three types of payment from the people or firm who worked their land. These are described below in an extract from a pamphlet on the coal industry written in 1919:

Source 68

(a) RENT—The price fixed upon for the use of the surface or ground on which a colliery with its buildings and rubbish tips is situated. The rent is an annual sum, generally for a term of years.

(b) ROYALTY—This is a payment which the land owner exacts for allowing the removal of the minerals from underneath the surface of the land. For practical purposes it is a kind of underground rent. It is generally calculated on a charge of so much per ton of coal raised, varying from 4d. to 2s. a ton, unless arrangements have been made for a lump sum royalty —called usually a dead rent.

(c) WAYLEAVES—Are payments extracted by the land owner for right of way. It is a tonnage charge on the conveyance of minerals

Source 67

DATED 15th JUNE, 1866.

CRAWSHAY BAILEY, Esq., M.P.,

TO

DAVID DAVIES and Others.

OF

COALS AND MINERALS

UNDER MAENDY, TON AND GELLY FARMS IN THE RHONDDA VALLEY, IN THE COUNTY OF GLAMORGAN.

TERM 60 YEARS,

FROM 29TH SEPTEMBER, 1866.

THIS INDENTURE made the 15th day of June, 1866, BETWEEN *Crawshay Bailey*, of Aberaman House, in the parish of Aberdare, in the county of Glamorgan, Esq., M.P., of the one part, and *David Davies*, of Llandinam, in the county of Montgomery, *Abraham Howell*, of Welshpool, in the same county, *Morgan Joseph*, of Ystradfechan, in the county of Glamorgan, *John Osborne Riches*, of Aberdare, in the same county, *Ezra Roberts*, of Tenby, in the county of Pembroke, and *Thomas Webb*, of Llandinam aforesaid (which last-named six persons are carrying on business at Ystrad, in the said county of Glamorgan and elsewhere, as coalmasters, in co-partnership under the name, style or firm of " David Davies & Co.," and are hereinafter designated or referred to as " The Lessees ") of the other part.

Source: Llandinam Papers, National Library of Wales.

over or under, the surface of land which is not part of the working area of a mine. This wayleave often amounts to some fraction of a penny, if not the whole penny, per ton on all coal raised from a colliery.

Source: J. Thomas, *The Economics of Coal*, 1919.

The income received in this way by Landowners could be considerable. In 1878 John Nixon had a survey made of how much his colliery company had paid since 1856 to their landlord, Lord Aberdare. These are the amounts that were paid under the terms of a lease signed in 1849:

Source 69

For the Upper Property 1856—1878:
£47,501.15.0. royalties
For the Lower Property 1858—1878:
£29,305.14.0. royalties

Source: South Wales Coalowners Association Records, National Library of Wales.

This of course was only for royalties—extra amounts were paid in rent and wayleaves. With this kind of income added to their existing wealth, the Landowners became even more rich and powerful. Lord Aberdare was able to build this fine house on his estate at Dyffryn near Mountain Ash:

Source 70

Source: W. W. Price Collection, Aberdare Public Library.

In 1925 it was calculated that the Marquis of Bute earned £115,000 annually from his mineral properties, Lord Tredegar earned £83,000 and the Earl of Dunraven £64,000. Perhaps it is not suprising that many people (including some Coalowners) were opposed to these men earning such fortunes simply because coal happened to be underneath their land.

Barriers

The ownership of coal by Landlords had two other harmful effects on the coal industry. As this map (Source 71) of royalty areas covered by the collieries of the Nixon, Taylor and Cory Company in the Merthyr Valley in 1878, shows, there could be many different royalty owners in one mining area.

Source 71 *(See page 35)*

To ensure that disputes did not develop between royalty owners as to who owned the coal on the boundaries of their land, large 'barriers' of coal were left unworked and this was obviously a loss to the mines working the area. For the same reason once a colliery had been sunk, rather than going to the furthest reaches of the coal seam and then working it back to the bottom of the shaft, the opposite happened and coal was worked from the bottom of the shaft until the royalty boundary was reached. This was a far more expensive way of mining and it also increased the dangers of mining. Why was this so?

Ownership and Management

The Iron Companies

The men who actually worked the early coal mines of South Wales were industrialists such as the Copper Works Owners and the Ironmasters. For them their coal mines were but one part of their total operation. Most of the coal being mined was used in their works, but they were always prepared to sell any surplus. This part of their business grew as the coal industry expanded after 1840, particularly from the 1860s when the old ironworks went into decline because of the increase in steel production. For example, the Merthyr Ironmasters increased their sale of coal from 166,000 tons in 1865 to nearly 350,000 tons by 1871. Because the royalties they had to pay were quite low (their leases had been drawn up in the late 18th century) and because they paid their miners lower wages, they were able to compete successfully with the 'sale-coal' owners. By the late 19th century many former iron companies such as Crawshays, Dowlais and Rhymney had become more coal, than iron producers.

Individual Owners

The single individuals and partners who opened up the successful steam coal collieries after 1840 (individuals like Thomas Powell, David Davies and John Nixon who were mentioned in the previous section of this book) came to the coal industry from a variety of backgrounds. Some were trained engineers or mineral agents who had worked already in the iron and coal industries—men such as W. T. Lewis who as Lord Merthyr was to become one of the most powerful of the Coalowners. Some were contractors—men like David Davies of

Source 71

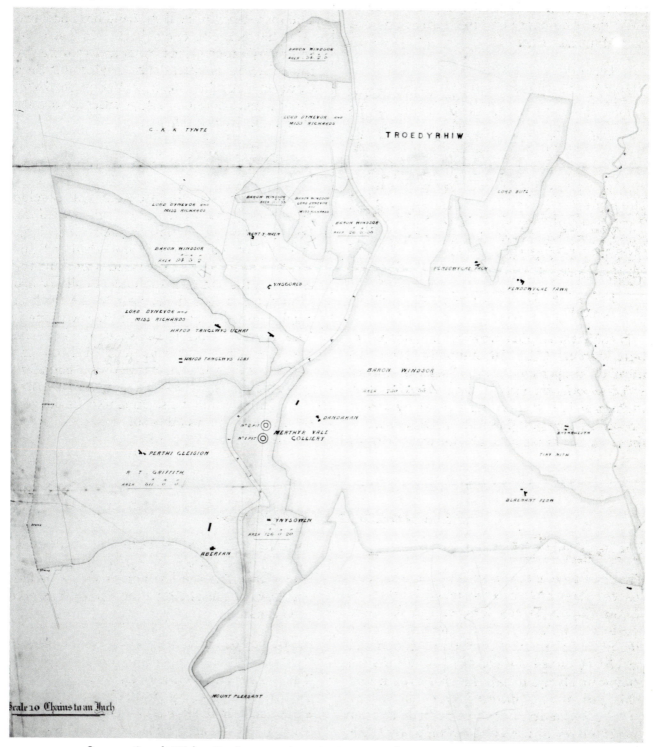

Source: South Wales Coalowners Association Records, National Library of Wales.

Llandinam who had made his name in building railway lines in Mid-Wales. Others were merchants and shipowners who after seeing the expansion of coal exports, decided to become involved in coal production as well—men such as George Insole and the Cory brothers. A few came from even more humble origins—Samuel Thomas, whose company eventually grew into the giant Cambrian Combine controlled by his son Lord Rhondda, started as a shopkeeper in Merthyr. Particularly in the anthracite coalfield of West Wales during this period, pits tended to be small scale concerns with the owners often being small farmers and sometimes even ex-miners who owned only one colliery.

The reason why individuals with quite modest amounts of money could set up as Coal-owners was because not much capital was needed to start mining operations. As pits became deeper and more equipment and miners were needed, the extra capital required was raised by putting back profits into the company and occasionally by raising mortgages or bank loans. These figures for David Davies' collieries in the Upper Rhondda show this steady type of growth and how the extra cost of paying miners was the main increase which Owners had to meet:

Source 72	Maendy	Parc	Dare	Eastern
Date when coal was first worked	May 1866	Aug. 1866	April 1870	July 1877
Total No. of men employed 1870	528	678	310	—
1880	810	832	354	460
1890	1,220	748	388	1,018
Gross Total of coal raised 1870	144,133	177,357	19,781	—
1880	277,788	248,460	190,605	157,390
1890	287,911	184,402	255,699	291,796
Gross Wages paid 1870 £60,000				
1900 £691,000				

Source: E. D. Lewis, *The Rhondda Valleys*, 1959.

Colliery Companies

The main way of increasing capital, however, was by the original single owner taking on partners or by forming *limited liability companies*. Here is an example of a partnership formed in 1858:

Source 73

The Penygraig Colliery, Rhondda Valley, was started in 1858 by Messrs. Moses Rowlands, mechanical engineer, Dinas; William Morgan, builder, Newbridge (Pontypridd); William Williams, clerk, Pontypridd, and John Crockett, jeweller, Pontypridd, afterwards known as the Penygraig Coal Company. Associated with the above, if not in actual partnership, were Mr. Evan Llewellyn, ironmonger, Pontypridd, and the celebrated old geologist, Richard Jenkins, advised Messrs. Rowlands and Co. where to start, and where to find the outcrop of the upper seams of coal—notably the No. 2 Rhondda.

Source: E. Phillips, *A History of the Pioneers of the Welsh Coalfield*, 1925.

Here are some details of a limited liability company (which became the main type of colliery concern)—D. Davis and Sons Ltd., which was formed in 1890 and owned pits in the Rhondda Fach:

Source 74

D. DAVIS & SONS, LTD.

DIRECTORS :
Frederick Lewis Davis (Chairman) ;
David Hannah, Jules Vasse, Thomas Vivian-Rees, Harry Leonard Warner and John Bell White.
SECRETARY AND GENERAL COMMERCIAL MANAGER :
T. Vivian-Rees.
Telegraphic Address : " FERNDALE, CARDIFF."
Telephone Number, 1192 Nat.
COLLIERY ENGINEER : David Hannah.

Capital and Debentures.

45,000 Ordinary Shares of £10 each, fully paid	£450,000
10,000 6% Cum. Pref. Shares of £10 each, fully paid	100,000
750 5% "B" Debenture Bonds of £100 each, fully paid	75,000
	£625,000

Annual Output about 1,750,000 tons.

Source: *South Wales Coal and Iron Companies*, 1911.

Although these companies issued shares to raise their capital, most of these shares were held by the Directors, who were in effect the Owners. Very few of these shares would be offered to the general public. So although by the end of the 19th century very few collieries were owned by a single man, ownership was still in very few hands. This was also because many Coalowners were directors of a number of colliery firms. Here for example, are details of some of the directors of the Ocean Coal Company in 1917:

Source 75

Mr. WILLIAM JENKINS is Director of:
Ocean Coal and Wilson's.
Deep Navigation Collieries Company.
Barry Railway Company (Aberconway Group).

Lieut.-Col. EDWARD JONES is Director of:
Ocean Coal and Wilson's.
Deep Navigation Collieries Company.
Mr. THOMAS EVANS is Director of:
Cardiff Coal and Shipping Exchange.
Ocean Coal and Wilson's.
Barry Railway Company.
Dinan Coal Company.
Sir H. WEBB is Director of:
Lillovet Holdings (Calgary, B.C.).
Deep Navigation Collieries Company.
Ocean Coal and Wilson's.

Source: G. Harvey, *Capitalism in The South Wales Coalfield*, 1918.

Source 76 is a photograph of the Board of Directors of the Bwllfa and Merthyr Dare Steam Collieries Ltd., in 1919 and it is followed by evidence given by a Coalowner to the Royal Commission on the Coal Industry, in the same year, on the work done by Directors.

Source 77

Directors have to appoint their agents and managers very often . . . then they have to meet regularly to examine all purchases, invoices, sign cheques and everything of that sort. Then their duty is to have a policy as to the development of the mine . . . We are constantly taking up new agreements and leases of all sorts and descriptions . . . My experience is the directors are a very important body in any colliery concern, especially in our complicated ones in South Wales . . . Our directors meet fortnightly and it takes them about three hours to get through their routine work . . . The salary of each of the 4 Directors is £400 a year . . .

Source: Report of the Royal Commission on the Coal Industry, 1909.

Source 76

BOARD OF DIRECTORS AND SECRETARY.
[*Photo by H. J. Whitlock & Sons, Cardiff, 1919.*

From left.—Mr. D. R. Llewellyn, J.P.; Mr. Thos. Leyson; the late Mr. Wm. Davies, J.P.; the late Mr. Rees Llewellyn. J.P. (*Chairman*); Capt. T. Ernest Malyon, T.D., F.C.I.S.(*Secretary*); Mr. F. W. Mander, J.P.; Colonel M. H. Grant; Mr. E. W. Arnott.

Source: A. P. Barnett and D. Wilson-Lloyd (Eds.), *The South Wales Coalfield*, 1925.

Coal Combines

By 1873 most of the major colliery companies in South Wales had been formed and here are the production figures of the ten largest companies for that year:

Source 78

Ebbw Vale Steel, Iron & Coal Co.	1,020,000 tons
Blaenavon Iron & Steel Company	915,613 tons
Powell Duffryn Coal Company	817,000 tons
The Dowlais Iron Company	800,000 tons
The Tredegar Coal & Iron Co.	564,608 tons
David Davies & Company	500,000 tons
Glamorgan Coal Company	500,000 tons
David Davis & Sons	485,000 tons
The Rhymney Iron Company	400,000 tons
The Aberdare Iron Company	454,000 tons

Source: South Wales Coalowners Association Records, National Library of Wales.

Notice how many of these are the old iron companies and that only one firm produced more than a million tons. There were a host of middle and small size companies as well, with the Swansea Valley Steam Colliery Company, for example, producing only 8,387 tons.

From 1873 up to 1920 some companies grew much more than others and as they did so they took over smaller companies and thereby production became concentrated in the hands of a smaller and smaller number of companies. These giant 'combines' as they were known dominated the coalfield by 1914. Amongst the biggest were the Cambrian Combine which controlled 7.3 million tons, United National with 2.4 million and T. Beynon and Company which produced 4.8 million tons. Altogether these giant firms (which also had interests in many other industries) controlled 40% of the total output of South Wales by 1914. Here are details of the various firms taken over by the Cambrian Combine, headed by Lord Rhondda, between 1910 and 1916, and their production figures:

Source 79

Lord Rhondda's group—	Output Tons.
Cambrian Collieries	986,000
Albion Steam Coal Company	375,000
Glamorgan Coal Company	905,000
Naval Colliery Company	595,000
Britannic Merthyr Company	230,000
D. Davis & Sons, Ltd., and Welsh Navigation	1,900,000
North's Navigation	1,219,000
Cynon	180,000
Celtic Collieries	160,000
Gwaun-cae-gurwen	310,000
Imperial Navigation	315,000
International	180,000
Total	7,355,000

Source: Report of the Commission Appointed to Inquire Into Industrial Unrest, 1917.

Profits

It was these large Combines, of course, which made the biggest profits. Whereas the Coal-owners tended to play down the size of their profits, the miners and their union pointed to examples of huge profits being made. It would seem that for every John Nixon (who died a millionaire) there were many coalowners who went bankrupt. This was particularly true after 1840 when companies were formed with too little money and the pits sunk produced little quality coal. Of the 53 companies formed in the coalfield between 1856 and 1867 only 7 still survived in 1875. Even those which did survive often had to wait many years more before they began to be in profit and even successful firms like Powell Duffryn and the Glamorgan Coal Company made little or no profit until the 1890s. From then on, however, most of the large companies made very high profits as the steam-coal trade of South Wales went through a continuing boom. Here, for example, are extracts from the balance sheets of D. Davis and Sons Ltd., in 1910.

Source 80

D. DAVIS & SONS, LTD.
Summary of Balance Sheet, December 31st, 1910

12 Years' Profits and Dividends

Dividends			Profits
Prefs.	Ordy.		
6%	10%	1910	£175,920
6%	10%	1909	90,685
6%	10%	1908	168,724
6%	10%	1907	229,699
6%	10%	1906	169,236
6%	5%	1905	60,647
6%	10%	1904	65,741
6%	10%	1903	62,775
6%	10%	1902	129,360
6%	10%	1901	138,919
6%	10%	1900	94,721
15%	8¾%	1899	149,057
			£1,535,484

Source: South Wales Coal and Iron Companies, 1911.

It is likely that on average, profits of about 10% a year were made in the period up to 1914. Obviously there were good and bad years and some companies made much bigger profits than this. It seems to have been precisely the attraction of making high profits which attracted businessmen into the coal industry, which was a high-risk business where it would be just as possible that you might fail. Why do you think this was?

It also has to be remembered that not all the profits made went into the pockets of the Coalowners for they had to be used for other purposes. The figures below show how some Colliery Companies in South Wales distributed their profits between 1899 and 1914. *Dividends* were amounts of money paid to people who held shares in the company. *Debentures* were a kind of loan on which repayments had to be made. *Capital* expenditure and *depreciation* was money spent (or lost) on maintaining and extending a colliery and its equipment.

Source 81

Colliery	Dividends	Debenture Interest	Debenture Redemption	Capital Expenditure	Depreciation	Reserve	Balance	Other	Total Profit
	£	£	£	£	£	£	£	£	£
Albion	279,579	6,472	57,750	58,477	0	0	16,638	1,933	421,049
D. Davis & Sons	1,134,921	183,813	240,480	450,772	0	200,000	81,432	0	2,291,427
Great Western	658,750	0	0	225,000	55,000	101,181	50,444	0	1,090,375
Insoles Ltd.	283,200	46,875	10,500	13,818	0	47,000	10,082	8,216	419,691
International	138,550	2,493	15,015	34,420	0	40,000	3,352	0	233,830

Source: R. Walters, *The Economic and Business History of the South Wales Steam Coal Industry, 1977.*

However, as the Directors of Colliery Companies owned most, and sometimes all, the shares, they received most of the dividends paid out to add to their salaries and fees as Directors. Obviously there were exceptions, but many Coalowners became exceptionally rich through profits they received during these boom years of the coal industry.

Managers and Officials

Source 82 shows Officials employed by the Onllwyn Colliery in the Dulais Valley, owned by Evans, Bevan and Co. brings us to the people who actually controlled the day-to-day affairs of collieries. In the early years of the industry there were owners who also acted as managers, but by the 1870s as companies grew and mining became more technical, nearly all mines had properly trained managers. In 1872, by Act of Parliament, it became the law for managers to undergo proper training to achieve a manager's certificate and the same Act laid down the duties of Managers and other officials. Here for example, are some of the duties of a Manager:

Source 83

1. He has the responsible charge and direction of the mine . . .
2. He has the control of all officers and of all other persons employed in or about the mine . . .
3. He shall lay out the ventilation of the mine . . .

Source: Mines Act, 1872.

Under Managers assisted Managers and had special responsibilities for safety in the mine

Source 82

Source: National Museum of Wales.

and the way that miners carried out their work. *Overmen* would be next in line and would take special responsibility for certain areas of a mine. *Firemen* had to have special qualifications in safety regulations. What do you think were the responsibilities of the *Weighers* and the *Master Hauliers?*

The way in which officials received their training varied. Many of them started life as ordinary miners and either through self-education (reading books, taking correspondence courses) or through evening-classes, studied to pass their certificate exams. Until the Treforest School of Mines (now the Polytechnic of Wales) was opened in 1913 there was nowhere in South Wales where men could study full-time for their certificates. This meant that many managers were brought in to South Wales from other coalfields, especially the North-East of England, where such training was available. As a Government Enquiry in 1917 reported, this could often lead to problems:

Source 84
The introduction into the district of managers and other officials who have no experience of the Welsh outlook—and no knowledge of the Welsh language . . . (leads to) misunderstanding and friction . . . the Welsh collier . . . is quick to resent any temper or violence of language towards himself on the part of those placed in authority over him.
Source: Report of the Commission Appointed to Inquire into Industrial Unrest, 1917.

So whilst managers and other officials had great power and authority over miners, because of this they were often the target of dislike. The evidence of one Colliery Manager makes this point very humorously:

Source 85
The old Tredegar manager often stated that a Colliery manager should retire from his job at least five years before his death, so that he would have time to prepare for heaven. There was no hope of his going there straight from his job.
Source: The Colliery Workers Magazine, April 1925.

The Lifestyle, Attitudes and Reputation of the Coalowners

Some Coalowners rose by their own efforts from fairly humble backgrounds to positions of importance. David Davies of Llandinam, for example, was the son of a small farmer in Montgomeryshire who through his own efforts, first in his trade as a sawyer and later as one of the first railway builders in Wales, accumulated the money which enabled him to become a Coalowner. Here from a history of the South Wales Coalowners written in 1919 is the similar story of Evan Evans who became a Coalowner in the Gilfach Valley:

Source 86
A farmer in the Neath valley, he decided to leave and seek his fortune in Merthyr . . . he began in the Merthyr collieries as a haulier, afterwards rising to be a first class collier. He was always steady, hard-working, and thrifty, and from the first saved money . . . he invested in a public-house and became an inkeeper in Merthyr. He made a great success of this and finally set up his own brewery . . . it seemed only fair that the money got from the colliers for drink should go back to them as wages for honest work . . . and he decided to speculate in coal mining . . .
Source: E. Phillips, *A History of the Pioneers of the Welsh Coalfield,* 1925.

Many early coalowners were Welshmen, unlike the ironmasters of a century before who had nearly all come from England. They lived among their workers in the new mining communities, spoke the Welsh language and shared the religious (Nonconformist) and political (Liberal) views of many of the miners. They often argued that they were every bit as interested in helping those who they gave work to, as in helping themselves. This is how Lord Rhondda (once D. A. Thomas) the head of the great Cambrian Combine, made this point in a letter he wrote in 1916:

Source 87
I have provided men with the means to pay for the food and clothing of themselves and their families . . . I say that I am out for the game and not for the stakes . . . By increasing the means of the people I have contributed more to the material happiness and wellbeing of Welsh colliery workers and their families than have all the miners leaders combined . . . Believe me, I am not out for the accumulation of wealth for its own sake . . . The only value of wealth is the influence and power it places in the hands of its possessor to do good . . .
Source: The South Wales Daily News, 14 February, 1916.

It is true that many did use some of their money to do good. They gave money for the opening of schools, chapels, workmen's institutes, libraries and hospitals in the new mining communities, for example. Many also became involved in charitable and social work, such as Lord Merthyr (W. T. Lewis). His work in this field is described here in a history of the Coalowners:

Source 88
The Miner's Provident Society of South Wales and Monmouthshire . . . was the idea of Lord Merthyr and to his efforts it owes great success. It was established in 1881 and up to 1907 the miners had contributed a sum amounting to £691,051—and the masters £278,870 . . . The society had been able to pay out in relief to widows, children, old-age pensioners and injured workmen—£868,474 . . . in spite of Lord Merthyr's somewhat terrifying presence there was no kinder heart.

Source: E. Phillips, *A History of the Pioneers of the Welsh Coalfield,* 1925.

The public work of the Coalowners also involved them in acting as Justices of the Peace, Poor Law Guardians, Councillors and sometimes M.P.s. D. A. Thomas, for example, was elected Liberal M.P. for Merthyr Tydfil in 1888 and he continued to serve the town up to 1910. For the last ten years of this period the second M.P. for Merthyr was the ex-miner and Socialist politician Keir Hardie. Thomas, however, always pushed him into second place in elections and like all Coalowners who were successful in politics, he proudly argued that this showed he had the support of the whole mining community. In general, the Coalowners were confident that they had the support and affection of their workers. In a book written on the life of one of them—Lewis Davis of Ferndale— by the minister of his chapel, the story is told of how he gave money to one workman who could no longer work because of illness. The writer tells how he visited this miner on his death bed and recalls that this is what he had to say about Lewis Davis:

Source 89
Will you please carry to my master my thanks. Tell him he has kept my home for my family and me for ten years, and, next to God, we owe him all. He has given us fifteen shillings every week . . . He has trusted his workmen and they had faith in their master; they honoured him as a prince . . .

Source: D. Young. *A Noble Life: Incidents in the Career of Lewis Davis of Ferndale,* 1899.

Lewis Davis in fact was one of the few important Coalowners by the 1890s who continued to live most of the time near to their collieries. Here is the home which Lewis Davis built for himself at Ferndale in the Rhondda.

Source 90

Source: D. Young, *A Noble Life: Incidents in the Career of Lewis Davis of Ferndale,* 1899.

By the end of the 19th century most Coalowners had bought themselves large houses in big estates of land near to Cardiff and Swansea and completely removed themselves from the daily life of the valley communities. Here for example are details of the many interests of Lord Rhondda (shown below with colliery officials at his Llanmaes Colliery) and the home he was able to own as a result of them:

Source 91

Source: National Library of Wales.

Source 92
Lord Rhondda, when he was appointed, in 1917, President of the Local Government Board, had to retire from the Directorates of more than thirty Coal, Iron, Steel, Shipping and Railway Companies. His interests were world-wide . . . He held large coal properties in the United States of America . . . and Canada . . . He was the owner of the famous Llanwern

Estate, with historic Llanwern House near Newport . . . the ownership of which made him the largest landowner in Monmouthshire, with the exception of Lord Tredegar.

Source: G. Harvey, *Capitalism in the South Wales Coalfield*, 1918.

David Davies returned to his native Montgomeryshire and built himself a mansion (Broneirion) there. Here is a photograph of it and it is followed by a photograph of David Davies about to set off hunting from his home towards the end of his life:

Source 93

Source: I. Thomas, *Top Sawyer: A Biography of David Davies of Llandinam*, 1938.

Source 94

Source: I. Thomas, *Top Sawyer: A Biography of David Davies of Llandinam*, 1938.

In June 1873, David Davies' son Edward celebrated his 21st birthday. Great celebrations were held at Llandinam in Montgomeryshire. 6,000 guests were invited and 3,400 of them were brought on four special trains from the Davies' pits in the Upper Rhondda. Here is a photograph of the scene at Llandinam on this occasion:

Source 95

Source: I. Thomas, *Top Sawyer: A Biography of David Davies of Llandinam*, 1938.

Such a lavish use of their wealth was a fairly rare incident for the Coalowners. They were usually very careful men whose religious views went against such displays. However, it is clear that their life style was now becoming totally different to that of their workers.

The other thing which began to distance them from their workmen was their whole attitude to them. There was nothing unusual at the time in a strict dividing line between 'master' and 'workmen'. But the Coalowners do seem to have been particularly hard employers. Times changed but the Coalowners did not seem to change with them and by the early 20th century it is clear that miners were becoming more and more hostile towards the great Coal Combines and their attitude to their workers. This sort of attitude can be seen in this extract from a book written by Alexander Dalziel, the Secretary of the South Wales Coalowners' Association and himself a Coalowner. The book dealt with the strike of 1871 in the coalfield and this is how he describes the miners at the end of it:

Source 96

The period of the strike resulted in a diminution (decrease) of the physical power of the workmen and fully two months elapsed before they could be said to have been restored to good working condition.

Source: A. Dalziel, *The Colliers Strike in South Wales*, 1872.

This treatment of miners as almost products rather than human beings can also be seen in the attitude the Owners had to the wages which should be paid to their workers. Here is how a newspaper cartoonist tried to show this:

Source 97

LOW WAGES.   MODERATE WAGES.   HIGH WAGES.

Work and Wages.
Source: The Western Mail, 12 March, 1902.

A further example is the attitude many Coalowners had to accidents in mines. They often blamed gas explosions on workers smoking their pipes. They always fought against paying compensation for deaths and injuries in the mine and a Government Mines Inspector noted in 1856 how difficult it was for a collier's wife to get a coroner's inquest to find a Coalowner guilty of neglect:

Source 98

All interests are against the survivors. The colliers, the jury . . . are subject to the influence of the proprietor of the colliery. The cost of an action . . . the difficulty of obtaining a solicitor . . . form an insuperable (can't be overcome) bar to the claim of the widow.

Source: Mines Inspector's Report, 1856.

They were always ready, however, to bring miners to court for breaches of contract and Colliery Rules, which if they were found guilty could lead to fines, losing their job and imprisonment.

Most Coalowners were totally against their workers forming trade-unions. For many years the 'discharge-note' was a powerful weapon which they used against trade-unions. Through this system, no worker could leave one colliery and start at another unless he had been given a note by his previous employer saying that he was a good and reliable workman. In general

they were prepared to use any means to break up organisations. In the strike of 1871, for example, led by the Amalgamated Association of Miners, the Coalowners brought in large numbers of 'blacklegs' from outside South Wales to break the strike. Their general attitude towards unions is shown below in Alexander Dalziel's view of the 1871 strike and twenty-two years later, Lord Aberdare in a letter (Source 100) shows how they were still prepared to use any means to oppose unions:

Source 99

It is with this section that the masters have most difficulty in dealing. It is composed of the noisiest and the laziest of them all—men who are neither willing to work, nor content that others should. They are the more rampant of the members of the Union—leading a life of idleness.

Source: A. Dalziel, *The Colliers Strike in South Wales*, 1872.

Source 100

We have had a lovely time since you left. Forty soldiers quartered at Mountain Ash, forty at Aberaman, forty at Aberdare, besides some twenty of the 14th Hussars. Their presence had a very quieting effect . . . The strike would not have lasted half the time, had not the weather been so fine . . .

Source: Letters of . . . Lord Aberdare of Duffryn, 1902.

What particularly annoyed the miners about this, was that the Owners had their own organisation which united them. The South Wales Coalowners Association was formed in 1873 and although not all Coalowners belonged to it (the Ironmasters in particular continued to compete rather than co-operate with other Owners) and there were divisions amongst them on many things, they were united in this body in opposing all attempts to increase miners' wages and in trying to get higher production from their workers. Wages were by far and away the highest part of the Coalowners costs and so their best means of increasing their profits was to keep wages down as much as possible. The Coalowners in South Wales were particularly concerned about wages because the amount of coal produced by each collier in the coalfield was much lower than in other British Coalfields as the figures in Source 101 *(See page 44)* show.

Source 101

Year.	Number of Persons Employed.			OUTPUT.			Production per person employed	
	South Wales.	Total for United Kingdom.	Proportion of South Wales in total.	South Wales.	Total for United Kingdom.	Proportion of South Wales in total.	South Wales.	United Kingdom.
1899	132,682	715,205	18·6	39,870,097	220,094,781	18·1	302	314
1900	147,652	766,901	19·2	39,328,209	225,181,300	17·4	268	300
1901	150,394	792,648	19·0	39,209,260	219,046,945	17·9	262	281
1902	154,571	810,787	19·0	41,305,583	227,095,042	18·2	268	285
1903	159,161	828,968	19·2	42,154,191	230,334,469	18·3	266	283
1904	163,034	833,629	19·5	43,730,415	232,428,272	18·8	269	284
1905	165,609	843,418	19·6	43,203,071	236,111,150	18·3	262	285
1906	174,660	867,152	20·1	47,055,969	251,050,809	18·7	271	294
1907	190,263	925,097	20·5	49,978,196	267,812,852	18·6	264	294
1908	201,752	972,232	20·7	50,227,113	261,512,214	19·2	250	273
1909	204,984	997,708	20·5	50,363,937	263,758,562	19·1	247	268
1910	213,161	1,032,702	20·6	48,699,982	264,417,588	18·4	229	260
1911	220,815	1,049,897	20·7	50,200,727	271,891,899	18·9	228	262
1912	225,483	1,072,393	21·0	50,116,264	260,398,578	19·2	223	245
1913	233,091	1,110,884	21·0	56,830,072	287,411,869	19·7	245	262

Source: The South Wales Coal Annual, 1915.

The Owners believed that the main reason for this was that colliers in south Wales were only prepared to produce enough to earn them sufficient wages in a week and not to produce as much as they possibly could in the time they were in work. H. A. Bruce in a letter he wrote in 1868 described why he thought miners in South Wales were against the introduction of a double-shift system which was used in other coalfields:

Source 102

The men are suspicious and believe that what is advantageous (an advantage) to the master must be injurious (harmful) to the men ... the Aberdare collieries are worked at a cost of nearly fifty per cent above those of the North.

Source: Letters of . . . Lord Aberdare of Duffryn, 1902.

The miners argued that the real cause of this situation was the difficult conditions which they had to face in South Wales collieries. The battle over this question, which increased with the growth of the giant Coal Combines on one side and the South Wales Miners Federation on the other, was to dominate the years from the start of the twentieth century up to 1914. There is no doubt that during this period the hostility of miners towards Coalowners increased considerably. One miners' leader, Noah Ablett, summed up in 1922 what these growing battles were all about as follows:

Source 103

The miner now realises that he is considered merely as a cog in the great mining machine: he doesn't know his employer, he only knows of some limited company. The character of the miners' demands during recent years has changed: the question of wages does not now receive any more attention than the question of status . . .

Source: N. Ablett, What we want and Why, 1922.

Further work on the evidence

1. Look at Source 67 and then try to answer the following questions:
   a. What words in this Source do you find it difficult to understand? Use the Glossary at the back of this book to see if you can find an explanation for what these words mean.
   b. What is the name of the Landowner who is leasing out his land?
   c. Who are the 'six persons' referred to and why are they leasing the land?
   d. The rest of this document (which you are not supplied with) goes on to deal with the *royalties* and wayleaves to be paid to the Landowner. Using Source 68 explain what these were.

2. Look at Source 77 and then answer the following questions:
   a. Name *three* things that the person giving this evidence says Colliery Directors do.
   b. This evidence is given by Hugh Bramwell, a South Wales Coalowner and Colliery Director. Do you think he is in a good position to supply this evidence? Explain your answer.
   c. On the basis of the evidence he gives do you agree with him when he says "directors are a very important body in any colliery concern"? Explain your answer.
   d. This evidence was given to a Royal Commission which was investigating the question of whether or not the coal industry should be nationalised (taken over by the State). What light does this throw on the value of the evidence given by Bramwell?

3. Source 86 comes from a history of the South Wales Coalowners which was first published in a series of articles in the newspaper, *The Western Mail*, in 1924. This newspaper was well known for supporting the Coalowners. Bearing this in mind, look at Source 86 and try to answer these questions:
   a. Does this Source provide us with first-hand information on how and why Evan Evans became a Coalowner? Explain your answer and try to decide whether

this is an example of primary or secondary historical evidence.
   b. What does the Source tell us about how Evan Evans got the money to become a Coalowner?
   c. What does the Source tell us about why Evan Evans became a Coalowner? Do you think this explanation is reliable? Explain your answer and consider other reasons he may have had.

4. Look at Source 88 (which comes from the same book as Source 86 which you have looked at in the previous question) and then try to answer the following questions:
   a. What does the Source tell you about the purpose of the Miners Provident Society of South Wales and Monmouthshire?
   b. What view does the author of this source give you on Lord Merthyr's role in this society? Do you think this view is reliable on the basis of the evidence you are given? Explain your answer.
   c. What part of the evidence seems to contradict the author's view that it was Coalowners like Lord Merthyr who played the most important role in this Society?

5. Source 103 comes from an article written by Noah Ablett, a well known miners' leader in South Wales in the early 20th century. Look at the Source and then consider these questions:
   a. What does Ablett say about the issues which concern the miners and the attitude he thinks the Coalowners have to the miners?
   b. Do you think Ablett is in a good position to give this evidence? Why might his evidence be biased? Explain your answers.
   c. What evidence would you try to look for in deciding whether Ablett's evidence was typical of what miners thought about the Coalowners?

6. In Sources 86—103 you were given various evidence on the South Wales Coalowners. Try to use that evidence now to:
   a. make a case *for* the Coalowners and
   b. make a case *against* the Coalowners.
   Remember to consider carefully the reliability of your Sources.

4.—The Miners
The Collier Boy

Going to Work

Let us begin this section by trying to put ourselves in the position of the young collier boy going to work for the first time. The picture below shows twelve-year old John Davies on his first day in work at the Ferndale Colliery in the Rhondda Fach in 1911.

Source 104

Source: C. Batstone, *Old Rhondda in Photographs*, 1974.

The journey he might have made to work would perhaps have been a fairly short walk. Sometimes, however, miners had so far to go to their pit that they would travel on one of the special miners trains—'cwbs' as they were known in Welsh. Many young miners would have had the same experience of getting to work as Will Paynter, here describing his journey to work from his home in Trebanog in the Rhondda Valley in 1917:

Source 105

There were no buses or other transport to take us the two and a half miles or so from Trebanog to the Coedely Pit . . . On the morning shift we were raised from bed at about 4.20 a.m. to dress and walk to the pit, collect the pit lamp, and be down the pit before 6 a.m. This shift would start to ascend (come up) at 2 p.m. which meant, with the uphill walk we had, getting home at around 4 p.m. . . . It was a state of affairs in which we were living only to work.

Source: W. Paynter, *My Generation*, 1972.

This first harsh fact of the hardness of the miner's life would not yet have affected the young schoolboys who might have looked forward to their first day in the pit with the same eagerness as Joseph Keating of Mountain Ash:

Source 106

All the boys in school looked forward with longing to the day when they would be allowed to begin work . . . my happiness was not so much in leaving school as in the idea of actually going to work underground. We saw the pit boys coming home . . . They adopted an air of superiority to mere schoolboys . . . They had experienced danger . . . They associated with big men and wonderful horses. They earned six shillings and ninepence every week . . . For me, the prospect of going to work in the mine contained more glittering romance than if its black mouth were the entrance to Ali Baba's cave of gold.

Source: J. Keating, *My Struggle For Life*, 1916.

Let's stay for a moment with the twelve-year old Joseph Keating and join him on the morning of his first day at work in the Navigation Colliery, Mountain Ash, in 1883:

Source 107

I was up at half past five . . . My mother put my food in a small tin box and filled a 'tin' jack with cold tea, and said: 'May the Lord bring you safe home!' as I left the house. I had on my duck trousers, pieces of string around below the knee known as Yorks, and my hobnailed working boots. I went to the pit-head in an ecstasy, with a thousand men and boys . . .

Source: J. Keating, *My Struggle For Life*, 1916.

In Sources 104 and 107 we can see the special 'uniform' of the 'collier-boy' and we have been told of his 'water-jack' and his 'tommy-box'. Along with his lamp, John Davies in Source 104, has the other essential for the new miner—his mandril. This was however, only one of the tools that would be needed by the collier as Bert Coombes, a Resolven miner, describes here:

Source 108

Shovels, mandrils of different sizes, prising-bars, hatchet, powder-tin and coal-boxes; boring-machines and drills and several other things. He valued them at eight pounds, and he was forced to buy them himself . . . Nearly every week he had to buy a new handle of some sort . . . so that his wages were not all clear benefit . . .

Source: B. L. Coombes, *These Poor Hands*, 1939.

The Colliery

With our young miner now dressed and equipped for work let us join him as he arrives at the colliery. In the 1880s most collieries were still fairly small concerns and even by 1900 the average colliery in South Wales employed 376 workers. Whatever the size of the workforce, what was seen on the surface was very little of the colliery compared to the size of the underground workings. Source 109 is a picture of a 'typical' colliery surface, the Bwllfa No. 1 Pit in the Cynon Valley in 1912 and Source 110 an account of some of the work which might have been going on in the various surface buildings by John Thomas, an Ammanford collier.

Source 110

Somewhere . . . you will find the Lampman in the lamproom busily engaged in trimming and cleaning the lamps . . . In the neighbourhood of the pit-mouth is the blacksmith's shop, so vital for the sharpening of the miners' tools . . . as well as to make . . . repairs to the rolling stock—broken tram axles etc . . . Then somewhere . . . is the busy tram oiler and greaser—In their respective engine-houses are the various enginemen for winding or haulage . . . At the saw mill we find the sawyer and pit carpenters busy preparing timber props of various sizes for use underground . . . Out on the pit rubbish tip . . . we find an army of men . . . busily heaving and unloading the rubbish of stone and slag. In the colliery office are the clerical staff . . . recording the output of each collier, preparing the colliery paysheet . . .

Source: J. Thomas, *The Economics of Coal*, 1919.

Below Ground

Our collier-boy is bound for the pit-top, however, and the cage which will take him below ground for the first time. Perhaps now his pride in his new found status as a collier-boy would be put to the test, because the journey down the pit (described in Source 111 by Frank Hodges of Abertillery as he made it in 1900) was one that continued to frighten many miners right up to the end of their working-days.

Source 109

Source: National Museum of Wales.

Source 111

We sank rapidly down out of the daylight—down; down in the abysmal (deep) blackness. The cage travels swiftly. About half-way down the engineman applies the brake. This checks the momentum and the queer sensation is experienced of coming back up again. Every miner experiences this. He knows, in fact, that the cage is still descending, but every physical sensation indicates that it is returning to the surface . . .

Source: F. Hodges, *My Adventures as a Labour Leader*, 1925.

Once pit bottom was reached fear might well have increased for it would be the almost total darkness which would now take him by surprise. It has been calculated that the light in mines at this time was no more than one seventeenth of that we would get from a candle held a foot away in a dark room. Here is a picture of pit bottom at Tirpentwys Colliery near Pontypool in 1908 and this is followed by Will Paynter's description of the darkness of the pit:

Source 113

It is hard to describe this darkness of the pit. It is absolute blackness, impenetrable and eerie (solid and strange). Sounds appear to be magnified, the creaks of roof movement sounding like cracks of doom and the falling of loose pieces of coal from the front of the coal-face become frightening crashes . . .

Source: W. Paynter, *My Generation*, 1972.

So our young miner was now face-to-face with the reality of the mine! We have still not, however, actually got him to the place where he is going to start his work and (as we will see later) he has not yet begun to earn any wages. This account by a professor at the University College in Cardiff explains why this was so:

Source 114

The pit bottom is high, roomy and comparatively safe . . . the miner . . . then starts on his way along one of the haulage roads to the district of the mine where his stall or working-place is situated. He makes his way along the narrow and low-roofed gateways, crouching

Source 112

Source: National Museum of Wales.

down as he walks and sometimes having to scramble over a fresh fall of roof until, after some minutes, he comes to a main haulage road—and a further walk of half a mile or so takes him to his place . . . The working places are often a mile or so from the bottom, and in older mines . . . they may be two or three miles from the shaft . . .

Source: H. S. Jevons, *The British Coal Trade,* 1915

Mineworkers

Underground Workers

Collier-boys and colliers were not the only mineworkers. On average nearly half the number of *underground* workers were not in fact colliers. We are not going to look at all these other underground workers—the Rippers, the Roadmen, the Hitchers, the Ostlers, the Spragmen, the Splicers, and so on—but we can look at two examples. We can also note that although the dangers they faced were just as great and the work they did was often as hard, they were not thought of as 'proper' miners by the colliers and they certainly were not paid as much.

Here, for example, is an account of the work done by an underground *haulier* from a report by Government Commissioners in 1842 and it is followed by a photograph of hauliers at work in a mine at Pontypool about 1910:

Source 115
The duty of the haulier is to drive the horse and tram from the face, where the colliers are picking the coal, to the mouth of the mine. He

Source 116

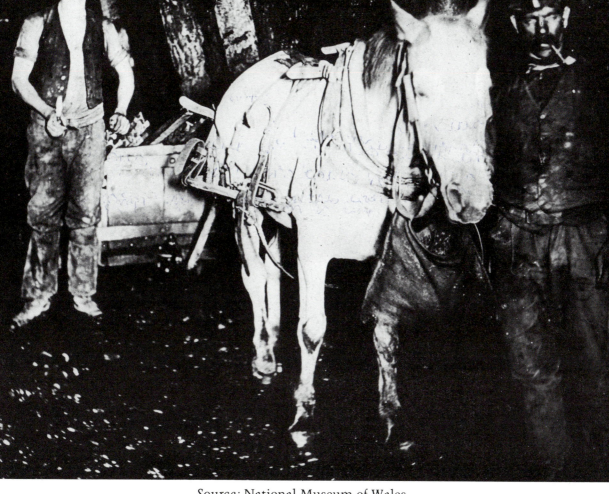

Source: National Museum of Wales.

has to look after his horse, feed him in the day . . . His occupation requires great agility in the narrow and low-roofed road . . . he frequently gets crushed . . .

Source: Report of Children's Employment Commission, 1842.

Whereas many hauliers would hope one day to become colliers themselves and thereby earn more money, this would not be so true of our second example—*repairers*. These men were highly skilled, took great pride in their work and would earn nearly as much as colliers. Here is a description of their work from a study of coalminers in South Wales made by a doctor in 1933:

Source 117

Their work consists in repairing and timbering the main roads and the roads leading immediately from the stalls. They keep the roads fit for haulage and the airways in good condition.

Source 118

They are usually the older men and they are skilled workers.

Source: E. M. Williams, The Health of Old and Retired Coalminers in South Wales, 1933.

Surface Workers

It is also important to remember that not all colliery workers were employed underground. Surface workers (as they were called as a group) were sometimes as much as one-fifth of 'all miners' but they are often forgotten in the history of coalmining. Many of the jobs done by surface workers have been mentioned already in Source 110. Some of these workers were craftsmen such as the *farrier*, a special kind of blacksmith who was in charge of shoeing the colliery horses. The photograph below shows a farrier at work at the Rhos Llandwit Colliery, Caerphilly, in 1885, with other craftsmen and surface workers looking on.

Source: H. C. Jones, *Old Caerphilly and District in Photographs,* 1979.

Another type of surface worker with a skilled and responsible job was the *Banksman*. His job is described here in the Special Rules of a Colliery:

Source 119
He shall have full control of the persons employed at the pit head, and shall constantly observe the condition of the cages, ropes, chains, catches and fans, and the gear used for lifting persons and things in the pit . . . He shall not permit more than eight persons in a single cage to descend a pit . . .

Source: Cadoxton Colliery Special Rules, 1874.

However, the majority of surface workers were not craftsmen or men in important positions. They were general surface labourers, many of whom were ex-colliers who through injury or old age were no longer fit enough to work below ground. Although their jobs were often very hard and the conditions they worked in unpleasant, they were the most poorly paid of all 'miners'. The photograph below shows surface workers on the screens at the Middle Duffryn Colliery in the Cynon Valley in 1911. Their job was to inspect the coal which was tipped from the trams brought from underground onto moving belts, picking out any stone or other rubbish and sorting the lumps of coal into different sizes. This job was just as dirty and dusty as working underground.

Source 120

Source: History of Powell Duffryn, 1914.

Children

Many children were employed both below and above ground at mines. In the early days of the coal industry children as young as six years old were employed underground. Some of them worked as door-keepers which meant opening and closing the underground doors which shut off sections of the workings and controlled ventilation. This is what 10 year old Elizabeth Williams, who worked at the mines of the Dowlais Iron Company, told Government Commissioners in 1842:

Source 121

We are door-keepers in the four foot level. We leave the house before six each morning and are in the level until seven o'clock and sometimes later. We get 2p a day and our light costs us 2½p a week. Rachel . . . was run over by a

tram a while ago and was home ill a long time . . .

Source: Report of Children's Employment Commission, 1842.

At the Esgyrn Colliery, Briton Ferry, Edward Edwards who was nine described his job as a 'trammer' to the 1842 Commissioners:

Source 122

I have been working here for three months and I drag carts loaded with coal from the coalface to the main road, a distance of sixty yards. There are no wheels to the carts . . . sometimes the cart is pushed on to us and we get crushed often.

Source: Report of Children's Employment Commission, 1842.

The drawing below, from the report published by the Government Commissioners, shows the door-keepers and trammers doing their work—which sometimes they did for up to twelve hours a day for as little as 18 pence a day.

Source 123

Source: Report of Children's Employment Commission, 1842.

As a result of this report an Act of Parliament was passed in 1842 forbidding the employment of children under 10 (later raised to 12) years old underground. However, despite the appointment of Inspectors to enforce the Act, there is plenty of evidence to show that children of below this age were still going underground in the 1860s.

Female Miners

As Source 121 suggests many of these children were girls and, of course, women were also employed below ground officially until the 1842 Mines Act. The number of them was never very great but the work they did in hauling the coal to the pit bottom and winding it up to the surface was every bit as hard as that done by men. Source 124 on page 52 shows women carrying coal in baskets out of a level in the early nineteenth century.

Source 124

Source: Report of Children's Employment Commission, 1842.

Women also continued working underground illegally after 1842 and legally on the colliery surface up to the 1920s. Source 120 shows women surface workers. Here is a short account by a woman from Treorchy of work done by women hauliers on the surface of Abergorchi Colliery in the 1880s and it is followed by a photograph of women employed in the washeries of the Ebbw Vale Colliery in 1896:

Source 125

The women were pulling the trams . . . coming up from the pit . . . bring it right out to the landing stage and then . . . tip the trams.

Source: Welsh Folk Museum, St. Fagans.

Source 126

Source: The South Wales Miner, 1968.

The Collier

Work

Colliers were then by no means the only type of miner, but they were the largest single group in the mine and carried out the basic job of mining the coal. The only training which a collier got was the training which he received as a young boy working as an assistant to an experienced collier—often his father or an elder brother. The way in which the job was learnt at first hand is described here by James Griffiths of Ammanford who began work as a colliers' lad in the anthracite pits of West Wales in 1904:

Source 127

It was in the Wythien Fach at Betws Colliery that I started work . . . I was sponsored by my brother Shoni . . . The Wythien Fach (Little Vein) was two feet seven inches thick and the stall would measure three yards . . . The job of the colliers' boy was to gather the coal, cut by his mate, into the curling box and carry it to the tram . . . The colliers' boy had to be careful to pick only the *lumps* of coal, as the . . . collier was only paid for the large coal in the tram. The tram would hold up to thirty hundredweight of coal, and when it was full it was the boy's responsibility to mark the tram, with chalk, with the collier's number. At eighteen years of age, having served five years of 'apprenticeship', I joined with another of my age to work our own stall on shares.

Source: J. Griffiths, 'The Miners Union in the Anthracite Coalfield' in G. A. Hughes (Ed.), *Men of No Property*, 1971.

The collier had other tasks to carry out in addition to hewing the coal. This description by a mining engineer, T. Foster Brown, in 1883, makes clear the total work expected of the collier:

Source 128

The collier of South Wales has to cut the coal and fill it into the trams; he has to get the rubbish, make and keep the working place safe and in order, he has to keep his stall road in travelling order, and do all the timbering necessary in the working place.

Source: Transactions of the South Wales Institute of Engineers, 1863.

Source 129 shows miners at a level near Pontypool in 1910 and reveals the cramped and difficult conditions in which the colliers work was often done. In 1900 one third of the coal seams being worked in South Wales were below 3' in height (below the level of the chair you are probably sitting on) and even in 4' seams the collier would be working on his knees and perhaps in water.

Source 129

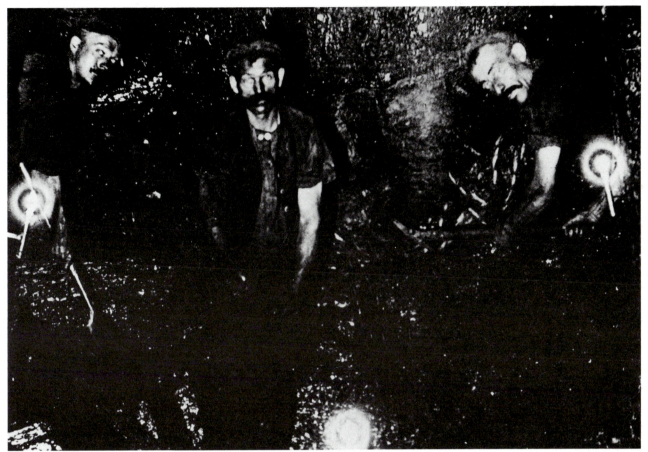

Source: National Museum of Wales.

Along with all the dangers of underground work the collier's task was of course, physically very hard and exhausting. This extract from a poem written in 1938 by Idris Davies, once a miner in the Rhymney Valley, describes the strain of the work and the conditions in which it was done:

Source 130

There are countless tons of rock above his head,
And gases wait in secret corners for a spark;
And his lamp shows dimly in the dust.
His leather belt is warm and moist with sweat,
And he crouches against the hanging coal,
And the pick swings to and fro,
And many beads of salty sweat play about his lips,
And trickle down the blackened skin
To the hairy tangle on the chest
The rats squeak and scamper among the unused props,
And the fungus waxes strong.
Source: Idris Davies, *Gwalia Deserta*, 1938.

The number of hours spent by the collier doing such hard work, per day and per week, did decrease as the 19th century went on. In the 1860s a twelve hour day, six days a week, would have been the average. By the end of the century this had fallen to about ten hours and in 1908 by Act of Parliament an eight hour day was introduced although overtime could be and still was worked. Even with this decrease the effect of long hours doing such physical work is clearly described by a miners' union leader from South Wales, Vernon Hartshorn, giving evidence to a Government Commission in 1919:

Source 131

The colliery starts winding coal at 7 o'clock in the morning. The men have to be down somewhere between 6 and 7 o'clock . . . They come up between 3 and 4 . . . So that we get the miner in his pit clothes from about 5 in the morning until, say, half past three when he ascends the pit, and by the time he gets home and has his food and a bath and gets out of his pit clothes again, it is half past four . . . I think it is true to say that during the whole of the winter months a miner never gets more than one or two hours of daylight on any day except Sunday . . . I know when I was a growing lad after I got home in the night and after getting my food . . . feeling too tired and stiff and lifeless to get a bath . . . In the morning when I was hauled out of bed, I felt it was like going to the gallows to get up at all . . .

Source: Report and Minutes of Evidence of the Royal Commission on the Coal Industry, 1919.

Part of the pride which the collier had in his status came precisely from the fact that his job was one which required great strength. Colliers were indeed proud of their work and the great skill they had to show in doing it. Edmund Stonelake, an Aberdare miner, talking about the early 20th century, explains how this pride was to a large extent due to the great control which the collier had over his work compared to other workers:

Source 132

Before the days of machine mining in South Wales each collier had his own working place, in much the same way as an allotment holder had his own plot. He worked his plot in his own way without interference from anyone; it was his own little domain (territory) he worked, and he had to live on what he got out of it . . . not even the manager dare tell me how I should work my place, and this was true of most colliers in South Wales.

Source: E. Stonelake, The Autobiography of Edmund Stonelake, 1981.

The fact that the collier did have this independence and control over his work is an important one to recognise and colliers in South Wales were well known for refusing to be influenced by Colliery managers and officials to speed up their work. The custom of controlling output was described by Alexander Dalziel, an official of the Coalowners Association, in 1871 as follows:

Source 133

In South Wales . . . the collier 'nurses' his work. He remains in the pit many more hours than the Northern workmen, and yet raises individually much less coal. All the rules of the pit, made by the men . . . are in restraint (restriction) of production. It is a point of honour with them not to 'race'.

Source: A. Dalziel, The Colliers Strike in South Wales, 1872.

As colliers were paid by the amount of coal they produced, this custom obviously resulted in harm to themselves. However, along with the great desire to protect their independence it was also probably a form of self-defence. In such a hard job, if you were to remain a collier for your working lifetime, then it was necessary to work at the pace, and for the number of days a week, that suited you best. Altogether the collier was a worker who seemed to value his control over his work and the many other customs of the pit, almost as much as he did the wages he received for his work.

Wages

Evidence on wages is incomplete and difficult to understand. In the case of miner' wages the difficulties are so great as to almost defy any understanding. Obviously, however, they were very important to the miner and his family. The collier was usually a pieceworker (that is he was paid for the *amount* of work he did). Other miners were paid for a day's work of so many hours. Below are the amounts paid each day to these workers as a result of the Minimum Wage Act of 1912. You can see again the great variety of mining jobs and the variation in wages paid for them:

Source 134

Day Wage Men	s	d
Rippers (not doing Timbering work)	4	0
Assistant Timbermen and Assistant Rippers	3	4
Roadmen	3	7
Hitchers (Leading)	3	10
(Ordinary)	3	6
Ostlers and Labourers	3	2
Underground Hauling Engineers, Electric, Steam and Compressed Air		
Main Haulage	3	4
Subsidiary Haulage	3	2
Underground Pumpmen, Electric, Steam and Compressed Air—Main		
Pumps	3	4
Small Pumps	3	2
Fitters if employed entirely underground	3	4
Electricians Ditto	3	5
Rope Splicers Ditto	3	10
Masons and Pitmen Ditto	4	2
Cog Cutters	3	5
Timber Drawers and Airway Men	3	10
Shacklers and Spragmen, and Watermen	3	2
Lamplockers, Lamplighters, Oilers	3	0
Coal-cuttermen	4	3
Boys under 15 years of age	1	6
Boys over 15 and under 16	1	9
Boys over 16 and under 17	2	0
Boys over 17 and under 18	2	3
Boys over 18 and under 19	2	6
Boys over 19 and under 20	2	9
Boys over 20 and under 21	3	0
Hauliers above 18 years of age—(1) Day Hauliers	3	11
(2) Night Hauliers	3	8
Tonnage Hauliers, above 18 years of age, for hauling coal	4	2
Riders above 18 years of age	3	9
Trammers above 18 years of age	3	3

Source: The South Wales Coal Annual, 1913.

As far as the collier paid by piecework is concerned, there are three factors to take into account in showing how he earned his wages:

1. He was paid so much per ton of *large* coal that he cut.

2. For other jobs that he had to do such as *ripping* the roof of the seam (to allow room for horses and trams to get in), *gobbing* (packing rubbish into the gap left where he had removed the coal) and *timbering* (putting up props to support the roof) he would be paid by the inch, foot, yard etc.

3. The amount for the two jobs above would be added together and then a percentage would be added to this total to give the total wage. Whereas the amount paid for the first two jobs would be decided for each different seam in each different colliery, the percentage was the same all over the coalfield and was meant to reflect the increase in the selling price of coal above a standard price agreed between the Coalowners and the miners in a certain year.

Let us look at just one Source here, which might help to clarify matters. Below is a section of a Price-List for one colliery—that is the amounts paid under the first two headings above:

Source 135

OCEAN COLLIERIES.

MAINDY PIT.—UPPER SEAM.

SCHEDULE OF PRICES

Payable for Dead and other Work, when properly and satisfactorily performed.

SEPTEMBER, 1882.

	DESCRIPTION OF WORK.	RATE.
		s. d.
Cutting ...	Cutting large clean Coal, including Ripping 18 inches of Top ...	1 11½ per ton.
	Note.—The price paid for the Large Coal covers the price of any Small Coal sent out in trams with the Large Coal.	
Headings	Wide Headings through face of Stalls, single turn ...	2 9¾ per yard.
	Do. do. in solid end of Slips ...	3 9¾ ,,
	Narrow Heading, including Ripping Height to 5ft. 6in. off rail, single turn ...	5 0 ,,
	Do. extra double ...	0 6 ,,
	Level Headings ...	1 10 ,,
	Heading Stall, measuring square off, and Heading Airway in Coal ...	2 6 ,,
Timbering	Timbering ...	1 10 per pair.
	Flat Collars ...	1 1 ,,
	Cogs, setting ...	1 10 each.
	Do. drawing out ...	1 4 ,,
	Road Posts, standing (repairing) ...	0 2½ ,,
	Posts, drawing out ...	0 1 ,,
Ripping .	Ripping and Gobbing Top, per yard, forward, 18in. thick, and not less than 5ft. wide, and in proportion for more or less thickness, but not for extra width ...	2 3 per yard.
	Cutting Bottom 12in. thick ...	0 11 ,,
	Cutting two Ribs in a Stall, when such a Stall is ordered to be driven that necessitates it ...	0 11 ,,
Gobbing..	Trimming Second Rippings, 18in. & upwards when first Rippings was of the usual thickness ...	3d. to 6d. ,,

Source: Rhondda Public Library.

Its not much easier to deal with the actual amount of wages which miners received in South Wales in the period up to 1920! Wages were certainly going up: one historian calculates that average wages of colliers were no more than 2 shillings and sixpence a day in 1800 but by 1914 they had risen to 9 shillings and four pence a day. However, precisely because colliers were pieceworkers, averages are almost meaningless. Conditions would vary from time to time in the same working places, resulting in the collier never being able to mine the same amount of coal each day. These conditions and the prices paid for work would also vary from seam to seam in the same colliery and from colliery to colliery across the coalfield. Also there would be deductions made from the miners' wages and he might miss a day's work through illness, injury, strikes etc. Therefore, even the same miner working in the same place might earn very different amounts from week to week. Even a wage slip like the one in Source 136 *(See page 56)* which at least (on the right hand side) show the deductions made from a man's wages, is therefore not a great deal of help.

One final point can be made on this question of wages. To really see what changes in wage rates actually meant you have to compare them with the movement of prices. Again the evidence here is very difficult to use but one historian has estimated that colliers on average were actually three times better off at the end of the 19th century than at the start, even allowing for price increases.

Conditions

We can be much more definite about the general conditions and dangers in which the miner worked underground. Although they improved as the 19th century went on they were always bad and South Wales was one of the most dangerous coalfields to work in because of its difficult geological conditions and its gassy deep mines. The miners' leader Noah Ablett gives this general description of the various dangers and difficulties the miner faced:

Source 137

The hewer down in the mine away from the sunlight and fresh air, sometimes in a temperature of up to 90 degrees, every movement of the day inhaling coal and shale dust, perspiring so abnormally (unusually) as few men in other industries can realize; head throbbing with the almost inhuman exertion (effort); the roof, perhaps, eighteen inches low, perhaps, twenty

Source 136

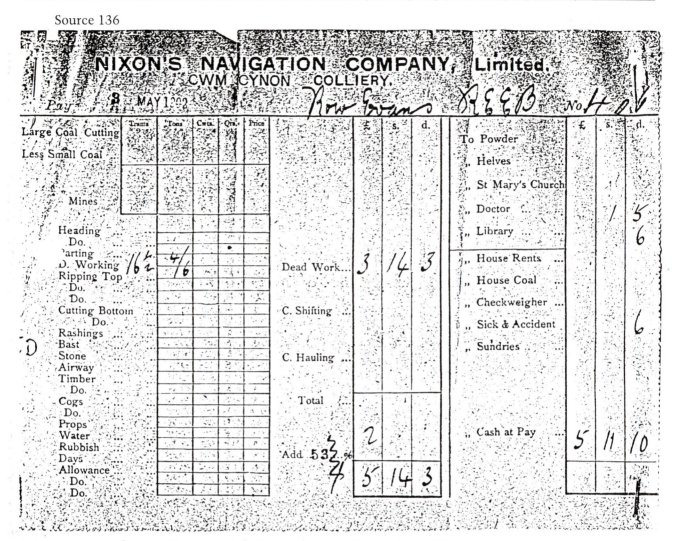

Source: Mountain Ash Comprehensive School, Local History Collection.

feet high; ears constantly strained for movements in the strata on which his limbs or his life is dependent, breathing always noxious (harmful) smells due to the absence of any kind of sanitation, and to gases . . . ; subject at any moment to the terrible list of mining diseases, most common of which is the dreaded nystagmus, which may, if neglected, lead to insanity; liable always to wounds and death from falls of roof . . . and ever and over all the sickening dread of the awful explosion . . .

Source: N. Ablett, *What we want and Why*, 1922.

Without these special dangers mining was a job which lead to general ill-health. Blood poisoning (from working in filthy clothes), rheumatism (from working in water), constant headaches (from the gas), ruptures (from cramped working positions) and many other ailments were accepted by the collier as part of his way of life!

Much less acceptable were the major mining *disasters* which occurred all too frequently in South Wales. These were usually caused by massive explosions of natural gas and sometimes by sudden inrushes of water from underground lakes. Three sources on pp. 57-59 show the effect of these terrible disasters. First a memorial leaflet listing all the major disasters in the North and South Wales coalfields from 1837 to 1927 (Source 138). Next a newspaper account of the disaster at Abercarn in September 1878 (Source 139) and, finally, drawings of the scenes at the Park Slip Colliery, Aberkenfig in September 1892 (Source 140).

The worst single colliery disaster ever to occur in Wales came twenty one years after the Park Slip colliery tragedy in which 112 miners were killed. In 1913, as the result of an explosion at Universal Colliery, Senghenydd, 439 miners were killed.

Sources 140 (a) and (b) on page 59 give us a glimpse of how appalling the tragedy of such a disaster was.

Source 138

In Loving Memory

of the

3508 MINERS WHO LOST THEIR LIVES

in

COLLIERY DISASTERS

IN NORTH WALES, SOUTH WALES, AND MONMOUTHSHIRE DURING THE PAST 90 YEARS.

	Killed.		Killed.
1837—May 10, Plas-yr-Argoed, Mold	21	1877—March 8, Worcester Pit, Swansea.	18
1837—June 17, Blaina (Mon.)	21	1878—September 1, Abercarn.	62
1844—January 1, Dinas	12	1878—September 11, Abercarn	268
1845—August 2, Cwmbach	28	1879—January 13, Dinas	3
1846—January 14, Risca	35	1879—Sept. 22, Waunllwyd, Ebbw Vale.	84
1848—June 21, Victoria (Mon.)	11	1880—July 15, Risca	119
1849—Aug. 11, Letty Shenkin, Aberdare.	52	1880—Dec. 10, Naval Steam Colliery	96
1850—Dec. 14, New Duffryn Colliery	13	1882—January 15, Risca	4
1852—May 10, Duffryn	64	1882—February 11, Coedcae	6
1853—March 12, Risca Vale	10	1883—February 1, Coedcae	5
1856—July 15, Cymmer	114	1883—August 21, Gelli	4
1858—October 13, Duffryn	20	1884—January 16, Cwmavon	10
1859—April 5, Neath Chain Colliery	26	1884—January 28, Penygraig	11
1860—December 1, Risca	146	1884—Nov. 8, Pochin Colliery, Tredegar.	14
1862—February 19, Gethin, Merthyr	47	1885—Naval Colliery	14
1863—October 17, Margam	39	1885—December 24, Mardy	81
1863—December 24, Maesteg	14	1887—February 18, Ynyshir	37
1865—June 16, Tredegar	2	1888—May 14, Aber. Tynewydd	5
1865—December 20, Upper Gethin	30	1890—January 20, Glyn Pit, Pontypool.	5
1867—November 8, Ferndale	178	1890—February 6, Llanerch	176
1869—May 23, Llanerch	7	1890—March 8, Morfa	87
1869—June 10, Ferndale	60	1892—August 12, Great Western Colliery	58
1870—July 23, Llansamlet	19	1892—August 26, Park Slip	110
1871—February 24, Pentre	38	1894—June 23, Cilfynydd	276
1871—October 4, Gelli Pit, Aberdare	4	1896—January 28, Tylorstown	57
1872—Jan. 10, Oakwood, Llynvi Valley.	11	1899—August 18, Llest Colliery, Garw.	19
1872—March 2, Victoria	19	1901—May 24, Senghenydd	82
1872—March 8, Wernfach	18	1901—September 10, Llanbradach	12
1874—April 5, Abertillery	6	1905—March 10, Clydach Vale	31
1874—July 24, Charles Pit, Llansamlet.	19	1905—July 5, Wattstown	119
1875—December 4, New Tredegar	22	1913—October 13, Senghenydd	436
1875—December 5, Llan Pit, Pentyrch	12	1925—April 26, Trimsaran	9
1876—December 13, Abertillery	20	1927—March 1, Cwm, Ebbw Vale	52

A sudden change; at God's command they fell;
They had no chance to bid their friends farewell;
Swift came the blast, without a warning given,
And bid them haste to meet their God in Heaven.

Source: National Museum of Wales

Source 139

THE COLLIERY DISASTER AT ABERKENFIG, SOUTH WALES.

FROM SKETCHES BY OUR SPECIAL ARTIST.

GENERAL VIEW OF NORTH'S NAVIGATION COMPANY'S COLLIERIES, INCLUDING THE PARK SLIP COLLIERY.

THE HOME SECRETARY VISITING THE HOUSE OF HENRY WHITE.

CARRYING AWAY THE DEAD.

ENTRANCE TO THE PARK SLIP COLLIERY: BRINGING UP THE LAST MAN ALIVE.

Source: London Illustrated News, September 1892.

Source 140

TERRIBLE COLLIERY EXPLOSION IN MONMOUTHSHIRE
LOSS OF NEARLY 300 LIVES

GREAT CONSTERNATION IN THE DISTRICT
THE MANAGER AND ENGINEER BAFFLED
RETURN OF THE EXPLORING PARTY
270 COLLIERS ENTOMBED IN THE WORKINGS

Abercarne, Wednesday night, Nine o'clock.... It was about five minutes to twelve when the inhabitants of the valley were startled by the reverberation of three distinct explosions, which were heard for a long distance off.... A dense volume of smoke issued from the mouth of the shaft, and fierce flames were clearly distinguishable....In a remarkably short space of time the roads leading to the pit were crowded with men, women, and children – wives, mothers, brothers and sisters who were hastening forward to ascertain what had really happened....

Searching parties were without delay then formed.... These gentlemen entered the cage, and were carefully let down to the bottom. But what a picture was there presented to their gaze!... Dead bodies lay in heaps on the roadways, dark, shapeless, charred masses, which a short time ago were moving about, animated with life. Here and there could be clearly seen the terrible results of the explosion. The brattices, of course, had been blown to pieces; overturned trams were strewed about, and by the faint light of the safety lamps could be seen, intermingled with the dead human bodies, those of the horses, who, along with the colliers, had met a fearful death.... The first exploring party remained down a long time, and I am happy to say that in the interval a portion of the miners were enabled to make their escape. Eighty-two of the poor fellows were crowded together at the bottom of the shaft struggling with each other to get up first. Some of them were severely burned, and the fearful look which hung about their faces as they were drawn up the shaft to the open air again will perhaps never be forgotten by those who were ready and willing to help them as they left the cage.... But the rejoicing on the part of some of those on the bank proved to be short-lived, for, alas, several of the 82 colliers, though brought up from the fiery tomb had received a shock to the system, and the after-damp had so effectively done its work, that shortly after death released them from their sufferings.... It will thus be seen that 373 men entered the pit in the morning; 23 afterwards left work, and after the explosion seven bodies were found, while 82 colliers were rescued. The number left in the pit, upon this calculation, is, therefore, 262, and no hope whatever is entertained that they are alive. The disaster is, perhaps, the most terrible one that has happened in South Wales and Monmouthshire."

Source: South Wales Daily News, 13 September, 1878.

Source 140(a)

Eight from one house

"Eight from one house": husband, four sons, two brothers, and one brother-in-law!

Can words paint or imagination depict the desolation of the woman bereft in one stroke of her whole household. Eight coffins in one home!

The hills around were dotted with groups here and there, and in the roadways along the valley there was movement and life and colour against a background of verdant-clad mountains, bathed in sunshine; but near the colliery, and especially the mortuary, the crowd was tense, voiceless, almost motionless. The numerous lady members of the Red Cross brigade ... busied themselves amongst the women who were waiting for news of husband, brother, father, etc., helping and comforting, and trying to console those to whom the certainty of bereavement had come.

Source: National Museum of Wales.

Source 140(b)

Source: Western Mail, 16 October 1913.

Naturally these major disasters, with the awful effect they had on single communities, captured a great deal of public attention. However, major disasters were not the typical cause of death in the mines, which was much more likely to result from isolated single incidents of roof-falls, the effect of gas, journeys of trams running wild etc. Edmund Stonelake of Aberdare gives this account of such an incident in his autobiography:

Source 141

In the mines it matters not how careful or skilful a man may be, sudden unforeseen accidents will occur. I had a man working with me one day in a perfectly timbered place. I was a few yards from him, holding conversation when without the slightest warning a huge stone weighing about half a ton crashed through the timbers and killed him instantly. Whilst men were trying to move the stone from his body, I recovered from the shock; I then caught hold of his legs and pulled him free, he was dead and his brains were on the floor.

Source: E. Stonelake, *The Autobiography of Edmund Stonelake*, 1981.

Non-fatal accidents, which sometimes would cripple or injure a man for life, were even more frequent. In 1892 for every fatal accident in South Wales there were 100 non-fatal accidents.

The effects of the *dust* which Noah Ablett mentioned in Source 137, were also a cause of disability and the early death of miners. However, it was a long time before the diseases caused by dust—pneumoconiosis and silicosis —were recognised as industrial diseases and compensation was paid. A doctor who made a survey of the health of retired coalminers in South Wales in 1933, here describes the effect of these dust diseases:

Source 142

The three main types of dust which the miner has to contend with in mining are coal-dust, rock-dust and shale-dust, and in the case of the steam coal miners, the stonedust used in dusting the mines as a precaution against explosions...The symptoms of pneumoconiosis are—dyspnoea (shortness of breath) . . . cough is almost always present . . . Sputum (phlegm) is, as a rule, scanty but may be copious (plentiful) and black . . . In late stages there may be signs of heart failure or tuberculosis . . . It is well known . . . that borers on a hard heading develop silicosis. One miner told me of a heading near Aberdare which eleven men were set to drive. As the money was good many of them worked double shifts. Before the heading was driven through, ten of the men had to give up work, and later died of silicosis . . .

Source: E. M. Williams, *The Health of Old and Retired Coalminers in South Wales, 1933.*

Ablett also mentions the eye condition *nystagmus* in Source 137. This was caused by working in conditions where there was not enough light and it was a disease which became more common as the 19th century went on because, ironically, the safety-lamp gave far less light than the flame from a candle. In 1912 a collier described the effects of nystagmus to a doctor making a study of it, as follows:

Source 143

Up to the last two years . . . I had no trouble with my eyes and always earned good money. During the last two years my eyes got weak, but I struggled on, hoping things would mend. I lost days and days, and on times a week. At the time it was not safe for me to go to the face without the help of another man. I could not recognise anybody . . . My wages fell to a pound a week, and the manager stopped me at last and told me that it was not safe to allow me to work any longer. If I could only have known before, I might have saved my eyes!

Source: T. Llewellyn, *Miners Nystagmus: Its Causes and Prevention*, 1912.

In British mines from 1868 to 1914, on average a miner was killed every 6 hours and seriously injured every 2 hours. This average would have been even higher in South Wales which was just about the most dangerous coal-field in Britain to work in. It also, of course, takes no account of the deaths and permanent disability caused by the diseases described in sources 142 and 143.

Miners Unions

Before 1898

It was not until 1831 that coalminers and ironworkers in South Wales were recruited into the first organised trade unions. Before this, miners often belonged to local combinations and clubs such as Friendly Societies (which are looked at in Section 5 of this book) and sometimes illegal organisations such as the infamous Scotch Cattle which often used violence and the threat of violence to achieve better wages and working conditions. In 1831 branches of the *Friendly Society of Coalmining* were set up on the coalfield—this was a trade union attached to the National Association for the Protection of Labour, which was based in the north-west of England. Here is an extract from the ceremony that took place when someone joined—why do you think there was such secrecy?

Source 144

Question: What is your name?

Is it of your free will that you come here to join this Friendly Society of Coal Mining?—I do.

1. I most solemnly and sincerely swear, with my hand on the Holy Book, and on my bended knee, that I never will tell who gives me this solemn obligation, or these witnesses present, as long as I live.—So help me God.

2. I will enter this Society and will pay according to the rules, or as the Committee thinks proper, or as far as lies in my power.—So help me God.

3. I never will instruct any person into the art of coal mining, tunnelling or boring, or engineering, or any other department of my work, except to an obliged brother or brothers or an apprentice.—So help me God.

4. I will never work where an obliged brother has been unjustly enforced off, for standing up for his price, or in defence of his trade.—So help me God.

5. I will never take any more work than I can do myself in one pay, except necessity requires me to do so; and if I do, I will employ none but an obligated brother, and will pay him according to the master's price, or according to his work.—So help me God.

Source: Cambrian, 12 November, 1831.

Despite this secrecy the Ironmasters by locking-out of work all those who joined the union were able to stamp it out in the autumn and winter of 1831. Repeated attempts were made to re-establish unions in the 1830s and 1840s as this leaflet from Aberdare in 1849 shows:

Source 145

Workmen, stop and read!—As there are so many different reports gone over the country, about the stoppage at Aberdare, we, the colliers of Aberdare, feel it our duty to make known unto our fellow-workmen, and all others, why we have ceased to work, and what is the reason of our present strike. On the commencement of last November, all the masters belonging to the sea-coal at Aberdare, gave us notice to leave our employment at the end of one month; at the expiration of the said notice, the terms that were offered us were, twopence per ton reduction, *and to bind ourselves to work on the said reduction of one year,* and the masters to have liberty to discharge six men in each month on giving them a month's notice; and six of the workmen, and no more, to have the power of giving notice within the same month, and therefore they would have power to manage the notice, so that the year would always be up on the slowest time on the sea-coal.

From the Colliers of Aberdare Sea-Coal.

Source: The Morning Chronicle, 1850.

However, it was not until the 1870s that trade-unionism established itself widely across the developing South Wales coalfield. Then, the Lancashire-based, *Amalgamated Association of Miners* built up a membership of 42,000 miner in South Wales. In two long and bitter disputes in 1871 and 1875, however, the A.A.M. was defeated. The defeat was partly due to the continuing hostility of the Coalowners to trade unions—'blackleg' labour was imported into the coalfield to replace strikers. It also resulted from the weakness of the union itself, as this newspaper extract of June 1871 indicates. It is followed by a print showing a mass meeting of A.A.M. members in Merthyr during the 1875 dispute:

Source 146

Colliers' Strike in South Wales.—The first instalment of the promised strike money was paid to the colliers by the agents of the Union on Friday. It amounted to 2s.2d. per man. Inasmuch as the men had been out of work for three weeks at the time of the first payment this ''advance'' amounts to a fraction less than 9d. per head per week. The colliers now are of one opinion, that the Union is nothing but a deception. In fact, most of the men are ashamed of themselves, that they have been so foolish as to expect 10s. a week and now at the end of three weeks only receive 2s.2d. It can truly be said that the Amalgamated Association of Miners received its death-blow on Friday in the Aberdare and Rhondda Valleys. Every member, we have no doubt, in this district repents the day he joined such a rotten concern.

Source: The Western Mail, 12 June, 1871.

Source 147

Source: London Illustrated News, May, 1875.

Following the collapse of the A.A.M. a number of separate District Unions were set up in South Wales and these represented the miners on the Sliding Scale Committee where together with the Coalowners they regulated wage levels. Many of these 'unions' were in fact little more than organisations set up and controlled by the Coalowners and they were totally opposed to strike action. Source 148 is an extract from the rules of such a 'union' in the Blaenavon area in 1891.

Up to the 1890s in all the coalfields of Britain miners were slow to join trade-unions, but thereafter unions did spread quickly with the formation of the Miners Federation of Great Britain. In South Wales, however, only 45,000 out of 120,000 miners belonged to unions in 1893. There seem to have been many reasons why South Wales was a backward area for trade-unionism at this time. The hostile attitude of

the Coalowners was certainly a factor as was the effect of the great waves of immigration into South Wales which took place at this time. Another reason seems to have been that colliers tried to dominate unions when they were set up, putting off other mine workers. In 1893, for example, hauliers took their own strike action to improve their working conditions. Source 149 shows drawings of some of the scenes from this strike.

The year 1898 was the major turning-point in the history of trade-unionism among the South Wales Miners. In a six months lock-out William Abraham (Mabon) led the District Unions in fighting for a wage increase of 10% and the abolition of the Sliding Scale. In Source 150 Mabon (on the right) is shown in a cartoon arguing the miners case with Sir. W. T. Lewis (on the left) the Coalowners leader in South Wales.

Source 148

RULES

OF THE

BLAENAVON ASSOCIATION

AND

COLLIERY

WORKMEN'S COMMITTEE

✕✕✕✕

BLAENAVON :

PRODERT AND CO , STEAM PRINTERS AND STATIONERS, HIGH STREET
—
1891.

RULES.

Name and Place of Business.

1. This Committee shall be called "THE BLAENAVON COLLIERY WORKMEN'S COMMITTEE," and be held at the White Horse Hotel, Blaenavon, on the first Wednesday in each month, or oftener if necessary, commencing at 7-30, (when the roll will be called), closing at 10 o'clock,

Objects and Constitution of Committee.

2. The objects of this Committee are to defray expenses of Sliding Scale, Tareing of Trams. Testing of Machines. Inspections of Workings, Seeking Clearance. Timber, Road Material, or any other appliance when deficient; also, settling disputes arising in any part of the workings, or in connection with Hauliers or Daymen, their hours of labour and rates of wages, and to protect them in accordance with Mines' Regulation Act.

Source: Big Pit Mining Museum, Blaenavon.

Source 149

The Collieries Strike in South Wales

1. March of strikers to the Ferndale pits: hooting those coming from work.
2. A striker and his dog.
3. Women and children bringing bread and cheese to the men at the Merthyr meeting.
4. Two thousand strikers passing up the main street of Merthyr.
5. Halt on the way to the Merthyr meeting.

Source: London Illustrated News, August, 1893.

Source 150

As Far Off as Ever.

EMPLOYER : "Let there be no misunderstanding. The price of coal MUST regulate the miners' wage !"
MINER : "No; distinctly I say no ! The miners' wage must regulate the price of coal !"

Source: The Western Mail, 14 February, 1898.

Despite great demonstrations by the strikers such as the one shown below in Merthyr Tydfil,

sheer starvation drove the miners back to work defeated in September 1898.

Source 151

Source: Merthyr Public Library.

Source 152   'THE FED'

Source: South Wales Miners Library, University College of Swansea.

Source 154

The fed . . . was a great deal more than a trade union. It was both an industrial and a social institution . . . It differed from the normal functions of trade unions because of its more intimate (close) involvement in the domestic and social life of the people. 'The Fed' was the single decisive union operating in the pits, the communities existed around the pit, and union branches were based upon it, hence the integration (joining) of pit, people and union.

Source: W. Paynter, 'The Fed' in G. A. Hughes (Ed.), *Men of No Property*, 1971.

1898 was more of a beginning than an end, however! The old District Unions were now in tatters, but the humiliation of defeat seemed to bring home the need for unity and in October 1898 a new union for the whole coalfield was set up—*The South Wales Miners Federation.* Source 155 is a newspaper report of the founding conference of the Union on 11 October, 1898.

Source 153

Federation Song.
(ARRANGED FOR VOICES.)

Words by W. B. JENKINS.   (Copyright.)   Tune, "Tredegar."   Music by ANNA LINCOLN.

It stands for all to see, And marks what we have won!

The hope of days to be! The rise of Labour's sun!

The home of which our fathers thought, And which with blood

and tears they bought, And which with blood and tears they bought.

To us, their children's sons,
They left their glorious gain.
Remember! victory runs
Through strife and toil and pain.
To them we raise a thankful song
And pledge ourselves : "We will be strong !"
And pledge ourselves : " We will be strong !"

Symbol of Unity !
Herald of Peace, strife-born !
With blood-dimmed eyes we see
The faint flush of thy dawn !
With trembling shout we hail with glee
The day of wider Liberty !
The day of wider Liberty !

Written in commemoration of the opening of the Tredegar Valley Miners' Federation Offices, Newport, Nov., 1915.

Source: South Wales Miners Library, University College of Swansea.

Source 155

Organisation of Miners
The New Union
Election of Officers
Framing The Rules
Echoes of The Great Strike

An important conference, which might be expected to have far-reaching effects upon the South Wales and Monmouthshire coalfield, was held at the Lesser Park Hall, Cardiff, on Tuesday. It was one of the largest and most representative meetings of delegates held for some time past, the circular issued to the various districts asking the men to appoint representatives to consider the draft rules of the proposed new organisation finding a ready response all over the coalfield. There were over 160 delegates present, and the proceedings which opened at 10.30 in the morning, did not conclude until a late hour in the evening. It was decided to exclude the representatives of the Press . . .

Source: South Wales Daily News, 12 October, 1898.

A remarkable turnaround now took place. From being the most backward area in Britain for mining trade-unionism, by 1899 the S.W.M.F., with 104,000 members, had become the strongest area. Ever since, the South Wales coalfield has maintained a reputation for strong trade-unionism among its miners. As a former President of the Union, Will Paynter, explains in Source 154, 'the Fed' played a much more important role in the lives of the people of the South Wales valleys than unions do normally. By 1914 the S.W.M.F. had nearly 200,000 members, making it the largest *single* union in Britain. Although the old District structure continued and the Agents (the 'Czars' of the coalfield as Noah Ablett called them) dominated the Executive Council of the union, the basic unit of the union's organisation was the Lodge, as a former Secretary of the Union, Dai Dan Evans, explains here:

Source 156

. . . the Lodge embraces all men, including craftsmen and surface workers, engaged at a mine. The only exceptions are overmen, deputies, shotfirers and members of high management . . . The lodge was the sole force standing in opposition to the employer and it negotiated all terms and conditions of employment, including:

  i. price-lists for pieceworkers
  ii. rates of wages for day-wage men
  iii. hours of work above and below ground
  iv. safety conditions

Source: D. D. Evans, 'Relationship Between N.U.M. and the Structure of the Coal-Mining Industry' in G. A. Hughes (Ed.), *Men of No Property*, 1971.

A powerful figure in the union's presence at each pit was the *Checkweigher* who was elected by all workers to represent their interests in the calculation of wages. The job of the checkweighman is explained here by Cliff Prothero, who held this position at the Cwm-rhyd-y-gau Colliery in Glynneath:

Source 157

My job was to check that the man who weighed the coal on behalf of the company put the correct weight in the book provided. When a tram of coal came on to the weighing machine, the gross weight would be taken, then the weight of the tram itself was deducted . . . The Company weigher would then enter all this information in his book and I would enter it in my book . . . At the end of the week my book would be checked against the weigher's book and then on the Monday morning I would issue a weight slip to each individual collier for him to know the tonnage of coal for which he would be paid.

Source: C. Prothero, *Recount,* 1981.

Source 158

Powerful as the Checkweighers, the Agents, the Executive Council members and other officials of the S.W.M.F. were, the union was also a very democratic one. All major decisions at local level and many decisions for the whole union, were taken by pithead meetings and ballots such as the one shown here in a Rhondda colliery.

Source: C. Batstone, *Old Rhondda in Photographs,* 1974.

Apart from the pithead ballot the most powerful voice in the S.W.M.F. were coalfield conferences (where every lodge was represented) in Cardiff. In such gatherings, which were probably the most representative meetings in the whole of Wales, matters great and small were decided by the miner's delegates as Source 159, a report of a conference in 1922 shows.

The S.W.M.F. 1898—1914

In the early years of the S.W.M.F. the policies of the union were dominated by the President, William Abraham (Mabon). In a speech in the United States of America in 1905 he outlined the policy that was known as 'Mabonism':

Source 160

We are working to elevate (raise) the working man, to give him an opportunity to prove himself worthy of all he asked for and all that could be given him . . . We have found a better way to fight out these questions than by strikes and lock-outs. The days of those weapons should be no more . . In South Wales our shrapnel and shot are facts and figures, and our battles are fought around a table.

Source: South Wales Daily News, 2 January, 1905.

This policy of believing that the miners and the Coalowners had the same interests at heart and should work together, led in 1903 to a *Conciliation Board* being set up where representatives of the S.W.M.F. and the Coalowners could meet to discuss wages and other questions.

Source 159

Annual Conference of the S.W.M.F.

REPORT OF PROCEEDINGS.

The Annual Conference of the South Wales Miners' Federation was held on Thursday, Friday and Saturday, June 25, 26 and 27. Mr. Enoch Morrell presided, supported by Mr. S. O. Davies (vice-president), Mr. Oliver Harris (treasurer), Right Hon. Thomas Richards (general secretary), and members of the Executive Council. There were 199 delegates present, representing 147,556 members.

The President, in briefly opening the proceedings, said it was unfortunate that since he had occupied the position of President of the South Wales Miners' Federation they had been in troublesome waters. This year they had the sad spectacle of thousands of good workmen who had been deprived of the opportunity of working to enable them to live respectably, and they had to be subjected to the demoralising effect of having to subsist on the dole.

General.

Resolutions were passed on general topics. Calling upon the M.F.G.B. to take action in opposition to the Dawes Report; that in the event of a Colliery closing down, the Federation use all its power to get the Government to have an inquiry as to the actual cause of closing. That all surgical appliances, such as limbs, false teeth, etc., the loss of which arise from accidents, shall be supplied by the employers. That our policy be directed towards the ultimate abolition of Capitalism. That if a workman is home ill, the employers should be compelled to re-employ him on his recovery. That the practice of unloading rubbish by Colliers should be abolished.

Source: The Colliery Workers Magazine, July, 1922.

However, from 1906 onwards a change of mood swept the coalfield. The first sign of this was the campaign to persuade all miners to join the union. This newspaper account in December 1906 of the campaign in the Maesteg area shows how bitter the feeling could be against non-unionists and the cartoon, Source 162, shows again the involvement of women.

Source 161

One of the non-unionists residing at Maesteg went to the door of his residence in his shirt sleeves and a number of women rushed upon him, tore his shirt off . . . and dragged him into the street. There some of them belaboured (set about) him with brooms, while others threw their dirty water upon him to the accompanying shouts of 'blackleg'. At length he pleaded for mercy, and said that any of the men could go to the colliery office for him and get £1 to pay his subscription . . . At Nantyfyllon . . . a number of workmen demonstrated in front of houses singing hymns all night. Landladies are turning out the non-unionist lodgers . . . Two young men were dragged out into the street by a shrieking mob of women . . . stripped of their upper garments and their faces were black-leaded . . .

Source: South Wales Daily News, 5 December, 1906.

Source 162

Peaceful Persuasion:
or, Strengthening the numbers of the Federation at Maesteg.

Source: The Western Mail, 15 December, 1906.

It was, however, between 1910 and 1912 that the South Wales coalfield became a hot-bed of militancy. The disputes of those years grew out of the problem known as 'abnormal places' which arose out of the wages system for paying colliers. The miners leader Noah Ablett explained the problem as follows:

Source 163

A working place with a good roof and a thick section of easily worked coal may change in one week. The roof may become very brittle and dangerous, the section of coal may become thin and the coal may be hard or stiff to work ... One man in a lucky place will produce with comparatively little effort three times the amount of coal produced by another man in the same seam using almost superhuman efforts.

Source: N. Ablett, *What We Want and Why,* 1922.

In the past when a collier's wages were low because he was working in a bad or 'abnormal' place, the Colliery Company would often pay an allowance to make up his wages. However, as seen in Section 3 of this book the large coal combines such as the great *Cambrian Combine* in the Rhondda were worried about the high wages bills in South Wales and they began to refuse to pay such allowances. In October, 1910, the 12,000 miners employed by the Cambrian Combine struck work and a similar dispute also began in the Cynon Valley. At the beginning of November the bitterness of the Cambrian Dispute flared up in the famous disturbances at Tonypandy which led to police and soldiers being brought to the area. Source 164 is part of a newspaper account of the events of 8 November in Tonypandy and Source 165 a photograph of Tonypandy Square after the riots.

Source 165

Source: South Wales Miners Library, University College of Swansea.

The Cambrian Strike ended in defeat for the miners, but the new militancy of South Wales played an important part in persuading the Miners Federation of Great Britain to call the first national strike of miners in 1912. This led to the setting up of a minimum wage for all miners. By 1914 'the Fed' had been transformed into one of the most militant unions in Britain

Source 164

THE WAR OFFICE AND THE CAVALRY.

ORDERS FOR THE MEN TO BE DETAINED AT CARDIFF.

TO BE READY IN CASE THEIR PRESENCE SHOULD BE WANTED!!

ONE SQUADRON LEAVES FOR THE RHONDDA.

METROPOLITAN POLICE SENT ON TO PONTYPRIDD.

The following official statement was issued from the Home Office on Tuesday night :—

A request was addressed last night by the chief-constable of Glamorgan to the local military authorities for the assistance of 200 cavalry and two companies of infantry in keeping order in the Cambrian Collieries.

The Home Secretary, in consultation with Mr. Haldane, decided to send instead a contingent of the Metropolitan police, consisting of 70 mounted and 200 foot constables, to the district to carry out the instructions of the chief-constable, under their own officers. This force was sent by special trains, and will arrive in the early evening.

In the meanwhile, the cavalry and infantry which had been despatched in response to the chief-constable's request have with. his concurrence, been detained—the infantry at Swindon and the cavalry at Cardiff, where they will remain for a few days in case their presence should prove to be necessary.

CAVALRY AT CARDIFF.

ANIMATED SCENES AT THE RAILWAY STATION.

The Great Western Railway station at Cardiff on Tuesday evening presented the appearance of an Army headquarters on a miniature scale. From 6.30 on military officers were arriving by train from various parts of the country and at once proceeding to the stationmaster's office, where Brigadier-general C. F. N. Macready, C.B., was in constant telegraphic and telephonic communication with the War Office and the chief-constable of Glamorgan (Captain Lindsay). The general came down from London in the afternoon, arriving at Cardiff by the 6.55 p.m. train. With him was Colonel M. C. Curry, D.S.O., and they were met by Lieutenant-colonel H. A. T. Phillips, R.G.A., commanding the troops in the Cardiff district, and Captain Bennetts, A.S.C., Pembroke Dock.

A quarter of an hour prior to the general's the officers arriving by each train. They all immediately waited upon General Macready, and at one time eight were in the station-master's room, the consultation lasting until eight o'clock. A quartermaster-sergeant of the Welsh Regiment from Cardiff Barracks was in attendance the whole time, and there were also a number of orderlies.

The railway officials were also present in full force, among them being Mr. J. J. Leaning, divisional superintendent; Mr. J. Carter, assistant divisional superintendent; Mr Hulin, the stationmaster, &c., while an interested attendant was Mr. C. A. G. Pullin, Mr. D. A. Thomas's private secretary.

When the Hussars arrived the orders for the officer commanding were that he must not proceed further than Cardiff until he received a communication from the War Office. He was also informed by telegram that General Macready was on his way from London to command operations.

It was very evident that even General Macready was under orders not to proceed further than Cardiff until receiving instructions from the War Office.

By the 7.30 train another batch of officers arrived from Bristol, and after acquainting the general of the fact they left the station.

At 8.3 the first contingent consisting of 200 foot police arrived from London. These men were under the charge of Superintendent Powell, and an hour and a half later a special arrived with 100 men and their horses. These forces were immediately despatched to Pontypridd, where further orders awaited them.

CAVALRY LEAVE FOR THE RHONDDA.

ALL FURNISHED WITH BALL AMMUNITION.

A squadron of the 18th Hussars arrived at Cardiff at 11.15, they having left Tidworth at 6.45. On Major Burnett, who was in command, reporting himself to Colonel Curry,

Source: The Western Mail, 9 November, 1910.

and more than that it had become the most important influence on the lives of the miners of South Wales. In large part this had been due to the work of Noah Ablett and other miners in the Rhondda Valleys who had joined together in a body called the Unofficial Reform Committee. As these extracts from the pamphlet 'The Miners' Next Step' published by the Committee in 1912, show, the union was moving a long way away from 'Mabonism' and towards a policy of the workers taking over the mining industry:

Source 166

THE

MINERS' NEXT STEP

BEING A SUGGESTED SCHEME FOR THE

Reorganisation of the Federation

Issued by the Unofficial Reform Committee

TONYPANDY

OBERT DAVIES AND CO., GENERAL PRINTERS, ETC.

1912.

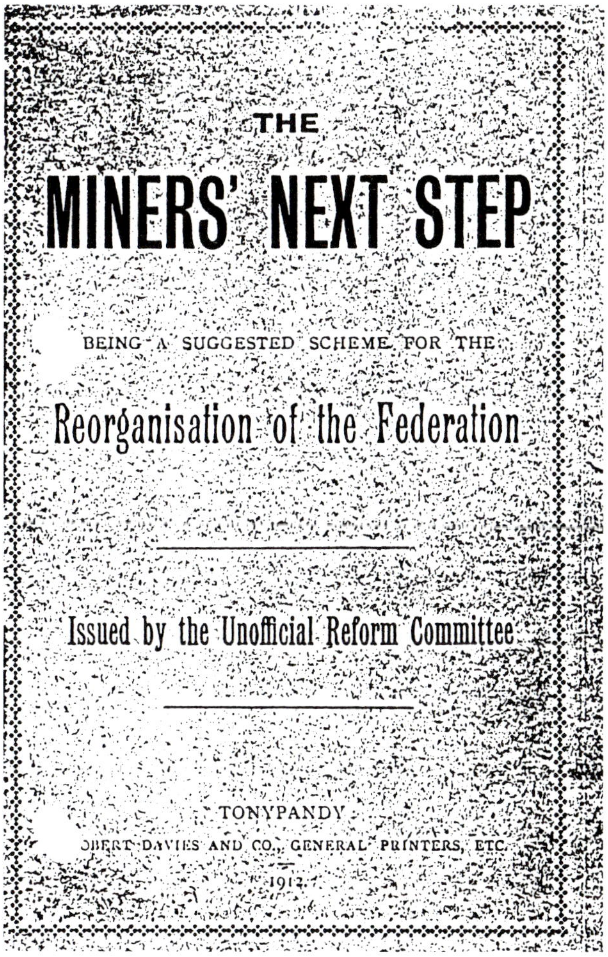

CHAPTER V

POLICY

I. The old policy of identity of interest between employers and ourselves be abolished, and a policy of open hostility installed . . .

XIII. That a continued agitation be carried on in favour of increasing the minimum wage and shortening the hours of work, until we have extracted the whole of the employers' profits.

XIX. That our objective be to build up an organisation, that will ultimately take over the mining industry and carry it on in the interests of the workers.

Source: The Miners Next Step, 1912.

Further work on the evidence

1. Look at Source 114 and then try to answer the following questions:
   a. What do each of these words or phrases mean
      i. 'haulage roads'; ii. 'stall'; iii. 'fall of roof'; iv. 'shaft'?
   b. Why is it important to understand what these words and phrases mean?
   c. Why is this Source important in understanding the way in which miners were paid their wages?
   d. Given what you are told about the author of this Source, what would you need to find out before you could be sure it was reliable information on the working conditions of miners?
2. Why is Source 130 different to the other evidence in this Section of the book? What would you need to know before you could regard it as first-hand information on the work of a collier?
3. Look at Source 131 and then answer these questions:
   a. Explain how it is that Vernon Hartshorn can claim that 'during the whole of the winter months a miner never gets more than one or two hours of daylight except Sunday'.
   b. Do you think this source is biased? Explain your answer.
   c. What other Sources in this section of the book seem to back up what Vernon Hartshorn says about the working hours of miners.

4. Look at Sources 132 and 133 and then try to answer these questions:
   a. In what way do these two sources differ?
   b. In what way do these two sources agree?
   c. Look back to Source 101 in Section 3 of this book. Does the evidence in that Source back up either of Sources 132/133?
   d. How by working in the way described in Source 133 would colliers lose wages? If this was so why do you think they worked in this way?
5. What evidence is there in Sources 137-143 to show the effect that each of the following things could have on the health and lives of the miners?:
   a. The presence of gases in mines.
   b. Roof falls underground
   c. The darkness of mines
   d. Dust in mines.
6. Look at Sources 161 and 162 and then try to answer these questions:
   a. Which of the methods used against non-unionists in Maesteg are shown in both Sources?
   b. What do you think the attitude of the cartoonist in Source 162 is towards the South Wales Miners' Federation.
   c. Why do you think women were so involved in the campaign against non-unionists?
   d. What other sorts of evidence might you look at to get a fuller picture of what was happening in Maesteg at this time?

5.—Coalfield Society I
The Creation of Coal Society

Population Growth

This section of the book deals with the mining communities of the South Wales valleys and the way of life that was led in them. In the second half of the 19th century there was a spectacular growth in the population of Britain as a whole, due to a declining death-rate and an increasing birth-rate. In Wales a population of 1,163,139 in 1851 more than doubled to 2,421,000 by 1911. A way of looking more closely at what was happening within Wales is to consider the census figures of population for Welsh counties. The map below shows the old counties of Wales and gives the census figures for each of them for 1801, 1851 and 1911. Study them and then answer these questions:

1. Did all the counties of Wales have an increase in population between 1801 and 1911?
2. Which counties lost population between 1851 and 1911?
3. In which counties did the greatest increase in population take place?

Source 167

Whereas in 1801 less than 20% of the population of Wales lived in the two counties of Glamorgan and Monmouthshire, by 1911 nearly 63% of the people of Wales were to be found in these counties. The reason for this shift in the balance of population was of course the growth of the iron and the coal industries in South Wales. This move from rural to industrial areas and the growth of new industrial communities happened all over Britain in the 19th century as a result of what we call 'the industrial revolution'. As a result of the tremendous growth of the coal industry a whole new society came into being in the valleys of South Wales. In the case of the Rhondda its population doubled between 1871 and 1881 and then trebled up to 1911. Most of the other valleys of the coalfield matched this rate of population growth.

The People and their Origins

Migration of people into South Wales was going on throughout the period 1851 to 1911 and altogether some 366,000 people moved into Glamorgan, Monmouthshire and Carmarthenshire between these dates. The peak of this migration occurred between 1901 and 1911 when 129,000 people moved into the area. Such was the incredible growth of South Wales at this time that it absorbed immigrants at a faster rate than anywhere in the world except the U.S.A.! You can work out in more detail where the people who migrated into the valleys came from by looking at the two maps on p. 72. The first map shows you the counties of England and Wales. The second map shows where people who lived in Glamorgan in 1911 were actually born: each dot within a county represents 500 people who were born in that county but lived in Glamorgan by 1911. By counting the dots see if you can answer these questions:

1. By 1911 of the people who lived in Glamorgan, but were born outside the county, did most of them come from Welsh counties or English counties?
2. Why do you think so many of the immigrants into Glamorgan came from Monmouthshire?
3. Which *four* Welsh counties (apart from Monmouthshire) supplied the highest number of immigrants? Why do you think this was so?
4. Which two English counties supplied the highest number of immigrants? Why do you think this was so?

Source 168

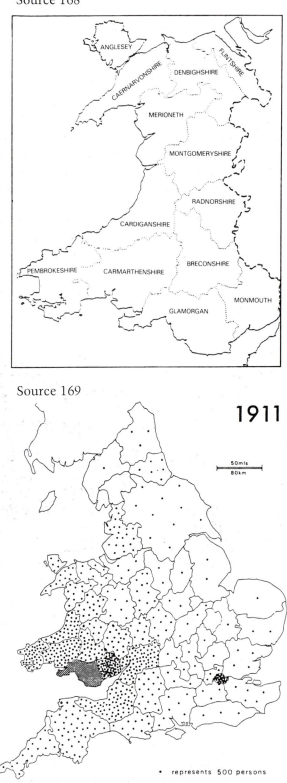

Source 169

1911

Source: A. H. John (Ed.), *Glamorgan County History*, vol. V, 1980.

Up to the 1890s the majority of the people entering Glamorgan had come from other counties in Wales. Many of the rural counties of Wales were actually losing population at this time and although many of the people who left these counties went to other parts of Britain and even other parts of the world (particularly the United States of America), the bulk of them moved to live and work in the new industrial areas of South Wales. Why did these people leave in such numbers? One reason, perhaps, is given below by a woman who moved to the Rhondda from Cardiganshire and who on a visit back to the county of her birth spoke as follows:

Source 170

We're fools to stay in a place like this. In Treorchy there's electric light. Just put your finger on the switch and the place lights up . . . Turn on the tap in the scullery and there's plenty of water . . . There are pavements to walk on . . . The street lamps are on all night. There are plenty of picture-houses for somebody to have some fun. If you haven't any dinner ready you just send the children round to the Bracchi (Italian) shop for fish and chips. On Saturday there are cheap trips to Cardiff. Oh yes, we're mugs to hang around here.

Source: W. J. Edwards, *Ar Lethrau Ffair Rhos*, 1963.

The actual journey from mid and north Wales to the south Wales valleys was made much easier by the spread of the railways. Here an agricultural labourer from Merioneth who came down to work in the mining village of Cilfynydd in 1906, described the experience of his railway journey and the first impression South Wales made upon him:

Source 171

Oh I remember that journey very well. It was on a warm day in the month of May and we were travelling through the Breconshire hills at a pretty slow pace . . . The train stopped for a good quarter of an hour at the station . . . waiting for a lady coming across the field from a village . . . But there was still no sign of the industries we had heard so much about. We had heard about the ironworks in Merthyr, to be seen before you'd see any coal mines, but anyhow we came to a certain point, we started to go downhill and lo and behold there was nothing but smoke in front of you for miles . . . So now of course I realised that I was in industrial South Wales.

Source: Interview with J. L. Williams, South Wales Miners' Library, University College of Swansea.

As source 169 showed, by the time this railway journey was being made in fact more people were moving to south Wales from outside Wales than from inside. Immigration from English counties was particularly high in Monmouthshire and the eastern part of Glamorgan, but was less high in western Glamorgan and Carmarthenshire. Why was this so? As these figures for the Rhondda show, England may well have been the main source of immigrants from outside Wales, but it was not the only one:

Source 172
Birth Places of Inhabitants of Rhondda Valleys 1891 and 1911

Birth Places			1891	1911
England				
Cornwall ...	...	...	485	749
Devon ...	...	...	841	1,141
Gloucester	...	...	2,236	2,875
London ...	...	...	316	1,681
Somerset ...	...	...	3,291	4,057
Yorkshire	...	...	159	225
Wales				
Anglesey ...	...	...	231	678
Brecon ...	...	...	2,437	2,921
Cardigan ...	...	...	5,829	5,505
Carmarthen	...	...	4,024	4,601
Caernarvon	...	...	905	1,937
Denbigh ...	...	...	281	481
Flint ...	...	...	140	177
Glamorgan	...	...	48,998	88,810
Meirioneth	...	...	780	1,172
Monmouth	...	...	4,985	4,720
Montgomery	...	...	2,481	3,030
Pembroke	...	...	3,186	3,656
Foreign Countries		...	358	638
Scotland ...	...	...		263
Ireland ...	...	...		929
Indian Empire	...	...		34
West Indies	...	...		22
Australia ...	...	...		63

Source: E. D. Lewis, *The Rhondda Valleys*, 1959.

The valleys of South Wales at this time became a 'melting pot' of different people and cultures. After the Welsh and the English, the next largest national group to come in were the Irish. In 1861 there were already 18,000 Irish in South Wales, the largest number being in Merthyr Tydfil. Joseph Keating of Mountain Ash shows how they still clung on to their national customs:

Source 173

When an Irish Catholic died . . . all who could attended the Wake. Our kitchen was crowded with men and women, young and old, till three o'clock in the morning. Two lighted candles were at my grandmother's head and another at her feet. On a table near her were the saucers of red snuff and tobacco, and a dozen long and short clay pipes. We played Cock-in-the-Corner, Hunt the Button, and told or listened to tales of leprechauns, giants and old hags . . . A few of the old people, on coming in, would kneel beside the corpse. As soon as their prayers were finished, they joined heartily in the game.

Source: J. Keating, *My Struggle for Life*, 1916.

In Dowlais and in Abercraf at the head of the Swansea Valley there were communities of Spaniards, in Merthyr there were small groups of Russians, Poles and Frenchmen. A nationality that were not large in number but which were very noticeable as most of them were involved in running cafes in the new valley towns were the Italians. They came mainly from Bardi in northern Italy and they followed the first family to come—the Bracchis—to the Rhondda and other valleys. Here is Julio Bracchi in his cafe in Tonypandy in the early years of this century.

Source 174

Source: K. S. Hopkins (Ed.), *Rhondda Past and Future*, 1974.

One observer in the 1930s noted how groups of migrants from different areas tended to stick together in their new homes in the Cynon Valley:

Source 175

People from the same districts in North Wales or England tended to settle together in communities in the mining valleys. There is a community of Corris people in Abercynon. They came to the coalfield from the slate quarries of Merionethshire . . . In Penrhiwceiber, too, there is a community of North Welshmen. Those who have migrated from Bristol or the Forest of Dean have settled along the main valley roads . . .

Source: E. M. Williams, *The Health of Old and Retired Coalminers in South Wales*, 1933.

For many reasons there was sometimes animosity between the different groups (anti-Irish riots were frequent events at one time as they were accused of accepting lower wages) but in the main these different peoples and cultures got on well together in the new valley communities.

The Nature of Coal Society

Language

Increasing immigration from outside Wales had a marked effect on the percentage of people in South Wales who could speak the Welsh language. By 1911 only 38% of the population of Glamorgan claimed to be able to speak Welsh and this percentage was concentrated in the older age groups of the population. However, this was only slightly below the average for Wales as a whole (40%) which had fallen from 54% since 1891 when the first census of language was taken in Wales. In the other two counties covering the area of the coalfield the figures were both higher (Carmarthenshire) and lower (Monmouthshire) than Glamorgan, as these figures from the 1911 Census show:

Source 176

	Total Population		English Only		Welsh Only		English & Welsh	
	1901	1911	1901	1911	1901	1911	1901	1911
Carmarthenshire	135,328	160,406	12,018	19,991	44,901	30,705	69,046	96,531
Monmouthshire	298,076	395,019	238,131	314,530	2,013	1,496	33,677	33,751

Source: Census of Population, 1911.

Immigration from outside Wales played a major part in the decline of the numbers speaking the Welsh language. Even in 1891, before the widescale immigration from outside Wales had begun, only 49% of the population of Glamorgan spoke Welsh. In addition (and as can be seen from Source 176) the actual *number* of Welsh speakers in the three South Wales counties was increasing because so many immigrants from rural Wales were Welsh speakers. Some historians argue in fact that had South Wales not provided a home for so many Welsh speakers, then these hundreds of thousands of people would have left Wales altogether and the Welsh language would have suffered an even worse decline. It seems that even among some Welsh-speakers the language was declining. Some people like Thomas Jones of Rhymney in Monmouthshire blamed this on the neglect of the language by schools:

Source 177

No Welsh was spoken or taught in school in my time and this fact tended to oust it from the home and the street. I have been told that we spoke Welsh at home until I was about six and that thereafter as the children went to school the family turned to English and reserved Welsh for the purposes of religion.

Source: T. Jones, *Rhymney Memories*, 1938.

Does Thomas Jones, however, suggest another reason why the language declined? This letter to a newspaper in 1902 also touches upon the same point:

Source 178

A good number of our Welsh parents cannot prevail upon their own children to learn the Welsh language upon their own hearths and among their own family and I admit that it is a most difficult matter in many instances in a town like Pontypridd where the English tongue is so predominant among all classes.

Even in the Welsh chapel after a Welsh service we find as soon as the service is over that most of the conversation takes place in English.

Source: *Glamorgan Free Press*, 11 June, 1902.

This decline of the numbers speaking the Welsh language, did not occur so much in the anthracite coalfield of West Wales where the language of work and life in general continued to be strongly Welsh. Why do you think this was?

Communities

What sort of places were the new communities of the South Wales valleys? Many of you using this book who live in the South Wales valleys know well enough just how different valley communities look compared to other areas. If you have travelled around South Wales then you will also know that to some extent every valley is different. However, we can start by looking at two pieces of evidence which give a fairly accurate view of the appearance of valley communities. The first is a photograph of the mid-Rhondda Fawr in the 1920s. The second is a written description of the South Wales valleys from the report of a Government commission in 1917.

Source 179

Source: H. V. Morton, *In Search of Wales*, 1932.

Source 180

All other British coalfields have fairly level or gently undulating (wavy) surfaces. In South Wales the coalfield used to be spoken of as the "hills" . . . but of more recent years "the valleys" . . . They are for the most part extremely narrow, with inconveniently steep sides, some of them indeed being so narrow at some points that there is scarcely space enough on the level for main road and railway in addition to the river itself. Nevertheless, it is into these valleys, shut in on either side by high mountains that the mining population is crowded, and it is in this same narrow space, and often right in the midst of the dwelling houses that the surface works of the collieries . . . have been placed . . . Streets run along the length of the valleys in monotonous terraces, instead of radiating from a common centre.

Source: Report of the Commission Appointed to Inquire Into Industrial Unrest, 1917-1918.

The density of population in the valley communities was extremely high. In 1911 in the Rhondda, for example, 23,680 people were crammed on average into each square mile where houses had been built. This was by far the highest density in England and Wales, where the average was 618 people per square mile. To set against this, however, it is important to remember that surrounded as they were by mountains, the valley communities of South Wales were much nearer to open countryside than was the case in other industrial areas of Britain. Here, for example is Tylacoch in the Rhondda in the 1920s, just a stone's throw away from the bustling mining village of Treorchy.

Source 181

Source: C. Batstone, *Rhondda Remembered*, 1983.

Many valley communities were almost semi-rural and quite isolated. This was particularly so in the western part of the South Wales coalfield. In the anthracite valleys the coal industry developed at a much slower pace and as a result the collieries and communities of West Wales were smaller than the rest of the coalfields and as was mentioned earlier this was an area where the Welsh language remained strong and ties with local agriculture were so close that there were men who spread their work between being a miner and working on their own small-holding or labouring on a farm. Together these differences made for a quite different way of life to the rest of the South Wales valleys as a doctor noticed in the 1930s whilst working in different areas of South Wales:

Source 182

On the whole, the wordly lot of the anthracite miner appeared to be better than that of the steam coal worker. Most of the mining villages were smaller and the cottages not huddled into untidy streets as they are in the Aberdare Valley. There is a great difference between this valley, with its coal mines in the main streets, and the clean open villages of Abercrave or Tycroes . . . In Cwmllynfell . . . the houses were nearly all of the semi-detached type . . . There did not seem to be the poverty and crowding which one saw in Mountain Ash or in Aberdare.

Source: E. M. Williams, The Health of Old and Retired Coalminers in South Wales, 1933.

The Domination of 'Coal'

East or West of the coalfield one thing is certain—the coal industry dominated the life of the people of the South Wales valleys. Census figures on occupations for Glamorgan between 1851 and 1921 (Source 183) show how much this was true in terms of work. What percentage of occupied workers were employed in 'Mines and Quarries' in (a) 1851 and (b) 1921?

Source 183

CLASS	MALES								FEMALES							
	1851	1861	1871	1881	1891	1901	1911	1921¹	1851	1861	1871	1881	1891	1901	1911	1921¹
1. General or Local Government	389	705	1,084	1,275	2,134	3,135	5,047	6,014	15	33	66	65	194	444	1,065	1,370
2. Defence	323	235	276	454	329	615	611	1,105	–	–	–	–	–	–	–	–
3. Professional Occupations	1,275	1,618	2,266	3,674	5,268	7,388	9,622	10,745	397	774	1,296	2,437	4,243	6,435	8,297	10,760
4. Domestic Offices or S	686	745	899	2,140	1,330	2,856	4,271	3,560	8,834	13,964	19,595	23,999	31,793	29,268	33,079	29,950
Commercial Occupations	608	1,411	2,326	4,464	7,684	11,248	15,886	19,179	51	12	27	44	128	527	1,404	7,596¹
Conveyance of Men, Goods and Messages	5,629	8,889	12,674	17,663	26,812	38,167	48,576	51,241	74	30	48	112	183	318	363	2,167
7. Agriculture	13,139	12,753	11,394	10,015	10,102	8,990	9,489	9,796	3,030	1,475	1,133	946	779	792	1,579	990
8. Fishing	98	92	288	171	113	107	229	374	–	6	14	18	33	3	28	10
9. Mines & Quarries	22,320	30,257	37,364	48,580	82,160	107,859	150,694	163,599	678	571	798	558	549	112	92	119
10. Metals, Machines, Implements & Conveyances	13,670	20,030	24,460	26,709	31,025	36,096	48,461	52,564	888	1,274	1,677	2,095	2,640	1,499	2,157	2,754
11. Precious Metals, Jewels, Watches, Instruments & Games	165	347	418	409	641	822	1,106	653	2	26	20	32	43	63	114	25
12. Building & Works of Construction	6,320	8,717	9,711	13,195	18,385	20,700	26,441	25,293	186	272	112	12	37	22	11	92
13. Wood, Furniture, Fittings and Decorations	1,310	1,466	1,601	1,840	2,204	2,870	3,921	3,776	24	60	63	71	104	128	281	181
14. Brick, Cement, Pottery & Glass	346	459	452	627	771	859	1,459	774	105	202	337	345	350	227	225	241
15. Chemicals, Oil, Grease, Soap, Resin, etc.	275	369	524	585	757	1,010	1,485	953	12	9	35	69	120	136	221	28
16. Skins, Leather, Hair and Feathers	318	364	370	408	506	507	594	455	8	9	8	13	23	24	35	46
17. Paper, Print, Books & Stationery	209	356	597	871	1,360	1,955	2,424	1,895	15	30	61	165	327	666	1,020	719
18. Textile Fabrics	1,099	1,215	1,557	1,705	1,971	2,168	2,169	383	331	285	468	672	1,214	2,254	3,133	763
19. Dress	3,982	4,344	4,482	4,383	5,330	6,263	7,749	4,029	5,696	8,343	8,663	8,450	12,812	13,532	15,376	8,766
20. Food, Tobacco, Drink and Lodging	3,291	4,527	5,646	7,004	10,414	15,049	21,156	6,644	1,941	1,986	2,174	2,582	7,575	5,564	10,906	6,575
21. Gas, Water, Electricity, Sanitary Work	22	102	195	281	563	1,115	2,022	1,518	2	1	–	–	1	–	1	9
22. Other, General & Undefined Workers	9,313	11,775	20,409	21,235	30,319	20,259	19,970	56,747	604	712	1,024	860	1,209	1,100	2,022	16,066
TOTAL OCCUPIED	84,787	110,776	159,912	167,488	240,178	290,016	383,182	421,097	22,893	30,074	37,619	43,545	64,155	63,114	81,409	89,227
23. Unoccupied etc.	40,300	57,059	70,623	98,640	35,769	46,962	62,575	54,554	92,115	128,345	158,563	208,710	178,624	245,444	320,998	366,298

Source: A. H. John (Ed.), Glamorgan County History, vol. V; 1980.

Many of the other occupations were dependent on the coal industry and in many valleys as much as 95% of the population either worked in or depended upon the coal industry. What might these have been? It was not just through employment that the coal industry exercised its domination over the lives of the people of the valleys. The graph (Source 184, p. 77) drawn by an historian, suggests other ways in which the coal industry could have an effect on people's lives? What were these effects?

'Women's Work'

Many of those people who depended on the mining industry, although they did not work in it, were the wives of miners. Although most women in the coalfield would have been in this position it is quite surprising how many women did work. Look at the 1921 figures in Source 183. What is the fifth largest occupation group in Glamorgan? Women still worked in the mining industry itself during this period,

Source 184

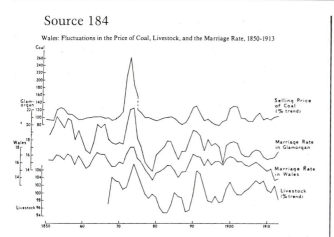

Wales: Fluctuations in the Price of Coal, Livestock, and the Marriage Rate, 1850-1913

Source: B. Thomas, 'Wales and the Atlantic Economy in B. Thomas (Ed.), *The Welsh Economy: Studies in Expansion*, 1962.

although the decline in their number is clearly shown in Source 183. Here is a photograph from the 1880s of some of these women who were employed as hauliers at the Abergorchi Colliery in Treorchy.

Source 185

Source: C. Batstone, *Old Rhondda in Photographs*, 1974.

Twenty years earlier some of the women who would have been employed under the heading 'metals' in Source 183, would have been the 'patch girls' of Tredegar. Source 186 is a photograph of these girls and Source 187 is a newspaper account of them and their work.

Source 187

Around the town (Tredegar) are what strangers call 'Black Mountains' which are the refuse and burnt coal tipped and heaped together from the ironworks . . . Women and girls are employed and wear a peculiar style of dress, consisting of a short frock and apron, tight to the neck . . . red worsted stockings and lace-up boots heavy with hob-nails, tips and toe-caps, that would pull the legs off some of the ploughmen of the Midland Counties . . . In the tempest and the storm, in rain and snow, in the

Source 186

Source: Manchester City Art Gallery.

sun and heat, exposed to all weathers, women and girls are employed on the tips in South Wales.

Source: The Bristol Mercury, 14 May, 1865.

Source 183 also shows that a number of women were employed in producing bricks. Brickworks would often be attached to collieries to meet the need for bricks for mineshafts and housebuilding. Source 188, p. 78 is a photograph of brickworkers at the Glamorgan Colliery, Llwynypia, in 1880 and Source 189 is a description of women brickworkers in Blaenavon in 1865.

Source 188 *(See page 78)*

Source 189

At the kilns were 10 girls . . . They did the whole of the work, with a Gaffer over them. They were all well-grown healthy lasses, aged

Source 188

Source: C. Batstone, *Rhondda Remembered*, 1983.

from 15 to 21; all wore coarse ragged smocks— 'pinnies' they call them . . . and strong laced boots, and kerchiefs around head and neck . . . One girl stood inside the kiln and took down the bricks; another wheeled the barrow full of bricks out to the tramroad close by; the third emptied the barrow and ranged the bricks in the trucks. There was much brick dust, and the girls were yellow from head to foot with it.

Source: Notebook of A. J. Munby, 22 September, 1865, Wren Library, Trinity College, Cambridge.

Source 183 also shows that the biggest single occupation for women at this time was domestic service. In fact after coalmining it was probably the next biggest area of employment for people in Glamorgan. However, most of the girls who worked as domestic servants had to leave Glamorgan and Wales. In particular a large number would have gone to London where it became fashionable to employ a Welsh parlour-maid. The hours of work and the wages received were much worse than anything these women who were still working at the mines would have experienced! Here are the sad memories of one South Wales girl in service in London of her first day:

Source 190

Mrs. Fox had told me to put on my black afternoon dress and white apron. I kept trying to staunch (hold back) the tears with the flannel and water in the washstand bowl. A black frock seemed to suit the occasion. I was in mourning for my lost self . . . My childhood was dead—and now I was the skivvy (servant) . . . I was given my supper in the tiny kitchen while the family ate in the living-room. It was strange to be considered not fit to eat in the same room as other human beings. It was a good supper . . . but loneliness and misery had taken away my appetite. How delicious, in comparison, seemed the remembered slice of marge-spread toast given me by Mam and eaten as a member of a family.

Source: W. Foley, *A Child in the Forest*, 1974.

Homes and Family Life

Homes

Source 52 in Section 2 of this book shows that when pits were sunk in South Wales after 1840, the first houses of the new mining communities were also built. These were often little more than the wooden huts shown in the photograph (Source 191) at Senghenydd, or three-roomed cottages of the type shown at Dinas, in the next photograph (Source 192).

In 1878 a survey was made of houses built at Merthyr Vale by the coalowners Nixon, Taylor, Cory and Company. Here is part of this survey:

Source 193

At Nixonville are the best houses. Built of brick . . . they contain 6 rooms and are chiefly occupied by the Overmen, firemen and best workmen . . . The cost was about £150 per house . . . At Cardiff Road . . . all built of stone . . . cost about £100 each . . . 5 rooms, 2 on the ground floor and 3 bedrooms . . . The manager and under-managers houses cost £423 . . . Altogether the amount expended by the firm in erecting cottages at Merthyr Vale up to the present time is £22,089 which equals about £105 per house. The rents received from 1869 to 1877 equal £3,202 . . .

Source: South Wales Coalowners Association Records, National Library of Wales.

In fact very few Colliery Companies in South Wales themselves built houses, as Coalowners preferred to leave this task to private builders such as those seen at work in building houses at Tallis Street, Cwmparc, Treorchy, in the 1890s (Source 194, p. 80).

Using stone quarried locally these 'speculative' builders quickly constructed a large number of houses—16,000 in the Rhondda alone between 1881 and 1914.

Source 191

Source: H. C. Jones, *Old Caerphilly and District in Photographs*, 1979.

Source 192

Source: C. Batstone, *Old Rhondda in Photographs*, 1974.

Source 194

Source: C. Batstone, *Old Rhondda in Photographs*, 1974.

Although these houses were of a better standard than these which had been built in the iron-making towns of South Wales a century earlier, little thought was given to overall planning as the terraces snaked their way down the valleys to become one of the unique things about the area's appearance. The photograph below shows a typical terrace development in the Rhondda. What problems arose as a result of houses being built near to rivers and hillsides in the narrow and tightly packed valleys?:

Source 195

Source: C. Batstone, *Old Rhondda in Photographs*, 1974.

Many of these new houses were rented (either from the Company or private landlords) but there was a very high percentage of home *ownership* in the South Wales valleys—as much as 60% in some areas and in the anthracite valleys even higher. A popular way for miners to raise the money to buy their houses was through what were known as *Building Clubs* and here is an account of how these operated:

Source 196
A number of miners club together and with the assistance of a secretary . . . arrange for a large number of houses to be built in one contract. Each member pays from £10 to £20 down and thereafter monthly instalments of from 10s to 25s for each "share", that is, house. When about one-fourth of the cost of each has been paid in, the club "divides", and each member takes over his house, which is allotted him by ballot, subject to a mortgage which he can pay off gradually . . . To meet the claims of these clubs men have had to save large sums from their wages to pay for the cost of their houses over a series of from 15 to 25 years, the usual rate of contribution being at the rate of from 15s. to 24s. per month.
Source: H. S. Jevons, *The British Coal Trade*, 1915.

Despite the tremendous amount of house-building which went on, it could not keep pace with immigration into the mining valleys and there was always a shortage of housing. This led to overcrowding. In 1911 in the Rhondda an average of 6 people lived in each house and this was much higher than the average for industrial areas in the rest of Britain. In the survey quoted in Source 194, it was found that some houses had 13 people living in them and many had 10 or more people. It was very common for lodgers to be taken in because of this shortage of housing and because their rent helped with family finances, and this obviously added to the overcrowding.

Family Life

Family life in mining communities was dominated by the pit. The shift system, partic-ularly in large households where many men were employed on different shifts, must have made it seem that miners were always either going to or coming back from work. The 'working day' of the house was thus a very long one and it was also true that in many houses beds were never empty because of the shift system. The piecework system of wages meant that the amount of money coming into the house was never predictable and of course there was always the dreaded fear of a husband or a son being brought home dead or injured. Perhaps the clearest example of how the pit intruded into the home was the case of bathing. There were no pithead baths in South Wales during this period, so once the miner returned from the pit his first task was to take a bath. Below a photograph and a written account by a miner, show how this was arranged.

Source 197

Source: South Wales Miners' Library, University College of Swansea.

Source 198

I was in lodgings . . . there were six or seven other miners lodging there. It was only a house with three bedrooms, so you can imagine that we were sleeping on a rota basis . . . I'd gallop home to be the first to have a bath. There were no bathrooms: all you had was an old zinc tub and the landlady would have a couple of buckets of water on the fire. If there were five or six of you together, first of all five of you would bath the top half of the body . . . and then you stepped back into the bath and washed the bottom part of your body . . . you'd get the women from next door . . . they'd come in here and they'd sit down in the kitchen and they wouldn't move—when even you were wash-ing the bottom part of your body.

Source: C. Storm-Clark. 'The Miners: A Test Case for Oral History', *Victorian Studies*, September 1971.

This account by a woman from Abergwynfi shows you how the pit dominated the life of the miner's wife:

Source 199

She gets up any time from 5 to 6 a.m., prepares breakfast and sends off, maybe, her son, next comes in another son from the night shift. She then prepares a bath for him, which means the lifting of a heavy boiler on and off the fire. He goes off to bed. Then the younger children get up and get ready for school. When they are safely off, she tries to clean up and clear a little bit of the pit dust . . . Then dinner has to be cooked and her husband got ready for the after-noon shift. Then her son returns again from the morning shift bringing with him some more dust. The same process has to be gone through again etc. He then goes off and she again turns around to clean and tidy up before tea-time and the children home from school . . . Just as she thinks she can have an hour or two to sew or read, she again has to be preparing water and supper for her husband returning from the afternoon shift and so it goes on day after day.

Source: E. Williams, 'Pit-Head Baths', *The Colliery Workers Magazine*, July 1925.

We can see here just how hard miners' wives had to work and why in valley homes 'Mam' often became the dominant person. The women of mining communities in South Wales were well known for being almost obsessed by the need for cleanliness in their houses. With dirt and dust always being brought into the home from the pit, it was a constant battle to keep up standards. Tidiness (being 'tidy') was even extended to the scrubbing of front door-steps and flagstones in the backyard. It was a mark of self-respect for women to work hard at this and the enjoyment and pride they took in this work can be seen in this account by a Rhondda housewife:

Source 200

I used to wash the path, we had flagstones, from the back door right down to the toilet. I used to love doing it . . . I used to love working. And I used to wash the pavement from the front door, right past the window right down to the drain . . . Beautiful, lovely . . .

Source: R. Crook, *Women of the Rhondda*, 1980.

Another major task in a house full of miners was washing—all done by hand and with filthy pit clothes to clean, terrific hard work. In source 201 a Pontypool woman is seen doing her washing using a dolly tub and a poss stick in the early years of this century.

Source 201

Source: National Museum of Wales.

There were also meals to cook, bread to bake, clothes to make and mend and so forth. 'Mam' not only reared the children of the large families that were common at the time, but also took most of the responsibility over them including discipline. This account by a Treorchy woman shows just how much 'mam' was often a person to be feared. The girl was fifteen and had already been away in domestic service in London, when one night she stayed out late with a boyfriend:

Source 202

I went out and I was at half past nine down by the Square. My friend said to me "May, I think your mother is down by the lamp". I said "Don't be so silly". There she was, flannelette nightie, with a big coat right over her, shouting "Dewch Mewn Yr Tŷ (Get in the House)!" Duw! You should've seen her. I had the finest clip across the ear, boyfriend or no boyfriend by the side o'me".

Source: R. Crook, *Women of the Rhondda*, 1980.

Whilst the importance and the hard work of the typical 'Mam' was part and parcel of valley life, not all women were tied to the home in the way that is sometimes suggested. Many women had jobs and even miners' wives would add to the family earnings by taking in washing, and wallpapering in other houses, for example. The effect of all this hard work on women is described here by one South Wales miner referring to his mother:

Source 203

Women get harassed, beyond endurance, nerves frayed, life is hard and unbearable. They become a bundle of nerves . . . Day after day they struggle on, lingering at a miserable existence without hope or colour. The woman sacrifices everything for her family . . . My mother died 56 years of age. I asked the Doctor 'Why? What was wrong?' I was told that there was nothing wrong organically. She was simply worn out . . . The constant repetition of work caused through lack of facilities in the house make them almost beasts of burden . . . The miners work seven hours themselves and work their women seventeen.

Source: H. Watkins, *Unusual Students*, 1947.

Furniture, Clothes and Food

Here is a description by an Ebbw Vale man of a 'typical' miner's cottage in the early 20th century:

Source 204

Horsehair sofas and high-backed chairs in the parlour . . . the mantle piece was made of slate . . . above it stood a wooden overmantel with a centre mirror and small statues with knick-knacks. On the wall enlarged photographs of parents, grandparents . . . Boer War generals or King Edward VII or Mr. Gladstone . . . Comfortable chairs were scorned as a weakness and arm chairs, like the beds, were made for spartans (people used to hard living). Iron bedsteads with brass decoration and wire mattresses cost £2.10.0d. double, £1.10.0d. single . . . Eiderdowns were too expensive, so extra warmth in winter was provided by heavy quilts made in West Wales or else home-made patchwork quilts . . .

Source: A. Gray-Jones, *A History of Ebbw Vale*, 1970.

The same source is also interesting for the fashions in clothes of the period. Look at the various photographs in this book which show the fashions described here, being worn:

Source 205

Men still wore Welsh flannel shirts . . . Best or 'Sunday suits' of dark cloth . . . No one went hatless; the bowler or cap for most people . . . Everyone wore boots; Shoes for men were considered effeminate . . . In the early 1900s infant boys still wore frocks until they were 'breeched' at three or four years of age, and until they were seven or eight might be decked out on Sundays in sailor suits . . . Older boys wore heavy nailed boots, long thick stockings, breeches fastened at the knee, waistcoats, belted jackets, caps . . . Female clothing was also heavy and cumbersome (awkward).

Women wore long frocks, dresses or shirts over corsets or stays and abundant underclothing. Highnecked blouses and 'picture' hats decked with flowers were in fashion in the summer. Generally the only difference between the clothing of women and girls was that the girls were allowed brighter colours . . . Shawls were much used . . . babies were carried 'Welsh fashion' in a large warm flannel shawl tucked around the mother's waist . . .

Source: A. Gray-Jones, *A History of Ebbw Vale*, 1970.

More information on men's fashions and the price of clothes can be gained from Source 206 *(See page 84)*, a newspaper advertisement of 1920.

The food eaten at this time was fairly basic and although the quantity of food eaten by people was less than we eat today, it would seem from recent studies by experts that the quality and balance of their diet was much healthier than ours today. One hot meal would be eaten each day when the miner returned home from the pit. Welsh *cawl* (soup) was popular or otherwise a meat and potato dinner. Our Ebbw Vale source is also very good for the food of the period 1900-1914 and its price:

Source 207

Milk was 1½d a pint, butter 10½d to 1/1d a lb, eggs 1d, sugar 1-lb for 3½d, tea 10d to 1/10d a lb, large loaves 5½d, small 3d, pork pies 2d, cooked ham 1/6d to 1/10d a lb, oranges ½d to 1d each—Gold Flake cigarettes were 10 for 3d, Lucky Star 6 for 1d. Bananas 2 for 1½d . . . ½d and 1d bars of plain chocolate . . . 1d ribbons of liquorice . . . ½d paper bags of sherbert . . . ice-cream in ½d or 1d wafers . . . Fish and chips shops selling fried fish 2d and 4d and chips 1d and 2d.

Source: A. Gray-Jones, *A History of Ebbw Vale*, 1970.

Shops

Although clothes were more often than not made at home and some miners had allotments where they would grow some of their food, shopping centres grew up in most valley towns and villages. Most shopping was done locally as it was expensive to travel to market towns such as Pontypridd, or large shopping centres such as Newport, Cardiff and Swansea. In some of the smaller and more isolated mining villages there was often a shortage of shops and this encouraged miners' wives to set up their own small business to earn some extra money, as Bert Coombes of Resolven describes in Source 208.

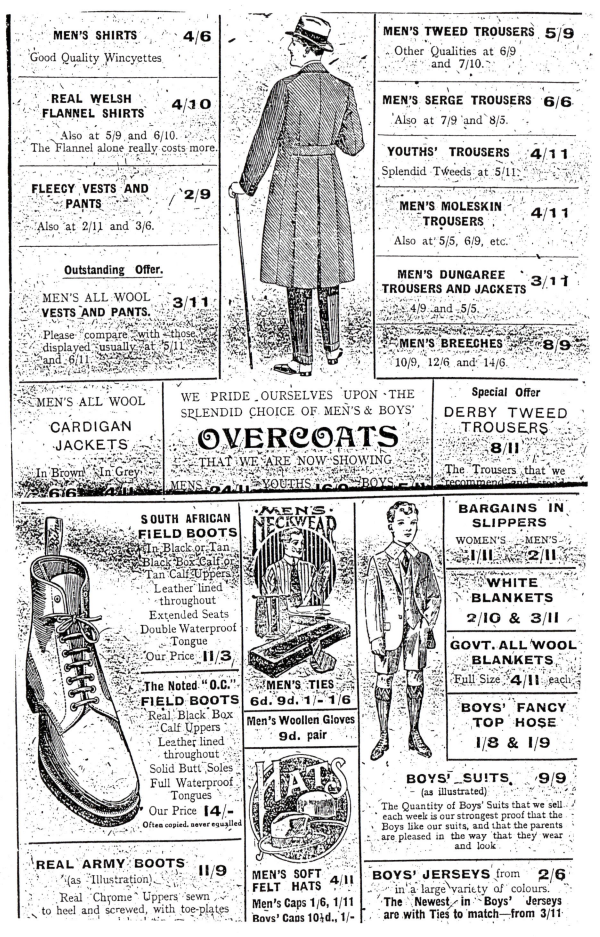

MEN'S SHIRTS   **4/6**

Good Quality Wincyettes

REAL WELSH FLANNEL SHIRTS   **4/10**

Also at 5/9 and 6/10.
The Flannel alone really costs more.

FLEECY VESTS AND PANTS   **2/9**

Also at 2/11 and 3/6.

Outstanding Offer.

MEN'S ALL WOOL VESTS AND PANTS. **3/11**

Please compare with those displayed usually at 5/11 and 6/11.

MEN'S ALL WOOL

CARDIGAN JACKETS

In Brown In Grey
6/6   4/11

WE PRIDE OURSELVES UPON THE SPLENDID CHOICE OF MEN'S & BOYS'

OVERCOATS

THAT WE ARE NOW SHOWING
MENS 24/11 YOUTHS 16/9 BOYS 5/11

MEN'S TWEED TROUSERS 5/9

Other Qualities at 6/9 and 7/10.

MEN'S SERGE TROUSERS 6/6

Also at 7/9 and 8/5.

YOUTHS' TROUSERS 4/11

Splendid Tweeds at 5/11.

MEN'S MOLESKIN TROUSERS   4/11

Also at 5/5, 6/9, etc.

MEN'S DUNGAREE TROUSERS AND JACKETS   3/11

4/9 and 5/5.

MEN'S BREECHES   8/9

10/9, 12/6 and 14/6.

Special Offer

DERBY TWEED TROUSERS

8/11

The Trousers that we recommend and

SOUTH AFRICAN FIELD BOOTS

In Black or Tan
Black Box Calf or
Tan Calf Uppers
Leather lined
throughout
Extended Seats
Double Waterproof
Tongue
Our Price **11/3**

The Noted "O.C."
FIELD BOOTS
Real Black Box
Calf Uppers
Leather lined
throughout
Solid Butt Soles
Full Waterproof
Tongues
Our Price **14/-**
Often copied, never equalled

REAL ARMY BOOTS   11/9
(as Illustration)
Real Chrome Uppers sewn
to heel and screwed, with toe-plates

MEN'S NECKWEAR

MEN'S TIES
6d. 9d. 1/- 1/6

Men's Woollen Gloves
9d. pair

HATS

MEN'S SOFT FELT HATS   4/11

Men's Caps 1/6, 1/11
Boys' Caps 10½d., 1/-

BARGAINS IN SLIPPERS

WOMEN'S   MEN'S
1/11   2/11

WHITE BLANKETS
2/10 & 3/11

GOVT. ALL WOOL BLANKETS
Full Size **4/11** each

BOYS' FANCY TOP HOSE
1/8 & 1/9

BOYS' SUITS   9/9
(as illustrated)
The Quantity of Boys' Suits that we sell
each week is our strongest proof that the
Boys like our suits, and that the parents
are pleased in the way that they wear
and look

BOYS' JERSEYS from **2/6**
in a large variety of colours.
The Newest in Boys' Jerseys
are with Ties to match—from 3/11

Source 208

Most of the selling was done in houses that had converted their front rooms into shops and hung outside signs advertising tea or salmon . . . my wife had caught the craze for shop-keeping, so I had made a counter and shelves . . . We had reared two bacon pigs, and we were selling the bacon and had peas and poultry out in the garden.

Source: B. L. Coombes, *These Poor Hands*, 1939.

In more populated areas proper shopping centres existed and as well as individual businesses, the first chain stores such as Hodges the outfitters and Home and Colonial foodstores developed.

Four sources on shops follow. The first two show individual businesses in the Rhondda in the late 1890s—why would a saddler (Source 211) have such a thriving business? The third is a street scene in Tonypandy in the early years of this century and finally there is a description of the scene inside a shop in Clydach Vale in the Rhondda.

Source 209

Source: C. Batstone, *Old Rhondda in Photographs*, 1974.

Source 210

Source: C. Batstone, *Old Rhondda in Photographs*, 1974.

Source 211

Source: National Museum of Wales.

Source 212

We lived for years behind and above our busy shops . . . It was a 'credit' shop . . . On a lectern desk panelled with a frosted glass screen lay an enormous black ledger, six inches thick, a double page for each customer. Its chronicle of strike-time debts was my mother's bible . . . The shop smelled of wholesome things . . . mounds of yellow Canadian and pallid (pale) Caerphilly cheese, rosy cuts of ham and bacon, wide slabs of butter cut by the wire for the scales . . . wall fixtures stacked with crimson packets of tea, blue satchels of sugar, dried fruit and peas . . .

Source: R. Davies, *Print of a Hare's Foot.*

By 1900 most shopping centres in the valleys would also have a *Co-operative Shop.* The idea of working people joining together to open shops was first developed in Britain by a Welshman, Robert Owen of Newtown. The first Co-operative in Wales was opened in Cwmbach, Aberdare in 1859 and by 1882 there were twenty-eight societies in South Wales. Like the Penygraig Society which was started by 46 people in 1891 and grew to have 6,200 members by 1937, they developed into big businesses which also went in for wholesaling and producing goods. The 'divi' (dividend)

which was paid back to members when there was a surplus on trade was a popular form of saving. Not only did many people believe that by supporting these societies they were getting a better quality of goods and a share of the profits, they also recognised the support which the societies gave to mining families during difficult times when money was scarce. Here are some details on the Aberdare Co-operative Society for 1902:

Source 213

IN THINGS ESSENTIAL, UNITY
IN THINGS DOUBTFUL, LIBERTY
IN ALL THINGS, CHARITY

*   *   *

THE WORKMEN'S CO-OPERATIVE
& INDUSTRIAL SOCIETY LIMITED
3, 4 & 5 Cardiff Street, Aberdare
Branches: 67 Gadlys Road and Bethesda Street, Merthyr
Bakery: Gadlys, Aberdare

Established 1869
Registered under the Industrial and Provident Societies' Act in June 1869.

Telegraphic Address.........Progress, Aberdare
Telephone.....................No. 21, Post Office
DEPARTMENTS:
Grocery and provisions; Drapery and Outfitting; millinery and Fancy Goods; Mantle; Furnishing; Boots and Shoes, and Butchering.

STATISTICS FOR THE YEAR 1902
Number of Members..........................1,604
Share Capital................................£22,331
Trade...£64,993
Net Profit.....................................£11,760

Average Dividend paid 3s 0d.

Source: Aberdare Co-operative Society Records, University College of Swansea.

Poverty and Public Health

Poverty

The 'Welfare State' that we have in Britain today did not begin until the early 20th century. In the 19th century if a miner was not in work (through illness, old age, unemployment etc.) he and his family had no automatic right to social security benefits as we do today. Therefore, even in fairly prosperous years there was always some real poverty. In such circum-

stances the poor would have to rely on help from their family and on 'tick' (credit) from shops. During periods of unemployment and strikes they often had to resort to picking coal from the tips and selling it, and soup kitchens where free meals were provided. Source 214 shows women picking coal at Aberdare during a strike in 1910 and Source 215 a soup kitchen at Beddau in 1912.

Source 214

Source: W. W. Price Collection, Aberdare Public Library.

Source 215

Source: D. Lewis, *A History of Llantrisant*, 1975.

If help and charity were not enough the only alternative was to 'go on the Parish'. This meant applying to the Poor Law Authorities for help. Each Parish set aside some of the money raised from the rates for poor relief which was doled out by Guardians, who were elected by the ratepayers. After the Poor Law Amendment Act was passed by Parliament in 1834 the Poor Law Unions (a number of parishes joined together) had to set up Workhouses. Usually those who applied for poor relief had to go into these Workhouses where conditions were harsh. Here, for example, is the food given in Swansea Workhouse in 1862:

Source 216
7 oz of bread and a pint of gruel for breakfast; dinner on three days of 4 oz of meat and either ¾ lb of potatoes or ½ lb of rice with 4 oz vegetables. One lb of pudding was given on two days and 4 oz of bread and 1 ½ pints of pea-soup on the other two. Supper was 7 oz of bread and 1 ½ pints of broth, with 2 oz of cheese and bread on two nights.

Source: J. E. Thomas, 'The Poor Law in West Glamorgan', *Morgannwg*, Vol. XV111, 1974.

Entering the Workhouse was called receiving 'in-relief' and usually the authorities did not believe in giving out-relief (money or food to people outside the workhouse) except in very few cases and then it would be no more than 2s. 6d. per week. By the end of the 19th century when there was a great deal of unemployment or a major strike, out-relief could be given only if work was done in return. This work was often very hard. Source 217 (p. 88) shows miners who had to work as stone breakers at Treharris during the miners lock-out of 1898.

Self-Help

Because of the poverty and hardship which might befall a miner as a result of an accident at work, some colliery companies set up their own Insurance Funds which paid sickness benefit for short periods. However, the main method chosen by working people to guard against the poverty which might come from

Source 217

Source: R. Page Arnot, South Wales Miners, 1967.

illness and old age, was to join a *Friendly Society*. People paid a weekly subscription to these Societies and in return they would receive assistance during difficult times. An extract from the rules of a society in the Dulais Valley provides more information on this.

Source 218 *(See page 89)*

These societies began in the early 19th century and were then organised on particular trades or areas and even individual public houses. After 1850 there was a tremendous growth in the societies and by the end of the century there were some 1,500 societies in Glamorgan and Monmouthshire alone, with nearly 250,000 members. By then it was the big national orders which were dominant—the Oddfellows, Hearts of Oak, the Ivorites. Not only were they a popular form of self-help, the societies were also organisations which people joined for the enjoyment that was had on 'club nights' and on processions and marches that were held. They were also very democratic organisations and gave training to many future community leaders. The societies did not pay very good benefits on the death of a member and with so many deaths from mining disasters taking place in South Wales, by the 1890s insurance companies such as the Prudential

and special insurance funds for major accidents (known as Permanent Relief Funds) were also active in the valleys.

Public Health

Today in our Welfare State, the availability of a free Health Service is taken for granted. Although conditions were better in the new valley communities which developed after 1850 than they had been earlier in the irontowns, there were still insanitary conditions which led to diseases such as cholera, typhus and diptheria, as this extract from a report of a Medical Officer of Health in 1893 shows:

Source 219

The river contains a large proportion of human excrement, stable and pigsty manure, congealed blood, offal and entrails from the slaughterhouses, the rotten carcases of animals, cats and dogs . . . old cast-off articles of clothing and bedding, and boots, bottles, ashes, street refuse and a host of other articles . . . In dry weather the stench becomes unbearable.

Source: Report of Medical Officer of Health for Rhondda Urban District Council, 1893.

Source 218

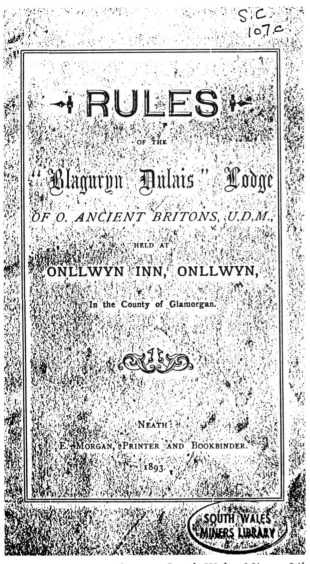

S.C.
107c

RULES

OF THE

"Blagwyn Dulais" Lodge

OF O. ANCIENT BRITONS, U.D.M.,

HELD AT

ONLLWYN INN, ONLLWYN,

In the County of Glamorgan.

NEATH:

E. MORGAN, PRINTER AND BOOKBINDER.

1893.

SOUTH WALES
MINERS LIBRARY

OBJECTS.

3.—It shall have for its objects the raising of funds, by entrance fees, subscriptions of the members, fines, donations, and by interest on capital, for the following puposes: insuring a sum of money to defray the expenses of the burial of deceased members and members' deceased wives; and rendering assistance to members when sick, and thereby unable to follow their employment; and for granting temporary relief to members in distressed circumstances. Every member shall pay or cause to be paid the sum of 2 - on each Lodge night.

ADMISSION OF MEMBERS.

4.—If any person wishes to become a member of this Lodge he must be proposed by a regular member on a Lodge night, and, if seconded, his name, age, occupation, and place of abode shall be entered in a book kept for that purpose. If the majority are of opinion that the person so proposed is fit to become a member he shall be admitted on the following terms, viz. :—

	s.	d.
From 16 to 20 years of age	5	0
„ 20 „ 30 „	7	6
„ 30 „ 35 „	10	0
„ 35 „ 40 „	12	6
„ 40 „ 45 „	15	0

CONDITIONS ENTITLING MEMBERS TO BENEFITS.

5(a)—After being a member for six months and upwards, having paid his contributions, entrance fee, together with fines, if any, he shall receive 5/- per week until he has received the full amount contributed, also an additional sum of one-half of the sum contributed, then to be reduced to 1/6 per week for the remainder of his illness.

(b) After he has been a subscribing member for twelve calendar months he shall receive the full amount which he has contributed in the sum of 10/- per week, also an additional sum of one-half of the sum contributed, then to be reduced to 1/6 for the remainder of his illness, and he shall not again be entitled until the expiration of twelve calendar months from the time he declared off the funds.

Source: South Wales Miners Library, University College of Swansea.

In particular, the rate of death of young children (the infant mortality rate) was very high in valley communities. In 1911 one of the highest rates in the whole country was in Aberdare where 213 children per 1,000 births, died, compared to an average for the whole of England and Wales of 122. The tragedy of so many young deaths is portrayed here in a newspaper 'cartoon': Source 220 *(See opposite column).*

Many of those who survived infancy still suffered badly from ill-health. Edmund Stonelake describes here the health of some of his classmates in a school at Pontlottyn in the Rhymney Valley at the end of the 19th century:

Source 221

Scabies, ringworm and tuberculosis also affected large numbers of children. I can clearly remember one boy whose head was

Source 220

Baby Graves.

MERTHYR'S YEARLY TOLL TO HER INSANITARY DWELLINGS.

This means that hundreds of human lives are being sacrificed year after year in Dowlais and the other bad districts by the failure of the capitalists employing labour to rescue that labour from foul and filthy dwellings which are death-traps and murder-holes. . . . . Merthyr does not destroy its refuse but it destroys its children.—"Human Wales," by GEO. R. SIMS.

Source: The Western Mail, 24 June, 1907.

almost covered with scab, and another who had a perpetual stinking discharge from his ears. I now know the scabby heads as ringworm. One boy of my own age, flatfooted, like a very old man, his face pale yellow, his large eyes protruding from their sockets and his breath smelled so badly that other boys avoided him and were unwilling to sit next to him . . . he died young . . .

Source: E. Stonelake, *The Autobiography of Edmund Stonelake*, 1981.

In the 1870s and 1880s Parliament passed laws to encourage local authorities to improve public health. Improvements did come but up to 1914 these were very slow and the effect of them was not to be felt for sometime.

Poor sanitation, lack of proper diet and bad housing were not the only causes of ill-health, of course. As we have seen in Section 4 of this book, work in the pit led to frequent injuries and crippling industrial diseases. The pit also led indirectly to deaths and accidents in the home. Midwives maintained that the main cause of premature births in South Wales was that expectant mothers had to lift heavy tubs of boiling water for their husband's bath. Children also suffered from this danger as one investigator reported in 1920:

Source 222

Many deaths of children occur by their falling into tubs and being scalded while the mother is preparing for the worker's bath. One of the coroners in South Wales has said "Every winter I hold more inquests on miners' children who die from scalds or burns than I do on miners who are killed underground".

Source: J. A. Lovat-Fraser. 'Pithead Baths', *Welsh Housing and Development Association Yearbook*, 1922.

Medical Facilities

With all the high incidence of ill-health and accidents there was a great need for medical treatment. Such treatment cost money, however, and it was often precisely those who were ill or injured who could least afford to pay. In such circumstances it is not surprising that wherever possible people tried to treat themselves and that the type of 'folk medicine' which Thomas Jones of Rhymney describes here, was so rife:

Source 223

Cow dung was used as a poultice for boils and carbuncles, and the water in which the blacksmith had cooled his red-hot irons was drunk as an iron tonic to strengthen the blood. Warm urine was believed to be a cure for a fresh wound and the juice of the house leek for earache. Whole pages of local newspapers were filled with standing advertisements of balms and balsams, pills and powders.

Source: T. Jones, *Rhymney Memories*, 1938.

When people were so ill that they had to receive hospital treatment they might if they were lucky belong to a Friendly Society which would pay for it, otherwise they would be forced into the dreaded fever hospitals of the Workhouses. Local Authorities were very slow to build hospitals—the first hospital in the Rhondda was not built until 1887 and then it only had 4 beds to serve a population of nearly 100,000 people! Even by 1914 when the population of Rhondda was 180,000 there were only 88 hospital beds in the valley. Matters had improved by this time as far as receiving medical treatment from a doctor was concerned. This was mainly because most Colliery Companies had employed doctors to treat their workers and their families. These medical schemes were paid for by deductions from the miners' wages and in time they were to be taken over and run by the miners themselves, for particularly where workers might be seeking compensation for an accident in the pit, there was a feeling that the doctor might not go against his employer, the Colliery Company. These *Miners Medical Schemes* led to South Wales having the most developed medical facilities for ordinary people in the whole of the United Kingdom by 1914. The quality of these medical schemes was praised and envied all over Britain. The Tredegar Medical Scheme became one of the models for the National Health Service created by a son of Tredegar, Aneurin Bevan, when he was Minister of Health in the Labour Government of 1945-1950. Despite such advances however, the death-rate and the infant mortality rate still remained much higher in South Wales than in many parts of the country. Prevention was obviously more important than cure!

Further work on the evidence
1. Look at Source 190. This is taken from an autobiography published in 1974 and it deals with the author's experiences as a domestic servant who had left South Wales in the 1920s to work in London. Consider the following questions about the Source:
   a. Do you think it is reliable, first-hand evidence on the experience of leaving South Wales to go into domestic service in London? Explain your answer.
   b. What sort of evidence do you think would be even more reliable than this?
   c. Do you think this single piece of evidence can give us a full picture of the way domestic servants were treated? Explain your answer and consider what extra evidence you would need to look at.
2. Source 207 provides evidence on the kinds of foodstuffs and other articles that people would have bought in the period 1900-1914, and the prices paid for them. The Source is taken from a history of Ebbw Vale, published in 1970, and the author does not make clear where he gets this information from. Consider these questions about the Source:
   a. What additional information do you need to have before deciding whether this is primary historical evidence?
   b. Is this sufficient evidence for a study of what a typical mining household might have spent on food and other household articles during this period? Explain your answer.
   c. What other sorts of evidence might give you more information on the amount and the quality of food that people ate at this time?

   d. Using the conversion tables at the back of this book and having found out what some of the articles mentioned cost today, make a comparison between the prices of food during this period and today.
3. Look at Sources 205, 206 and 211 and then try to answer the following questions:
   a. Which of these Sources do you think gives the clearest description of the fashions worn by boys and men at this time? Explain your answer.
   b. Which of the fashions worn by boys and men that are mentioned in Source 205 can you pick out in Source 211?
   c. Using Source 206 try to work out what it would have cost to clothe the boy shown in the foreground of Source 211. Using the coversion tables at the back of this book then try to make some comparisons with what you would pay for your clothes today.
4. Look at Source 218 and then consider the questions below:
   a. Having read carefully through the *objects* of this Friendly Society make a list of these objects in your own words.
   b. What part of the evidence in this Source would support the claim that this Friendly Society was a democratic body? Explain your answer.
   c. Why do you think older people had to pay more to join this society than younger people?
   d. What information does the Source lack on the payments which members had to make to the Society?

6.—Coalfield Society II
Popular Culture and Pastimes

Self Entertainment and Hobbies

For much of this period when people did have the time for entertainment they provided it for themselves. This was particularly true of children and Thomas Jones of Rhymney describes here some of the street games that were popular during his childhood in the 1880s:

Source 224

We bowled iron hoops on the pavement, spun tops, stalked on stilts, blew soap-bubbles out of saucers by means of a clay pipe, played marbles, leap frog, I spy. At the back of the house we played rounders and cricket and . . . 'bat and catty'. We flew kites and banged bladders about, which we got from the slaughter house. Girls skipped and hopped on the pavement and played duckstones . . .

Source: T. Jones, *Rhymney Memories*, 1938.

Source 225 is a photograph of 'bat and catty' (or 'catty and doggy' as it was also called) being played at a tournament in Tonypandy in the 1920s. Obviously adults enjoyed it as well.

Source 225

Source: C. Batstone, *Old Rhondda in Photographs*, 1974.

Carnivals and visiting Circuses were also very popular with children in valley communities. Source 226 *(See page 93)* is a typical carnival parade at Pontycymmer in the Garw Valley in 1908.

Miners also made a great deal of their own entertainment and 'hobbies' were a passion with them. Amongst such popular pastimes were rabbit-snaring, pigeon-fancying, whippet racing and keeping allotments. What is there about all these which may have made them particularly popular with miners and which also indicates something about the physical lay-out of the mining valleys?

Theatres, Cinemas and Outings

Organised entertainment first appeared in the 1870s when portable theatres were put up near public houses. Travelling actors would perform and seats for the performances were 2d. or 3d. By the 1890s permanent theatres such as the Theatre Royal in Tonypandy, shown below Source 227 *(See page 93)* were being opened.

In the same street was the Empire Theatre of Varieties and Source 228 is the souvenier programme which was produced to mark its opening in 1909. What was meant by an 'Empiroscope' (probably their word for 'Bioscope')?

Source 226

Source: R. G. Keen, *Old Maesteg and the Bridgend Valleys in Photographs*, 1979.

Source 227

Source: C. Batstone, *Old Rhondda in Photographs*, 1974.

Source 228

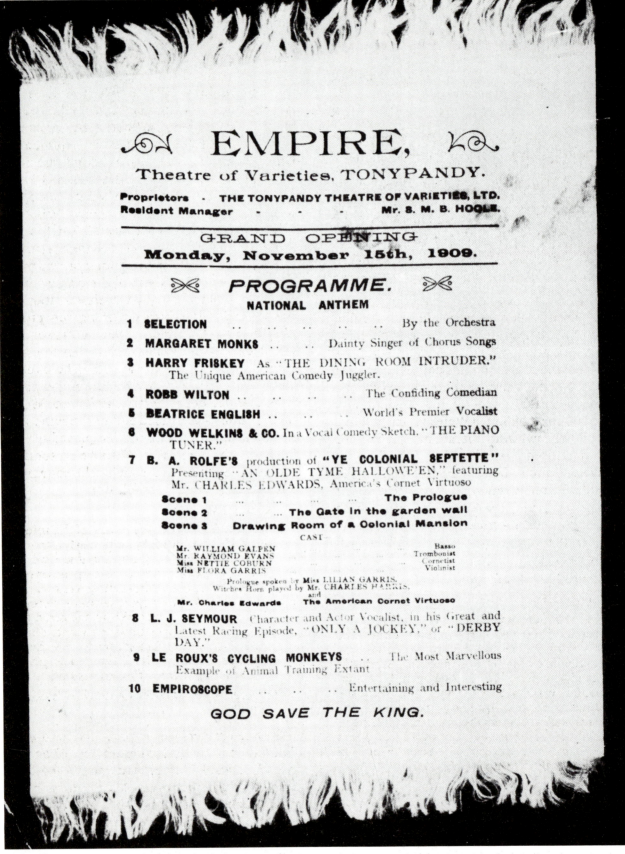

Source: C. Batstone, *Old Rhondda in Photographs*, 1974.

By 1914 the Cinema had arrived as well. Here at Treherbert in the Rhondda, the Saturday morning children's matinee (known as the 'Penny Rush') is about to start:

Source 229

Source: K. Hopkins (Ed). *Rhondda Past and Future*, 1974.

In a period when miners did not receive 'holiday pay', long holidays were rare events for a mining family. When they were taken, it would be to the seaside resorts and spa-towns of Mid and North Wales, or to relatives in the countryside. Much more common were day-trips to the coast of South Wales (usually Barry Island, Porthcawl and Aberavon) by coach or train, organised by chapels, schools and collieries. Source 230 is a photograph of the 'Rhondda Butterfly' charabanc about to set off on such an outing and the account which follows by a Bedlinog man off on a trip to Barry Island, shows the excitement of children on these occasions.

Source 230 *(See page 96)*

Source 231

We were off, under the bridge, waving to people—Then they were lost to sight and there was nothing for it but to wait for the sandwiches and pop to appear . . . Stomachs already crammed with food would then be further overloaded with sweets . . . home-made lumps of toffee . . . Spanish . . . soda water. The sea was glimpsed for the first time . . . After a solid year of village life . . . it was like a sight of Araby . . . we stampeded like a herd of buffaloes to the water's edge.

Source: W. H. Davies, *The Right Place, The Right Time . . . 1972.*

Sport

Like other industrial areas of Britain in the late 19th century, the South Wales valleys were obsessed with organised sport. Games such as rounders and quoits were very popular and,

especially in the Rhondda, handball had a great following. Boxing and foot-racing were sports which attracted gamblers. Thousands of spectators attended the many 'Powderhall' sprints and there were a suprising number of professional or semi-professional runners in the valleys. Boxing varied from the bare-fist fights organised on local hillsides which went on for as long as it took for one man to be beaten unconscious, to more organised and controlled contests. South Wales produced a number of boxing champions during this period, the most famous of whom were Freddie Welsh of Pontypridd who became world lightweight champion in 1914 and the legendary Jimmy Wilde of Tylorstown, who in a career of 864 fights lost only 4 and became flyweight champion of the world in 1916. The most popular of organised sports by the 1890s, however, were association and rugby football. Rugby was first introduced into South Wales by boys returning from public schools in England and the few public schools which existed in Wales itself. Despite this upper-class background it soon took hold in the South Wales valleys, with many rugby clubs being founded in the 1870s. In 1881 the Welsh Rugby Union was formed and in the same year the first international match was played against England, which ended in Wales being soundly beaten. A Bedlinog man explains the popularity of rugby in the valleys as follows:

Source 232

Possibly it was the very nature of the miner's work which made rugby particularly attractive . . . mining was tough, rough and hard . . . These qualities were to develop a sense of cameraderie (fellowship) among workers, who tended to take their sport far more seriously than others . . . taking part in the game gave the miner an opportunity of gaining more social prominence as a player for was he not rubbing shoulders with the elite and surpassing (overcoming) them at their own game.

Source: W. H. Davies, *The Right Place, The Right Time . . . 1972.*

Although miners were to be found in most of Wales' teams during this period (the 'Rhondda' type of forward—strong and robust—became famous) they often lined up along with schoolteachers, doctors and ministers of religion! In the early years of international rugby, valley clubs such as Treorchy, Treherbert, Penygraig and Llwynypia provided a steady supply of internationals. However, by 1914 it was the clubs on the South Wales coast—Newport, Cardiff, Swansea and Llanelli

Source 230

Source: K. Hopkins (Ed.), *Rhondda Past and Future*, 1974.

—which were beginning to dominate first-class rugby. They drew most of their players from valley communities, however, and some valley clubs such as Pontypool, Maesteg and Ebbw Vale (shown here in the 1900-1 season) were not far behind the big clubs.

Source 233

Source: K. Thomas, *Old Ebbw Vale in Photographs.*

1901-1912 was Wales's first 'golden age' in international rugby when Wales won the triple-crown six times and the first rugby 'superstars' appeared—W. J. Bancroft, Evan and David James of Swansea and especially A. J. Gould of Newport. Perhaps the most famous game of these years was the 1905 victory over the all-conquering New Zealand 'All Blacks' which was watched by 50,000 spectators in Cardiff. It did much to confirm rugby as the national game of Wales. Here is a souvenir photograph of the Welsh team in that match:

Source 234

Source: B.B.C. Hulton Picture Library.

In North Wales soccer was much more popular than rugby and it was probably the migration of so many North Walians into the South Wales coalfield, along with Englishmen, which made soccer so popular in the valleys. At first Merthyr Town, formed in 1907, were the 'big' team and they were admitted to the Third Division of the English League in 1918. Cardiff City F.C. was founded in 1910 and within ten years had been admitted into the Second Division of the Football League, winning promotion to the First Division in their first season and in 1923-24 only failing to become champions by .024 of a point. Thousands travelled by train from the valleys to see Cardiff City, Newport County and Swansea Town play and by the 1920s in many valley communities soccer had outstripped rugby in support. Even small villages such as Ynysddu in Monmouthshire could boast three successful teams. Source 235 *(See opposite column)* shows one of them, Ynysddu Town AFC, in 1920.

Source 235

Source: K. Thomas, *Old Ebbw Vale in Photographs.*

The Public House

Because they did not yet have their own club-houses many of the early rugby and soccer clubs would have been founded, met and even changed before matches, in a local public house. Indeed if anything rivalled sport in popular activity and entertainment at this time it was 'the pub'. Villages in the mining valleys had a tremendous number of public houses and beer-shops per head of the population and before licensing laws were introduced they were open the greater part of the day. Here is a photograph of the New Inn, Ton Pentre, a fairly typical valley pub of the period, and it is followed by a description of a pub at this time by Bryn Lewis, whose father kept the New Inn Hotel in Clydach Vale.

Source 236

Source: K. Hopkins (Ed.), *Rhondda Past and Future*, 1974.

Source 237

There was over eighteen pumps in the big bar alone and there was a small bar that men in working clothes weren't allowed in. On a Friday pay day, we'd have 23 people serving behind the bar, and when the hooter went for the men to come up we'd start drawing the pints of beer and put them under the counter. . . There was a lot of drunkenness and nearly every Saturday night a lot of fighting . . . Women were only allowed in the 'Jug and Bottle' . . . only about half a dozen women came in altogether to drink . . . I never saw women drink until I went to London in 1926 . . . Colliers would drink eleven or twelve pints, and the beer was stronger then . . . They played dominoes, rings, bagatelle . . . quoits . . .

Source: Interview with Mr. Bryn Lewis, South Wales Miners' Library, University College of Swansea.

Why was drinking so widespread? Drinking beer was as popular in the rural areas of Wales as it was in the valleys and it was much preferred to drinking water, milk or tea. This letter sent by a miner to a newspaper in 1881 gives some help in finding an explanation for this:

Source 238

How would these very good people (who want pubs to be closed on a Sunday) like to live days, weeks and months underground without a sign of the sun, and then on a wet Sunday to keep within doors all the sunless hours, except while attending divine worship? Oh, these very generous people have their nice cosy clubs or homes which they enjoy every day. But the collier has to live in discomfort in a small house.

Source: The Merthyr Express, 30 July, 1881.

Drunkeness was one result of this, though the amount of it was often exaggerated by campaigners against pubs and drinking (the Temperance Movement). In 1881 in Glamorgan the place with the highest number of convictions for drunkeness (Pontypridd) had 9.1 convictions for every 1,000 of its population. By the end of the 19th century drunkeness had declined a great deal. Some of this was due to the campaigning of the Temperance Movement, but it also had much to do with the supply of purer drinking water, the building of halls and libraries where people could meet and the growing popularity of open-air sport.

Music

A particularly strong part of the popular culture of the valleys was a love for music and especially for participation in the making of music. Perhaps choirs more than anything else have earned Wales her reputation as 'the land of song' and mass choirs became part of people's

image of the communities of the South Wales valleys. The growth of this choral tradition dates back to the 1870s. In 1872 and 73 the famous 'Cor Mawr' won choral competitions held at Crystal Palace, London, under their conductor Griffith R. Jones (Caradog), a colliery blacksmith from Aberdare. In the Rhondda the Treorchy Male Voice Choir and the Rhondda Glee Society were the two great choirs which grew up. Source 239 *(See page 99)* is a photograph of the Glee Society taken to mark their appearance at Windsor Palace to sing before Queen Victoria in 1898.

Brass and Silver Bands became just as famous. In the Rhondda the Parc and Dare Band (based at Treorchy) and the Cory Band (based at Pentre) became, and have remained, the two great names. All over South Wales, Colliery Companies, individual Coalowners, Friendly Societies, Chapels and Miners' Unions, helped Bands to form. Here is a picture of one band (a silver one) from Gwaun-Cae-Gurwen in the Amman Valley (West Wales) which was formed in 1902.

Source 240

Source: South Wales Miners' Library, University College of Swansea.

The Tonic Solfa system helped the members of Choirs, Bands, Opera Societies and Orchestras to read music. Thousands of people learned music through this and two other indications of this passion for music in valley communities were the pianos so often to be found in miners' homes and the naming of sons Haydn, Handel etc., after great composers of that name. Why were so many miners involved in Choirs and Bands and why did mining villages take so much pride in their local choir or band winning a competition?

The Eisteddfod

The competitions in which these bands and choirs participated were often ones organised

Source 239

The Rhondda Glee Society.
As they appeared at Windsor Castle before Her Majesty the Queen. Feb.

Source: C. Batstone, *Old Rhondda in Photographs*, 1974.

by the *Eisteddfod* movement. The Eisteddfod had its roots deep in Welsh history but it was in the 1820s that it was revived and by the end of the 19th century it was a form of mass popular entertainment in most of Wales. The National Eisteddfod was revived in 1858 and with the coming of the railways people flocked to the National and the other large eisteddfodau (known as semi-nationals) to support their local choirs, poets and writers. The standard of literature in these competitions was not necessarily very high, but the opportunity they gave to ordinary people to express and enjoy themselves was perhaps the important thing about them. It was not at national or semi-national level that the Eisteddfod movement was at its strongest, however, for in most valley communities hardly a week would pass without a Church, Chapel, Friendly Society or some other organisation, holding a local eisteddfod. Here is part of the programme for

the 2nd Annual Eisteddfod of the Mountain Ash Cottage Hospital in 1896:

Source 241

PROGRAMME.
Literature, &c.

	£	s.	D.
An Elegy to the late J. W. Jones. (Full particulars may be had on application to Mr. David Williams, Clothing Mart, Mountain Ash). Prize	5	5	0
Essay, "The Rise and Progress of Mountain Ash." Prize, given by D. T. Phillips, Esq., Solicitor, Mountain Ash	3	3	0
The successful Elegy and Essay to become the property of the Committee.			
Recitation, "Y Groes Ddu." Prize, given by J. Griffiths, Esq., Butcher, Mountain Ash	1	1	0
Recitation, with Musical Accompaniment, "Curfew must not ring to-night" (Stanley Hawley). Prize, given by the Publishers, Messrs. Robert Cocks & Co., 6, New Burlington Street, London	1	1	0

* * * * * * * * * * * * * *

Vocal Music Competition.

Chief Choral Competition (open to all comers), not under 120 voices—"When His loud voice in thunder spoke" ("*Jephtha*," *Handel*). Published by Messrs. Novello, Ewer & Co., 1 Berners' Str

Source: Mountain Ash Comprehensive School, Local History Collection.

Religion

The Rise of the Chapels

The strength of the musical tradition and the Eisteddfod movement in the South Wales valleys, owed a great deal to the influence of religion in people's lives. The century up to 1850 had seen the Church of England (the 'established' or official Church) fall into disfavour with many of the Welsh people. The reasons why this happened are many and complicated. What is certain, and as can be seen here in these figures for South Wales taken from the Religious Census of 1851, is that the various *Nonconformist* groups which were set up replaced the Church of England in majority popular support:

Source 242

SOUTH WALES

Population, 593,607

RELIGIOUS DENOMINATIONS.	Number of places of Worship and Sittings.		Number of Attendants1 at Public Worship on Sunday, March 30, 1851			Number of Places open for Worship at each Period of the Day on Sunday, March 30, 1851; and Number of Sittings thus available.					
						Places of Worship open.			Sittings.		
	Places of Worship.	Sittings.*	Morning.	Afternoon.	Evening.	Morning.	Afternoon.	Evening.	Morning.	Afternoon.	Evening.
TOTAL -	1863	435,556	205,936	88,481	200,604	1256	735	1076	332,012	142,145	297,928
PROTESTANT CHURCHES:											
Church of England -	615	129,491	47,907	25,286	19,695	434	294	129	98,068	56,665	46,816
Independents - -	367	103,997	64,662	17,116	59,079	266	104	269	87,129	23,279	80,217
Baptists:											
Particular Baptists	264	69,690	39,597	11,468	46,946	197	73	203	56,315	13,877	58,980
General Baptists,											
New Connexion -	3	414	255	..	252	3	..	2	414	..	330
Baptists (undefined)	30	5817	3164	561	3023	23	5	24	5287	650	5117
Society of Friends -	7	714	98	39	..	7	4	..	714	614	..
Unitarians - -	25	4890	1904	703	730	16	8	7	3394	1505	1312
Wesleyan Methodists:											
Original Connexion	168	31,313	9973	4304	17,082	93	63	138	23,478	7449	28,467
Primitive Methodists	37	4152	1133	1128	2553	14	21	29	2203	1976	3850
Bible Christians -	1	140	..	..	120	..	..	1	..	..	140
Wesleyan Methodist											
Association - -	1	258	52	72	98	1	1	1	258	258	258
Wesleyan Reformers	2	120	40	..	115	1	..	2	120	..	120
Calvinistic Methodists:											
Welsh Calvinistic Methodists - -	302	77,949	32,099	25,291	47,054	167	138	240	49,127	31,560	67,820
Lady Huntingdon's Connexion -	1	650	450	..	600	1	..	1	650	..	650
Brethren - -	1	200	90	..	173	1	..	1	200	..	200
Isolated Congregations -	12	1541	789	390	959	7	5	7	535	590	1011
OTHER CHRISTIAN CHURCHES:											
Roman Catholics -	7	1938	2540	381	376	7	4	4	1938	1522	1358
Latter Day Saints -	18	2170	1149	1721	1726	16	14	16	2070	2170	1170
Jews - - - -	2	112	34	21	23	2	1	2	112	30	112

Source: Census of Religious Worship, 1851.

The Church of England did regain some of its following in the latter part of the 19th century, but it was the Nonconformist Chapels which were to dominate the religious life of the new mining communities in the South Wales valleys. Chapel building in South Wales went on at a remarkable pace in the second half of the nineteenth century: it has been calculated that in Wales as a whole, a chapel was built every 8 days! Some of these chapels were hurriedly and cheaply built at first and later the original buildings would be replaced by grander structures designed by architects. Here, for example, is Carmel Chapel, Ebbw Vale, originally built in 1821 and then re-built in 1829 and 1865:

Source 243

Source: K. Thomas, *Old Ebbw Vale in Photographs.*

The Denominations

Evidence for Maesteg in 1926 shows the various chapels which were set up in one valley community. The list which follows of Chapels in the Maesteg area (Source 244, p. 101) shows the main denominations (groups of chapels) and in some cases it gives the number of seats in particular chapels. In 1926 Maesteg had a population of about 28,000. Bearing this in mind and having looked closely at the Source, try to answer the questions which follow.

1. What are the four largest groups (denominations) of chapels?
2. How many seats are there in all (for the chapels where seating is given)?
3. What proportion of the population of Maesteg could be seated in the chapels for which we are given the number of seats?
4. Although obviously not all the seats in the Chapels would have necessarily been filled on any Sunday, compare the percentage you have arrived at in Question 3 to the

Source 244

	Seat.
Bethania (Welsh), Bethania st. Rev. Edward Iorwerth Jones	1000
Bethel (English), Church street, Rev. Owen Jones	500
Caer Salem, Nantyffyllon	500
Calvaria (Welsh), Cwmvelyn, Rev. Benj. Jones	600
Hope (English), Caerau	200
Noddfa (Welsh), Caerau road, Caerau	550
Zion (English), Castle street	500
Tabernacle (Welsh), Station street	620
Salem (Welsh), Nantyffyllon	1150
Ainon (Welsh), Llangynwyd	
Calvinistic Methodist—	
Tabor, Commercial street, Rev. William Thomas	700
Jerusalem (Welsh), Picton street, Rev. David John Morgan	600
Libanus, Bridgend road	800
Hermon, Caerau, Rev. William Edwards	
Moriah, Llangynwyd	
Trinity (Welsh, Forward movement),Nantyffyllon	
Congregational—	
Canaan (Welsh), St. Michael's road	575
Carmel (Welsh), Commercial street, Rev. William Rice Bowen	750
Castle street (English)	250
Dyffryn (Welsh), Spelter	400
Garth road (Welsh) (Ebenezer), Rev. Rees Walters	300
Llangynwyd (Bethesda) (Welsh)	
Noddfa, Troedyrhiw-Garth, Rev. Rees Walters	
Saron (Welsh), High street, Nantyffyllon	700
Siloh (Welsh), Nantyffyllon	800
Soar (Welsh), Zoar place, Rev. David Roberts	600
Zion (Welsh), Caerau road, Caerau	600
Presbyterian (English), Hermon road	
Wesleyan (Welsh) (Penuel), Hermon road	
Wesleyan (English), Castle st. (Bridgend Circuit)	
Wesleyan (Welsh),Horeb (Treorky Circuit),Troedy-rhiw-Garth	
United Methodist, Caerau road	

Source: Kelly's Directory of South Wales, 1926.

percentage of people in your History class who attend Church or Chapel today.

To take another example, in the Rhondda in 1905 there were 151 chapels which could seat up to 85,000 people—nearly 75% of the population. As in Maesteg the most popular Nonconformist Chapels (denominations) were known as the 'Big Four'. These were the *Calvinistic Methodists*—the largest in Wales as a whole, but they had most of their strength in rural Wales. Then there were the *Congregationalists* (known usually as the Independents or in Welsh as the Annibynwyr) who were particularly strong in South Wales, the *Baptists* and the smallest of the four, the *Wesleyans*. There were other groups and sects as well, of course. One of these was the Salvation Army, which has always had a presence in valley communities. Here Source 245 *(See opposite column)* is one of their famous bands in Pentre, Rhondda, in 1912.

The Influence of the Chapels

With their great popular following the Chapels and their Ministers had a powerful influence over the lives of mining communities in the 19th century. They involved themselves in

Source 245

Source: Treorchy Comprehensive School, Local History Collection.

politics. They were a source of great strength for the Welsh language. Most of all they were a great influence in the everyday lives of many people; there was great respect for the Sabbath and attendance at Chapel and Sunday School. Families kept their best clothes for Sunday; many people prepared the Sunday dinner on Saturday to keep most of Sunday free for chapel. People looked forward to the sermon and after chapel would talk about the oratory and 'the message'. There were chapel choirs, bands and drama groups; the holding of local and district eisteddfodau; the development of the highly popular public singing festivals known as *Gymanfa Ganu*; the organisation of *Penny Readings* where children would make their own entertainment through reading stories to each other, and much else besides.

In the 1860s the Chapels were at the forefront of the *Temperance Movement*, for they saw alcohol, public houses and drunkeness as a great evil which undermined the Christian way of life. In the campaign which led to the Welsh Sunday Closing Act of 1881 that closed public houses in Wales on a Sunday, they carried out many canvasses of people's views on drink. Source 246 *(See page 102)* is the result of one of their canvasses held in Mountain Ash in 1878.

The chapels also supported Temperance Societies such as the Band of Hope, the Rechabites and the Good Templars. They encouraged their members—especially children —to join them and to 'take the pledge', described here by a young boy from Bedlinog:

Source 247

The Chief Ruler then turned to us and asked us to note what we were going to pledge ourselves to do . . . Then solemnly we repeated this pledge "I promise to abstain (forgo) from all intoxicating liquor, to do all I can to promote

Source 246

CANVASS OF HOUSEHOLDERS AT MOUNTAIN ASH ON THE QUESTION OF STOPPING THE SALE OF INTOXICATING LIQUOR ON SUNDAYS, 14 MAY 1878

| | | | | Percentage of Each 'Class' | | |
Occupation	For	Against	Neutral	For	Against	Neutral
Colliers	438	12	15	94.2	2.6	3.2
Labourers	194	18	6	89.2	8.2	2.6
Mechanics	84	13	8	79.6	12.6	7.8
Tradesmen	58	5	5	85.2	7.4	7.4
Widows	50	—	2	96.1	—	3.9
Engine drivers and Firemen	35	2	—	94.6	5.4	—
Unemployed	29	5	2	80.6	14.8	5.6
Colliery Managers, Overmen and Weighers	26	3	—	89.7	10.3	—
Railway Employers	10	—	1	91	—	1
Ministers	7	—	—	100	—	—
Professionals	6	1	2	66.7	11.1	22.2
Publicans	3	5	1	33.3	55.6	11.1
Farmers	1	1	—	50	50	—
TOTAL	941	65	42	89.9	6.1	4

Source: Lord Swansea Collection, National Library of Wales.

total abstinence, to abide by the rules, to obey the officers and ever strive to be a faithful Rechabite." We were then given our sashes which hung like horse collars over our necks and shoulders . . .

Source: W. H. Davies, *The Right Place, The Right Time . . .* 1972.

The importance of the Chapels in the lives of many families and the great influence which the Minister and his sermons had, is seen here in the views of a Glynneath miner:

Source 248

A sermon was not some talk given on a Sunday evening and then forgotten about, it was talked about by groups of people during the week and attempts made to put it into practice not by church members only but by others who got to know of the sermon. The church building was the centre of much activity where friendship could be formed and cultivated and where conversation would always be helpful. Furthermore there was nowhere else to go in the village so we went to the chapel where we also had much fun which we made ourselves. I have no regret that I had to attend chapel so often because it gave me a firm foundation and an outlook on life. It gave me to understand that we are so dependent upon other people and that "Man is not an island unto himself" but is a member of a community and must be

concerned with other people and the conditions under which they live.

Source: C. Prothero, *Recount*, 1981.

Chapels were democratic organisations, which gave working people one of the few opportunities they had at this time to express themselves and their views. They were built with the savings of the people, and it was the members who selected and paid the Minister, elected the Deacons and generally decided the activities of the Chapels. They helped to strengthen the old idea of the Welsh people as 'Y Werin'—a classless, cultured and respectable people.

Criticism and Decline

Great as the influence of the Chapels in the mining valleys was, we must be careful not to over-exaggerate their importance. The 1851 census of religious worship (see Source 242) showed that at least half the population of Wales did not attend any church or chapel. After civil marriages (i.e. in registry offices) were introduced by a law of 1837, Wales had one of the highest percentages of marriage outside Churches and Chapels. The appearance of Clubs in valley communities in the 1880s (which could open on Sundays) and the kind of evidence provided by a Pontlottyn miner, shows that many people were not influenced by the temperance views of the Chapels. Pontlottyn was a village on the border between Glamorgan (where after 1881 pubs were closed on a Sunday) and Monmouthshire (where they were still open):

Source 249

On the West bank of the river the Act was in operation and all the public houses are closed on Sundays; on the East side they were open. People residing on the West bank had only to cross a very short bridge to get as much beer as they required . . . Promptly at noon there marched a continuous procession of men, and women, from the dry area to the wet area carrying every kind of vessel that would hold liquid. This traffic kept moving throughout the opening hours . . . After closing hours . . . men moved to a quarry, consumed the beer, fell asleep and remained prostrate and helpless until they awoke a few hours later . . .

Source: E. Stonelake, *The Autobiography of Edmund Stonelake*, 1981.

The Chapels also had their critics. The very strict values of the Chapels did turn people away from them. Ministers and Deacons were often opposed to their members attending theatres, sports matches and trade-union meetings, let alone going to pubs or gambling. Members could be expelled for courting in public. One person who turned against the Chapels for such reasons was Will Paynter, later a President of the miners' union in South Wales. He describes here the reaction of his Minister to him leaving the Chapel, and his own response:

Source 250

I remember coming home from the pit one afternoon to find the minister waiting for me. I was tired, hungry, in sweaty pit clothes, and certainly in no mood for a discussion on religion. He tried his best to get me to . . . return to the chapel. Finally he got down on his knees, pulling my mother and me down with him, and prayed for my salvation. He then told me the story of a similar experience he had of a lad like me refusing God, and how on the day following his talk with him, he saw this young lad's body being carried from the pit: Mother started to cry and I became very angry, yanking the minister to his feet, telling him . . . I would never respond to such methods.

Source: W. Paynter, *My Generation*, 1972.

By 1914 the 'Big 4' Chapels were losing members. We certainly should not exaggerate the decline of the Chapels and their influence during the period we are looking at, for there were still 400,000 chapel members in Wales in the early 1920s. However, by the early years of this century it is clear that the influence of Nonconformity in South Wales was declining. There was a great 'religious revival' in 1904-05 led by an ex-miner from Llwchwr, Evan Roberts. For eighteen months people returned to the chapels in droves and it was shown that there was still a great passion for religion in the

valleys. Within a matter of years, however, the Chapels admitted that most of these 'converts' had left.

The Chapel and the Community

Many people who came to live in the valleys built their views and values largely on their religious beliefs and faith. The chapels helped them maintain and develop these in their new surroundings—it gave them a quick sense of belonging, a quick sense of direction. Chapels were also right at the centre of many of the musical, dramatic and social activities which sprang up. Chapel was particularly important for women, who had few other opportunities for social life in the valley communities. For children who were scrubbed sparkling clean and decked out in their 'Sunday best', 'Chapel on a Sunday' might be the highlight of their week. Perhaps this social and community role of the Chapels is best summed up in the annual Chapel Walks or Processions, such as this one below at Pontycymmer in 1908, which were so much a part of the valley scene:

Source 251

Source: R. G. Keen, *Old Maesteg and the Bridgend Valleys in Photgraphs*; 1979.

Education

Sunday Schools

Churches and Chapels also played an important part in the development of education in Coalfield communities. Until the 1870s *Sunday Schools* organised by Churches and Chapels provided much of the education which people received. Source 252 is a photograph of the Sunday School classes at Nebo Baptist Chapel, Pontygof, Ebbw Vale in 1900 and the account of a Sunday School class in the

Rhondda in the 1880 which follows (Source 253), shows what went on in such classes which involved adults as well as children.

Source 253

Near the fire . . . is seated a large class of children of both sexes, engaged in learning the Welsh A.B.Ch. In another class are older little ones, learning to read Welsh . . . Those in the pews are struggling to learn the Welsh Bible . . . In the great pew . . . are the advanced students and their teacher . . . Another class is composed of the advanced scholars of the

Source 252

Source: K. Thomas, *Old Ebbw Vale in Photographs.*

women . . . The Clerk . . . jots down the record of the number of verses each one has related from memory . . . Then the classes . . . recite before the entire school the Ten Commandments . . .

Source: O. Morgan, *History of Pontypridd and the Rhondda Valleys*, 1903.

Day-Schools

Until 1870 the Government took very little responsibility for education and schools, before then, were either set up by individuals or by organisations like the Church and Chapels. Some of the first day-schools (ones attended from Monday to Friday) were set up by Iron and Coal Companies, which would then deduct money to pay for them from their workers' wages. Thirty-four colliery schools were opened in Glamorgan and Monmouthshire between 1860 and 1886. The standard of education in them varied a great deal. A Church of England minister visited one of these schools at Hirwaun in March 1856 and this is what he reported:

Source 254

I found that the miserable schools connected with the works in this place are still great obstacles . . . The workmen are obliged to pay out of their wages towards the support of schools, one superintended by a drunken man who is in the habit of cursing and swearing at the children . . .

Source: Journal of William Roberts (Nefydd), Blaina. National Library of Wales.

Perhaps this minister was a little biased as he was trying to start a Church School (known as 'National' schools) in the area. Indeed there was tremendous competition between the Church and the Chapels (with their 'British' schools) to open day-schools in the new mining villages and this helped to provide schools more quickly. The Church was richer, however, and built more schools despite the fact that far more people were chapel-goers. In 1870 Parliament passed an Act which allowed School Boards to be set up in areas where there were not enough day-schools already, using money from the rates to build new schools. By the end of the 1870s, therefore, new *Board Schools* began to appear as well. Source 255 *(See page 105)* shows the first pupils at the Beddau Board School in 1878.

By 1900, all children from the ages of about 4 to 12, received a basic education in elementary (what we call primary) schools. What is known about these schools? Classes were very large and partly because teachers had so many children to deal with, discipline was very harsh and most learning was done by rote (memory) in the basic subjects of Reading, Writing, Arithmetic and Scripture. Source 256 is a photograph of Treorchy Girls School in 1913 and Source 257 an entry from the school log of a Maesteg Infants School in 1895 showing the work done by different classes on one day.

Source 255

Source: D. Lewis, *A History of Llantrisant,* 1975.

Source 256

Source: K. S. Hopkins (Ed.), *Rhondda Past and Future,* 1974.

Source 257 *(See page 106)*

Secondary Schools

In 1881 there were only 4,000 children over the age of 12 in school in the whole of Wales. Some of these were in the Higher Grade Schools which School Boards had set up in some areas, but most went to fee-paying Grammar and Public Schools. In 1889 the Welsh Intermediate Education Act was passed which allowed most local authorities to set up 'County Schools' which could educate pupils up to the age of 18. However, although there were scholarships to be won to these new Secondary schools, most

places were fee-paying. Not many parents in mining communities could afford this as can be seen in the case of the Rhondda, where in 1891 there were still only 487 pupils in the two secondary schools. In 1902, nearly all the places in these schools became free and although most children in South Wales still left school by the age of 12, a growing number of pupils attended the County Schools and sat for the examinations of the Central Welsh Board. Source 258 lists the examination subjects and regulations for the Central Welsh Board Junior and Senior Certificate (today's equivalent of the GCSE) in 1911. Consider these points:

Source 257

216

The Goods which I ordered before the
holidays have Not yet come. We want
many things badly.

Oct. 4th

Attendance still very low. Fever increasing
in prevalence.

7th

Mabon's Day. Flannel Fair, Baptists' Tea,
and Foundation Stone of Church laid.
Compelled to give a holiday.

Syllabus for Oct. 18th

	Reading	Writing	Arith.	Occupation	Obj Less
1st class	Blackie 39 to 46	Names	Add. of 10s	Mats 4" pat. Embroidery	Bl.bd Apple
	Moffatt's 18 to 23	Dictation of Letters	Sub. of 10s	Button sewing	Owl
2nd class				Hemming Knitting	sewing Forms & Col.
	Word Building to page 6, & preceding every Reading Lesson from page board				
3rd class	Cards 13 to 18	o a s x	Dict. of units	Mats	B.L. Pencil
		b h k	Bld. bd. add.	Word Build from	Apple
		y z qu	+ subt. to 7	ax, at, ed, en,	Owl
				en, eg, it, id	Herring
	Needle Thimble + Hemming Drills			ir, im, ip, ij, ec	Forms & Colour
5th class	Alphabets Cards 3 letters	m c i s	Mental to 6	Cubes	Rabbit
	Needle + Thimble Drills		Figure making	Stick laying	Parts of Body Butcher's Shop
Babies	1st column & alphabet	1 6 7	Mental to 3	Letter making	Dolls Kitchen articles Ditto

Source: Merthyr Colliery School, Maesteg, Infants Department Log Book, 1895.

1. What subjects on the list are not available in your school today?
2. What subjects that you can study today are not on the list?
3. What do you notice about the option choice compared to the one in your school today?

Source 258

Section A	Scripture Knowledge	Literature
	English Language	History
Section B	Arithmetic	Mathematics
Section C	Latin	Spanish
	Greek	German
	Welsh	Italian
	French	
Section D	Physics	Elementary Science
	Chemistry	Mechanics
	Botany	Applied Mechanics
	Elementary Biology	Geology
	Geography	
	Agriculture	
Section E	Book-keeping	Drawing
	Shorthand	Hygiene & Domestic
	Theory of Music	Economy
Section F	Woodwork	Needlework
	Metalwork	Cookery

Pupils presented for examination must take at least five subjects from Section A-D and, as a rule, one at least from each of the first three sections.

Source: Central Welsh Board Regulations, 1911.

Adult Education

As we have seen the desire for self-education was part of the appeal of the Eisteddfod and, particularly through the Sunday Schools, of the Chapels. There were also Literary and Debating Societies, Mechanics' Institutes and Scientific Societies in many parts of the coalfield. The Chapels and the Coalowners encouraged and supported such organisations as they believed they turned men away from public houses and trade unions and so encouraged them to become better and more 'respectable' work-men. Local Authorities organised adult evening classes with first-aid and mining classes being particularly popular. In the early twentieth century the Workers Educational Association and the Extra-Mural classes organised by University College Cardiff and the University College of Wales, Aberystwyth, added to the growing enthusiasm for adult education.

Many miners however, who shared this love of education became suspicious of education which they felt was organised for them by their 'betters' and designed to keep them in their place in society. In the early 1900s they formed the 'Independent Working-Class Education Movement' which was designed to educate working-men to be more effective in their trade-union and political work. The teachers and organisers of these classes were often working men who had won scholarships from the South Wales Miners Federation to leave their jobs as miners to study for a year at Ruskin College, Oxford and the Central Labour College in London. This movement helped to produce a new generation of miners' trade-union leaders and M.P.s like Aneurin Bevan and James Griffiths, who both held important positions in the 1945-51 Labour Government. The classes were organised sometimes by the *Plebs League* (later the National Council of Labour Colleges) and otherwise by the S.W.M.F. itself. Source 259 is part of the syllabus of classes organised by the Western District of the S.W.M.F. in 1921. It shows you the type of subjects taught in these classes.

Source 259

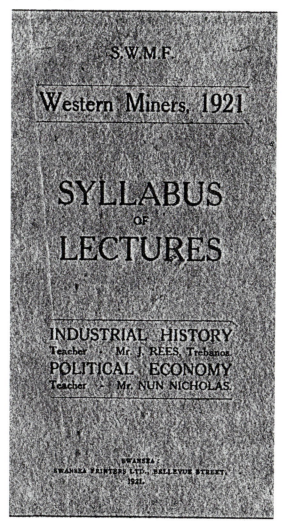

Source 259 *(Continued)*
Political Economy.
———o———

Lecture 1.—Political Economy: Scope, Objects, Categories, Schools.

(1)—*Object:* To arrive at an understanding of the various relations which men mutually enter into in order to produce the requirements of life, together with the social phenomena arising therefrom, and the formulating of same into general propositions, or Laws.

(2)—*Scope:* Is therefore limited to an analysis of the facts and phenomena of Production, Circulation and Distribution of material " wealth."

(3)—*Schools:* Represent the various attempts made at different times and at different places to formulate and explain these Laws. The Chief Schools are :—
  (a)—Ancient
  (b)—Mercantile
  (c)—Physiocrat
  (d)—Classical
  (e)—Ricardian Socialist
  (f)—Marxian
  (g)—Utility, or Psychological.

(4)—*Categories:* Goods, wealth, use-value, commodities, value, exchange-value, money, price, capital, rent, profit, interest, surplus-value, etc.

Source: South Wales Miners' Library, University College of Swansea.

Miners' Institutes

By the early years of the twentieth century many adult classes were being held in the Miners' Halls and Institutes which had grown up in most of the towns and large villages of the coalfield. These institutions provided the community centres which the new mining communities had lacked for so long, and in their size, their architectural style and their attraction, they equalled the Chapels as the focal points of mining villages. Source 260 *(See opposite column)* for example shows the front view of one of the most impressive of them, the Parc and Dare Workman's Hall in Treorchy.

Sometimes Coalowners made contributions towards the building of these Institutes but usually they were paid for out of weekly deductions from every miner's wage packet at local collieries. The history of the Ferndale and Blaenllechau Workmen's Hall and Institute serves as a good example of the efforts that were made to found such institutions and of the facilities they provided. In 1884 a one-room Library was opened paid for by 1 penny a month deductions from the earnings of miners working at the collieries of D. Davis and Company, who gave a sum equal to one-third of these deductions and paid the yearly rent on the property. During the 1898 Strike the Company withdrew these allowances and the miners now

Source 260

Source: The Valley, BBC Wales, 1982.

had to run the building from voluntary contributions. This did not prevent them buying larger premises in 1904 for £2,000 and within 4 years paying off £1,000 of this cost. When larger halls appeared in the nearby villages of Maerdy and Ynyshir, the Ferndale Hall Committee decided to improve their Institute. They persuaded the Company to restart deductions and by December 1909 they were able to open a brand new Hall and Institute on the old site. This was one of the biggest Institutes in the coalfield and its size and facilities can be seen from this description of the new building given in the Souvenir Programme of the opening:

Source 261
In the centre of the front is the Refreshment Room . . . a screen divides it from the Supper Room . . . the Institute Lounge and main Institute rooms. On the first floor is the Billiard Room with five full-sized tables . . . and Refreshment Bar. On the next floor are the Reading and Reference Rooms . . . The third floor contains a large Games Room . . . The Hall provides seating accommodation for fifteen hundred people . . . The lesser Hall is capable of seating nearly 350 persons . . . Descending the Swimming Bath is reached . . . Along one side run the Dressing Boxes and behind those the Rifle Range . . .

Source: Souvenir of the Opening of Ferndale and Blaenllechau Workmens Hall and Institute, 1909.

In the Ferndale and most other Institutes there would also have been a Library, and as there were no public libraries in the valleys until the 1920s, these were a very important part of the facilities offered by the Institutes. Here is a photograph of the Oakdale Institute Library in its heyday when with up to 23,000 books it was one of the largest public libraries in the whole of Britain and a section of the printed catalogue of the Parc and Dare Institute Library in Treorchy follows.

Source 262

Source: G. H. Hoare, *The History of the Oakdale Institute*, nd.

Source 263

Sociology (Section D).

1	Ancient Society	...	Morran
2	The World of Labour	...	Cole
3	The Rise of Democracy	...	J. Clayton
4	Labour Strife in the South Wales Coalfield		D. Evans
5	Creative Revolution	...	E. & C. Paul
6	The State	...	W. Paul
7	Robert Owen	...	
8	Defence of Terrorism	...	L. Trotsky
9	Social and Industrial Reform	...	
10	Evolution of the Idea of God	...	Grant Allen
11	Sunlight and Shadow	...	J. B. Gough
12	The Great Illusion	...	Norman Angell
13	Savage Survivals	...	J. Howard Moore
14	Stories of the Cave People	...	M. Marcy
15	Philosophical Essays	...	Dietzgen
16	Prolet-Cult	...	E. & C. Paul
17	Life in Ancient Britain	...	Ault
18	Marxian Economics	...	Untermann
19	The Fruits of Victory	...	Norman Angell
20	The Class Struggle	...	Kautsky
21	Revolutionary Essays	...	Burrowes
22	Revolution (1789 to 1906)	...	Postgate
23	The Poverty of Philosophy	...	Marx
24	Labour International Handbook	...	
25	Industrial Problems	...	Richardson
26	Pioneers of Evolution	...	Edward Clodd
27	The History Sheet	...	
28	Capital Punishment	...	J. C. L. Carson
29	Legal Position of Trade Unions	...	
30	Capitalist Production	...	Marx
31	Practical Politics	...	
32	Production	...	George Belt
33	The Municipal Manual	...	Lauder
34	A History of Economic Doctrines	...	Gide & Rest
35	Oxford House Papers	...	
36	A Handy Book of Parish Law	...	Holdsworth
37	Essays and Lectures	...	Huxley
38	The Dawn of History	...	J. L. Myres
39	Big Navies and Cheap Labour	...	
40	Capital, Vol. 1	...	Marx
41	do Vol. 2	...	do
42	do Vol. 3	...	do
43	Pithead and Factory Baths	...	

Source: South Wales Miners' Library, University College of Swansea.

These libraries, financed and controlled by the miners themselves, had a great influence on the people of the mining communities, many of whom received their education from them. They contained a wide selection of serious and light reading. The passion for education and the great richness of the tradition of adult education which grew up in the South Wales mining valleys is captured in a story told by a Tredegar miner, Archie Lush. Through adult education classes he was able to win a scholarship to Oxford University in 1927:

Source 264

This tutor saw me . . . and he gave me a long list of books to read. When I told him I had read (them) . . . he just didn't believe me. And he said "Well where would you get these books" because I was this working-class . . . student. And I said "Tredegar Workmen's Library" . . . I had read them and I was able to tell him what was in them.

Source: Interview with A. Lush, South Wales Miners' Library. University College of Swansea.

Politics

At the beginning of our period, politics was dominated by the middle and upper classes. It was only great Landowners and Industrialists who had the right to vote and who became Members of Parliament. In Merthyr Tydfil, for example, only 1 out of every 57 men, on average, had the right to vote and of course no women had that right. The 1867 Reform Act, however, extended the right to vote to male working-class householders and by 1919 all men over the age of 21 and women over 30, could vote in elections. By then the rapidly expanding South Wales coalfield also had a greater number of Parliamentary constituencies, with just about every valley having the right to elect an M.P.

The Liberal Domination

The party which benefitted most from the working people of South Wales being given the vote was the Liberal Party which almost totally dominated Welsh politics in the period up to the First World War. Some of the first Liberal M.P.s elected in South Wales were Ironmasters and Coalowners. They tended to be the 'Whig' type of Liberal—not all that different in politics and religion to the churchgoing landowners who made up the Tory Pary. In the 1868 General Election however, when for the first time working men had the vote, a great change began to take place in Welsh politics. At Merthyr Tydfil the sitting M.P., H. A. Bruce (a Liberal landowner and industrialist), lost his seat to another Liberal, Henry Richard. He was a 'Radical' who wished to see society reformed in the interests of working people and, like the vast majority of the voters, a Nonconformist in religion. Soon, in nearly all the South Wales constituencies, men like Henry Richard were elected as M.P.s. This extract from a newspaper report of a speech made by Henry Richard during the 1868 Election, shows you some of the views which these Radical M.P.s held:

Source 265

"Mr. Richard at the Temperance Hall.

On Wednesday evening last Henry Richard, Esq., the popular candidate, addressed a crowded and most enthusiastic meeting at the Temperance Hall, in this town. Mr. Richard, accompanied by several friends, were drawn in an open carriage to and from the place of the meeting by a large body of working men and some hundreds of others bearing torchlights. The greater part of the houses along the route were also beautifully illuminated. Near the Blaengwawr Colliery, too, a monster bonfire was seen blazing away, lighting up the whole valley . . .

Amongst those present were noticed . . . the principal ministers of the neighbourhood . . . Mr. Richard began . . . "The people who speak this language (the Welsh), who read this literature, who own this history, who inherit those traditions, who venerate those names, who have created and sustained and worked those marvellous organisations—the people forming three fourths of the people of Wales— Have they not a right to say We are the Welsh nation? Have they not a right to say to those small propertied class, but say it calmly and respectfully, and yet with energy and emphasis, We are the Welsh nation; and not you? This country is ours and not yours, and therefore we claim the right to have our principles and sentiments and feelings represented in the Commons House of Parliament (applause). It should be observed that up to this time the representation of the people of Wales has been almost entirely in the hands of the propertied class of whom I am speaking . . ."

Source: *Aberdare Times*, 14 November, 1868.

By 1885 the Liberal domination of Welsh politics was almost complete—in the General Election of that year, 30 out of the 34 Parliamentary seats in Wales were won by the party. The reasons for the unpopularity of the Conservatives (who after the 1906 General Election did not hold a single seat in Wales) can be seen in this account of the 'Treorchy Riots' of 1874:

Source 266

"In the Glamorgan Election of 1874, Mr. C. R. M. Talbot of Margam and Mr. Henry Vivian (Lord Swansea afterwards) were the Liberal candidates and Mr. Guest, father of Lord Wimborne, was the Conservative champion. The two Liberal candidates had already addressed meetings in the valley when the Conservatives organised a great horseback procession to escort Mr. Guest from Llantrisant to the Rhondda. This display was resented by the miners, and the Pentre colliers, who happened to be idle that day, got from forty to fifty horses out of the pit and organised a counter-demonstration. The two forces met near the Cardiff Arms Hotel, and in the mêlée that ensued, the Conservatives were forced to take refuge in the schoolroom and soon to take flight towards Pentre. A few were thrown into the river and there were heavy casualties. The Riot Act was read, and twenty to thirty people arrested. Of these, thirteen were sent to gaol."

Source: W. Morris. 'Reminiscences of the Rhondda', *Rhondda Leader*, 19 July, 1919.

What were the policies which made the Liberal Party so popular with the people of Wales during this period? There were three main specifically 'Welsh' issues:

1. As the vast majority of the Welsh people were Nonconformists they wished to see an end to the Church of England as the official or 'established' Church in Wales and the system of paying *tithes* whereby the people had to pay a tax to the established Church.
2. They wanted to see an end to the great power of the Landlords (who were mainly Conservative and Churchmen) over their tenants (who were mainly Liberal and Nonconformist).
3. They wanted more independence or 'home rule' for Wales in matters such as education and religion.

Under popular leaders such as David Lloyd George and T. E. Ellis, the Liberals were able to unite the working people of rural and industrial Wales around these policies.

Lib-Labs

However, in areas such as the South Wales mining valleys, issues such as wages, working conditions, housing and public health gradually became to be seen by people as being more important than the old issues and the Liberal Party did not keep pace with these changes. This was probably because Liberal politics at local level was dominated by people such as Ministers of Religion, Solicitors and shop-keepers. The first working-man to win import-ance in the Liberal Party in Wales was William Abraham (Mabon) the miners' leader. In 1885 he won the new Parliamentary seat of Rhondda as a Liberal. Here is a photograph of Mabon followed by a newspaper account of his election campaign in 1885:

Source 267

Source: National Library of Wales.

Source 268
RHONDDA DIVISION OF GLAMORGAN
THE POLLING.
FEARFUL RIOTING.
THE MOB CHARGED BY POLICE.
MANY PERSONS INJURED.
GREAT DESTRUCTION OF PROPERTY.

Our Pontypridd correspondent writes:

Up to the time of writing there is a continuous stream of workmen, dressed in what they call "clean clothes", from Tre-herbert to Heolfach, a distance of between three and four miles. All seem actuated with but one impulse, viz., to return "Mabon" to Parliament as their representative. The enthusiasm is truly remarkable, and the behaviour of the vast multitude is all that could be desired. I have visited all the polling booths in the locality, and found everything going on quietly. At the entrance into each I found a number of genuine working men checking the names of each voter entering the booth so that they should know who had voted and who had not. The majority of voters polled early. Early in the day Mr. Fred Davies, accompanied by a number of young ladies drove through the valley, as far as Treherbert, and back in a carriage drawn by a gallant pair of greys. He was greeted everywhere with tremendous cries of "Mabon, O Mabon for ever!" and prolonged "Boos!" from the population. Presently Mabon who knows the idiosyncracies of his brethren well, appeared coming up the valley on foot. He was hailed with unbound enthusiasm, and Welsh cries of "Here comes our man on foot. He can walk, he can!" He was lifted on the brawny shoulders of the toilers of the valley and carried in that way a considerable distance."

Source: The Western Mail, 3 December, 1885.

By 1906 Mabon was to be joined in the House of Commons by two of his fellow leaders of the South Wales Miners' Federation, Thomas Richards and William Brace. They too were elected as Liberal M.P.s and because of their background as working men and trade-unionists they were part of the group of M.P.s known as the 'Lib-Labs'. Why were they called this?

The Rise of Socialism

In the same election, however, two other working-men and former miners' leaders were elected to Parliament to serve South Wales seats and they were not Liberals. By the end of the 19th century a new political movement had grown up in Britain—*Socialism.* In 1893 the Independent Labour Party was formed and along with the other main socialist group, the

Social Democratic Federation, it slowly began to gain support in the South Wales Valleys, especially during the great miners' lock-out of 1898. These groups believed that socialism would only be achieved if working men and women were elected to Parliament to represent their class in an independent party. They succeeded in 1900 in persuading a number of trade unions to join them in setting up a new body called the *Labour Representation*

ranks. In local government in South Wales, as well as in Parliament, the Labour movement was beginning to threaten the domination of the Liberal Party. However, during this period we should not exaggerate the rise of the Labour Party or its difference to the Liberals. Even by 1914 the Labour Party still had far less support in elections than the Liberals. Also many of the Labour men shared the same background and views as the Liberals. They were often strong

Source 269

Source: South Wales Miners Library, University College of Swansea.

Committee to achieve this. One of the candidates put up by the L.R.C. in the General Election of 1900 was the Scottish miner Keir Hardie who fought the seat of Merthyr Tydfil and was elected to become Wales' first 'Labour' M.P. Source 269 is a photograph of Hardie speaking to an open-air meeting at Dowlais Top during his campaign in 1900 and Source 270 is a poster from the 1910 Election showing the policies he stood for.

By 1910 the L.R.C. had been re-named the *Labour Party* and after a ballot of miners in 1908 the South Wales Miners Federation decided to affiliate to the new party. Mabon and his fellow 'Lib-Lab's' rather reluctantly were forced to leave the Liberal Party and join the Labour

supporters of Nonconformity, Welsh-speakers and in many ways 'radicals' who ten years earlier would have been keen Liberals, and many of whom (like Mabon, Richards, Brace) were still 'Liberal' in thought and deed, if not in name.

A new type of leader was appearing, however, within the Labour movement with very different views to the 'Lib-Lab's'. The rise of militancy which happened within the S.W.M.F. from 1910 onwards (which we looked at in Section 4 of this book) also had an effect in politics. A new, much more socialist and militant, generation of miners' leaders began to emerge to challenge the old leadership of Mabon and his supporters. Although these

Source 270

TRECH GWLAD NAC ARGLWYDD

Source: Labour Party Photograph Library.

younger men worked within the Labour Party they had doubts whether socialism could be achieved only through electing people to Parliament. They argued that direct action taken by the mass of working people through their trade unions was likely to lead to Socialism being achieved much more quickly. Their views were known as *Syndicalism* or *Industrial Unionism* and they were heavily influenced by the ideas of Marxism which many of them had learnt in adult education classes. This movement was particularly strong in the Rhondda Valley and Source 271 *(See page 114)* shows a section of a newspaper they published in 1920. Why was it called 'The Workers' Bomb'?

Perhaps the real decline of the fortunes of the Liberal Party in South Wales came during the 1914-18 War. Although the Labour Party itself was divided on the issue of support for the War, disillusionment with the long and bloody struggle and the effect of the many industrial disputes of the post-war world seem to have persuaded many old Liberal supporters to change to the Labour Party. In the General Elections of 1918 and 1922 the South Wales coalfield steadily changed from electing

Liberal, to Labour, M.P.s and by 1923 the Labour monopoly became as great as the Liberal had been previously. That election led to the first ever Labour Government taking power and the new Prime Minister, another Scottish 'exile' in South Wales, was the newly elected Labour M.P. for the mining seat of Aberavon, Ramsey Macdonald.

Women and Politics

The rise of the Labour Movement was to see women much more active in politics than they had been before. The campaign for 'votes for women' led by the Suffragette Movement was mainly associated with middle and upper-class women but it did have growing support from working women and men in South Wales up to 1914. Although in the mining industry women were being driven out of work as it was thought unbecoming for them to work even on colliery surfaces, in many other areas of employment the importance of women as workers (in and out of the home) was beginning to be recognised and the work done by women during the 1914-1918 War also played a part in women over 30 being granted the vote in 1918. In the Labour and Co-operative movements women began to play a major role. Source 272 describes their activities in the Rhondda and Source 273 an excerpt from a newspaper article by a Labour Councillor and miners' leader from Pontllanfraith, which shows, however, that women still had a great deal of male prejudice to overcome, even within the Labour movement:

Source 272

The first Women's Section was formed at Ton Pentre, Rhondda, in 1918 with the help of the local Trades Council. I was appointed Secretary. There were twelve women present. At that time the South Wales Miners' Federation were agitating for shorter hours and higher wages. When discussing this matter, the women felt that the time was long overdue to get something done to lighten the burden of the miner's wife.

I wrote a letter to the Miners' conference saying we whole-heartedly supported their demands and while doing so, thought the time had come when shorter hours for miners' wives should have some consideration. We also made the request that the question of pit baths should be a part of their campaign. This letter was read to the conference and interest was aroused as well as some opposition. The Press gave this matter much publicity and I had

Source 271

The Workers' Bomb

TO DESTROY IGNORANCE AND PREJUDICE.

No. 2.   DECEMBER, 1920.   ONE PENNY

Source: South Wales Miners Library,
University College of Swansea.

Notice to Correspondents.

Copy for the Press. if unsealed, may be sent
at the following rates :—

Not exceeding 1-oz.	...	½d.
"	"	2-oz.	...	1d.
"	"	4-oz.	...	1½d.
"	"	6-oz.	...	2d.

NOTICE.

A MEETING of "The Workers' Bomb" Press Society
will be held at the Aberystwyth Restaurant. Llwynpia.
on SUNDAY, DECEMBER 12th, 1920, at 2.30 p.m. sharp.
All interested please make every effort to he present.

All Communications, and all monies, to be
addressed to The Editor, " The Workers'
Bomb." 58, Tyntyla Rd., Ystrad-Rhondda.

The Workers' Bomb

DECEMBER. 1920.

The "Bomb." The enthusiastic
reception accord-
number is highly gratifying, which
augurs well for the success of the paper.
and proves that the venture was justified.
Repeated efforts at co-ordinating the
various Socialist and Communist bodies
in the Rhondda have failed, chiefly
through " geographical control." In the
BOMB we have a means of, partially at
least, making good such a desirable end,

for here is a common platform which
can serve all sections of the Labour
Movement, and become, if we so use it,
a powerful weapon in our hands. The
days of compromise and half measures
are relegated to a past epoch in the de-
velopement of working-class conscious-
ness; the occasion for mild propa-
gandist clap-trap and vague meaningless slogans and generalisations is spent.
Our fight has been a mere masque of
mock-heroics. In justice to our cause
and the tremendous issues at stake, let
us cry " curtain " on it. Leaders have
talked for decades, and the sum of it all
may be aptly stated in the words of the
man in *John Ploughman's Talk* who
took to shearing the sow : " much noise
and little wool." We are in dire need of
leaders who are out to get what we tell
them we want, and not what they think
we ought to be satisfied with. If they
are out for anything less than what we
demand, let us give them the "bird," in
other words, scrap them ruthlessly, for
they are mere camouflaged tools in the
hands of the capitalists. The BOMB
exists to blow this game of sham histri-
onics, if not to blazes, well out of the
way, we shall then, at least, know where
we are.

many lively discussions with some of the
miners' leaders.
Source: E. Andrews, *A Woman's Work is
Never Done*, 1948.

Source 273

I want to state that I find that in practice it is
not always wise to establish separate sections
for Women. In large Centres I would favour the
establishment of Women's Sections, but in the
smaller villages I would unite both sexes in one
party. In a number of instances this has
become necessary in my area to save the
organisation of the women becoming defunct.
To a large extent, women are passing through
a period of apprenticeship in the Labour

Political movement, and in the smaller
villages there is a tendency to depend too much
on one or two to carry on the work, and if they
are absent from the meetings, the whole
atmosphere becomes too much of the
''gossipy'' character, whilst if they meet
jointly with the men, this weakness does not
exist. I know I am touching a very tender spot
in dealing with this aspect, but as I know from
experience that I am dealing with a weakness
from the point of Women's Organisation, I feel
I ought to point it out, and I shall personally act
accordingly in my area.

Source: The Colliery Workers Magazine,
February 1925.

Further work on the evidence

1. Look at Source 232 and then try to answer these questions:
   a. What do you think the author means when he says that one of the reasons why miners enjoyed playing rugby was that 'taking part in the game gave the miner an opportunity of gaining more social prominence'?
   b. Describe two of the other reasons which the author gives for the popularity of rugby among miners.
   c. Can you think of another reason to do with the nature of their work which might have made playing games like rugby attractive to young miners?
   d. In what way do you think the growth of the new mining communities themselves might have been a reason for the popularity of games like rugby as spectator sports?

2. Look at Source 246 and then attempt the following questions:
   a. Which occupational group in Mountain Ash has given the most support to the Sunday closing of public houses? Why do you think this was so?
   b. Which group has given the least support and why do you think this was the case?
   c. What other information would you need to have so as to be able to decide whether this Source is reliable information on the views of the population of Mountain Ash towards Sunday closing of public houses? Do you think the word 'householder' is a clue to this? Explain your answer.
   d. By itself is this piece of evidence sufficient to reach a conclusion that the vast majority of people in Wales in 1878 were in favour of Sunday closing? Explain your answer.

3. Look at Source 265 and then consider these questions:
   a. What two groups of people mentioned in this newspaper account appear to be strong supporters of Henry Richard? Why should this be so?
   b. To what groups of people is Henry Richard referring when he says 'We are the Welsh nation; and not you'?
   c. Do you think that the newspaper (*The Aberdare Times*) which this Source is taken from, is biased towards Henry Richard? Explain your answer and point to words and phrases which lead you to your conclusion.

7.—Coal Society in Crisis
Introduction

The story of the coal industry in South Wales between 1840 and 1914 and the way of life within the new mining communities of the South Wales valleys is one of the expansion, growth and great vitality of this 'Coal Society'. A typical example of this overall development might be said to be the *Powell Duffryn Coal Company*. Thomas Powell was one of the original pioneers of the sale-coal trade in the Cynon Valley and in Monmouthshire in the 1830s and 40s. Eventually the pits that he founded became part of the giant coal combine, the Powell Duffryn Company, which flourished with the expansion of the South Wales steamcoal export trade. The Company dominated the lives of the people in the mining communities which grew up around its collieries in the Cynon and Rhymney valleys. To the miners and their union, the South Wales Miners Federation, the initials 'P.D.' were sometimes said to stand for 'Poverty and Death' rather than 'Powell Duffryn' due to the animosity that grew up between the Company and its workers. Perhaps one thing that might have united them, however, would have been the hope and the confidence that the growth of the coal industry which had gone on unchecked throughout the late 19th and early 20th centuries, would continue. In 1914 Powell Duffryn issued a brochure in which the future of the company was looked at as follows:

Source 274

THE FUTURE

The present position of the Company and its remarkable growth are an index of their prospects in the future. The advent of oil as a motive power need not be taken seriously for many years, if ever; and with the natural growth of manufactures in all parts of the world, the extension and development of railways, the expansion of the mercantile marine and the increase of trade generally, the prosperity which Powell Duffryn coals now enjoy is bound to continue. Great as the output is, it is small compared to the quantity still unworked, the approximate figures of their reserves being:

Rhymney Valley:
New Tredegar
  and Elliot Pits   94,000,000 tons.
Bargoed   86,000,000 tons.
Penallta   100,000,000 tons.
Pengam   90,000,000 tons.
                          370,000,000 tons.
Aberdare Valley   78,000,000 tons.

Or sufficient to furnish an annual output of 4½ million tons for 100 years.
Source: History of Powell Duffryn, 1914.

However, this optimism was to be false. Today there is no Powell Duffryn Coal Company and hardly any of the pits that the Company once owned have survived. The mining communities which grew up around their collieries still survive but to many people they are communities in 'crisis', having lost the pits which gave them their need to exist and therefore having no reason to continue to exist into the future. It could be said that the fortunes of Powell Duffryn since 1914 are also a mirror-image of what has been happening to the South Wales Coalfield and its valley communities.

The two sources below show just how much all the trends which affected South Wales before 1914 seem to have gone into reverse since then. What do they suggest about the general experience of the South Wales coal industry and of mining communities like the Rhondda since 1920?

Source 275

EMPLOYMENT AND PRODUCTION IN THE SOUTH WALES COALFIELD

	Number of Men Employed	Tons of Coal Produced
1890	109,935	29,415,000
1920	271,161	46,249,000
1950	102,000	24,314,000
1983	22,071	6,562,000

Source: H. Francis and D. Smith, *'The Fed': A History of the South Wales Miners in the Twentieth Century*, 1980.

Source 276

POPULATION FIGURES
1921, 1951 and 1981

	1921	1951	1981
Wales	2,656,474	2,598,675	2,791,000
Glamorgan	1,252,481	1,202,581	1,290,000
Cardiff	200,184	246,000	265,000
Rhondda Valleys	162,729	111,389	81,955

Source: Census of Population, 1921, 1951, 1981.

The 1914-18 War and After

The War and the Coalfield

Source 275 shows that the amount of coal mined in South Wales had actually increased significantly by 1920 from the amount produced in 1890. However, the 1920 figure was in fact 10 million tons lower than in 1913 when the peak production figures of the coalfield (56,830,000 tons) were reached. This was because during the 1914-18 World War although there was a high demand from the British Navy for the steam-coal of South Wales, there were not enough miners available to produce all the coal that was needed. In addition the anthracite coalfield lost most of its export market due to the war at sea.

The shortage of manpower was due to the war. Although in August 1914 the South Wales Miners' Federation had proposed an internat-ional miners' strike to stop the outbreak of war and there continued to be an anti-war move-ment in the coalfield, there was mass volunteering in South Wales in 1914 and 1915 and thereafter additional miners were conscripted into the armed forces. Scenes such as this parade at Mountain Ash in 1915 and support by the S.W.M.F. for the war effort (as shown in Source 278) were, therefore, common during the war years:

Source 277

Source: Mountain Ash Comprehensive School, Local History Collection.

The Navy's need for coal and the shortage of miners to produce it, put the South Wales miners in a very strong bargaining position. A sharp rise in the price of food during the War years led to the S.W.M.F. putting forward regular wage demands on behalf of its members and there was a strongly held view that Coal-owners were making record profits because of the great demand for South Wales coal and

Source 278

South Wales Miners' Federation.

NOTICE.

The Workmen's Representatives on the Conciliation Board having had an application from the Admiralty that the August Holidays should be curtailed as much as possible, unanimously decided to strongly recom-mend all Workmen to limit the holidays to ONE DAY, viz., MONDAY, AUGUST 2nd.

The Representatives urge upon every Workman to return to work ON TUESDAY NEXT, that the Coal supplies to the Navy and the Coal necessary for the transport of the Troops and the Manufacture of Munitions shall be interfered with as little as possible.

(Signed),

General Secretary.

Source: Records of the South Wales Miners Federation, University College of Swansea.

therefore could afford to meet these demands. The Coalowners, however, refused the miners demands for a new wage agreement in July 1915 and 200,000 South Wales miners began a strike. They found themselves opposed not only by the Coalowners but by the Government, the news-papers and even the Miners' Federation of Great Britain, as it was believed that a strike would stop the supply of coal to the Navy. At first the Government threatened to imprison those who did strike but when the men remained solid this proved impossible. In the end the Government intervened and the S.W.M.F. was granted most of its demands. It was the Welshman David Lloyd George, Minis-ter of Munitions, who settled the strike on the Government's behalf. He is shown in Source 279 *(See page 118)* addressing a S.W.M.F. Conference in Cardiff at the end of the strike.

State Control of the Coal Industry

Disputes between the Coalowners and the miners' union in South Wales continued, however, and to ensure that no further strikes would endanger the supply of coal to the Navy, in 1916 the Government took over control of the South Wales Coalfield. A year later the rest

Source 279

Source: South Wales Miners Library, University College of Swansea.

of the British coalfields were also taken over by the Government and after the war the future management and organisation of the coal industry had to be decided upon. To help the Government come to a decision a Royal Commission was set up to investigate the matter and to make recommendations. The miners' unions gave evidence to the Commission advising that the coal industry should be *nationalized*—taken over permanently by the state and run on behalf of the nation as a whole. Here is part of the evidence given to the commission by James Winstone, the President of the S.W.M.F.

Source 280

Men would feel that they had control or some control over their own energies, and that they were not merely at the will and direction of another being. They would be in a better position than the horse that they have to drive, or the machine that they have to attend. As I have said on a previous occasion, it is that desire that cannot be crushed that is making itself felt in the ranks of labour at the present time, and has given rise to more unrest than anything else.

Source: Report and Minutes of Evidence of the Royal Commission on the Coal Industry, 1919.

Here is part of the evidence to the Commission of Hugh Bramwell on behalf of the South Wales Coalowners Association:

Source 281

I think that nationalisation . . . will absolutely sterilise (get rid of) the accumulated knowledge of all directors in the country of colliery companies . . . If that knowledge is to be swept away I do not believe any central authority can accumulate it, and no body of experts can know the actual conditions of every mine in the country. The country will be losing if they lose the directors of colliery companies . . . The whole of the directors fees paid in the coalfield is £1,000 per 1,000,000 tons and that works out at under 1d a ton. A central authority will cost a lot more than that.

Source: Report and Minutes of Evidence of the Royal Commission on the Coal Industry, 1919.

In 1919 the Royal Commission issued its report and to the shock of the Coalowners it was in favour of nationalization. Here are some of the crucial extracts from its report:

Source 282 *(See page 119)*

Source 282

COAL INDUSTRY COMMISSION ACT, 1919

REPORT

BY

THE HONOURABLE MR. JUSTICE SANKEY, G.B.E.
(*Chairman*).

TO THE KING'S MOST EXCELLENT MAJESTY

MAY IT PLEASE YOUR MAJESTY.

I HAVE the honour to present a further Report in pursuance of the Coal Industry Commission Act, 1919.

1. RECOMMENDATIONS

I

I recommend that Parliament be invited immediately to pass legislation acquiring the Coal Royalties for the State and paying fair and just compensation to the owners.

II

I recommend on the evidence before me that the principle of State ownership of the coal mines be accepted.

5. METHOD OF PURCHASE AND CARRYING ON OF THE COAL MINES

XXXV

It is suggested that the State should purchase all the collieries, including colliery buildings, plant, machinery, stores and other effects in and about the colliery at a fair value subject to the next paragraph.

Source: Report and Minutes of Evidence of the Royal Commission on the Coal Industry, 1919.

The 1921 Lock-Out

After first appearing to accept the Report, the Government eventually changed its mind and in 1921 the coal industry was handed back to the control of the Coalowners. Instead of negotiating nationally with the Government, the miners' union now had to return to district agreements negotiated for each coalfield. The South Wales Coalowners argued that wage rates had increased far too much during the period when the industry was controlled by the Government and they now demanded that the miners accept lower wages or they would refuse to employ them. The S.W.M.F. set out the Coalowners demands in Source 283 *(See opposite column).*

On 1 April 1921 a lock-out of 1 million miners in Britain who refused to accept such terms began. It lasted for 3 months until by the end of June 1921, when support promised by Transport Workers and Railwaymen had not been given, the South Wales Miners' Feder-

Source 283

EFFECT OF THE COAL OWNERS' PROPOSALS.

The following is the position that will be created if the Owners' Proposals are put into operation in the South Wales Coalfield. The Prices and Costs are for the month of February, and are based on information received from Official Sources:—

Selling Price of Coal—35s. 10.03d. per ton.

	s.	d.
Standard Wages Cost (1921 Standard) per ton	13	11.92
Owners' Profits at 17 per cent. of Standard Wages per ton	2	4.54
Other Costs (Stores, Timber, Royalties, Salaries, etc)	14	4.50
Total	30	8.96

	s.	d.	
Selling Price	35	10.03	per ton.
Total Costs	30	8.96	per ton.
Surplus	5	1.07	per ton.

5s. 1d. on 13s. 11.92d. equals 36.37 per cent. This would mean 36.37 per cent on the New (1921) Standard Rates. The effect of this change on the wages of the workmen would be as follows:—

Colliers—Present wage, 17s. 10.2d. per Shift. New wage (7s. 4d. plus 36.37 per cent.), equals 10s. per Shift. **A reduction of 7s. 10.2d. per Shift, or 44 per cent.**

Labourers—Present wage, 14s. 9.5d. per Shift. New wage (5s. 4d. plus 36.37 per cent.), equals 7s. 3.28d. per Shift. **A reduction of 7s. 6.22d. per Shift, or 50.82 per cent.**

The grades of workmen whose wages vary between those of Colliers and Labourers would suffer reductions varying between 44 per cent. and 50 per cent.

Source: Records of the South Wales Miners Federation, University College of Swansea Library.

ation accepted defeat after a Coalfield Conference narrowly voted to return to work under the Owners' terms. During the lock-out one crucial question in South Wales became the position of safety-men and whether they should continue working, as can be seen in the newspaper report (Source 284) and photograph (Source 285).

Source 284

"From early morning the miners of Mardy, Tylorstown, Ferndale and the surrounding districts congregated in the public squares and formed themselves into three huge processions, each of which was headed by its own colliery band. Shortly after nine o'clock they started off making for the United National Collieries at Ynyshir and Wattstown in the lower Rhondda Fach where safety men were still at work. They gathered force as they proceeded, until they numbered fully 5,000 strong. The men wore red rosettes and had red ribbons in their hats. They marched four abreast with military precision. On arriving at the colliery offices they assumed mass formation and whilst negotiations proceeded the crowd began to sing 'The Red Flag' with considerable fervour. Eventually the management agreed to the immediate withdrawal of thirty six officials from the pit. The demonstrators marched back up the valley, the bands playing 'Land of My Fathers' and 'Men of Harlech'.

Source: The Western Mail, 14 April, 1921.

Source 285

Source: The Western Mail, 14 April, 1921.

The Coal Industry in the Inter-War Years

Recovery and Collapse

The settlement of the 1921 Lock-Out was by no means the end of industrial disputes in the South Wales coalfield in the 1920s, but soon a more pressing, and in the long-term more damaging, problem confronted the coal industry. In 1921 a recovery began in the world economy and the coal industry appeared to be beginning to return to its pre-war boom conditions. By 1923 coal production in South Wales had risen to 54 million tons, the second highest figure ever recorded in the coal-field's history. However, as the following 5-yearly figures for the next twenty years show, this proved to be merely a lull before the storm and within two decades the production of the coalfield was to be halved:

Source 286

Year	South Wales Coalfield Tons Produced
1923	54,252,000
1928	43,312,000
1933	34,355,000
1938	35,293,000
1943	25,116,000

Source: H. Francis and D. Smith, *'The Fed': A History of the South Wales Miners in The Twentieth Century*, 1980.

Between 1921 and 1936, 241 mines were closed in South Wales and the number of working miners fell from 270,000 to 130,000. This sort of decline was taking place in all of Britain's coalfields but it was particularly marked in South Wales. What were the reasons for this overall decline and the greater extent of it in South Wales? Certainly part of the reason was that oil, which was cheaper, cleaner and easier to handle, replaced coal in many of its former uses. However, although the use of oil was increasing it was not a major reason for the decline of the coal industry in the 1920s and 30s. The major reasons for the collapse of the South Wales coal industry during this period are bound up with the growth of the industry up to 1920. Two of the most important features of that growth were:

1. South Wales *exported* most of its coal.

2. Due to geological difficulties it was more expensive to mine coal in South Wales than in most other coalfields in Britain.

The two Sources which follow provide other clues for the decline of the coal industry in South Wales after 1921:

Source 287

South Wales Coal Exports
to Certain Countries

Destination	*1913*	*1931*
Russia	540,467	6,063
Germany	294,632	44,201
France	7,245,887	5,567,827
Argentine Republic	3,194,761	1,734,368
Chile	444,278	5,788
Canada	16,650	656,093

Source: The South Wales Coal Annual, 1931.

Source 288

Average Price Per Ton of Coal Produced in
Certain Coalfields in Britain 1921

Coalfield	*Price*
South Wales	23sh. 7d.
Yorkshire	18sh. 3d.
Scotland	20sh. 9d.
Durham	19sh. 10d.

Source: Report and Minutes of Evidence of the Royal Commission on the Coal Industry, 1925.

Why did the countries mentioned in Source 287 want less coal from South Wales? What in Source 288 suggests why South Wales suffered a greater decline than other coalfields in Britain? By 1929 South Wales, which once supplied almost one-third of the world's coal exports, supplied only 3%.

The General Strike and Miners' Lock-Out 1926

The decline of the industry in South Wales particularly hit the smaller coal companies. The giant Combines which had developed before 1920 were able to fare better as they were not totally dependent on the coal industry. In fact these Combines grew in size by taking over some of the smaller companies and in 1935 the process went even further when two of the largest Combines—the Ocean Coal Company and Powell Duffryn—amalgamated to form the largest coal company in the United Kingdom. These powerful companies believed that it was the high cost of producing coal which had particularly caused the decline of the South Wales coal industry and they were determined to push these costs down. The main factors in these high costs, they believed were the short working hours, low productivity and high wages of their mines. They attacked these things partly by closing down their least productive collieries and using the strong position they found themselves in, as so many miners were unemployed, they offered less wages and demanded high productivity from those miners who were in work.

In 1925 the Coalowners across the British coalfields asked their miners to accept cuts in wages and an extra hour on their working day as a way of producing coal more cheaply and making it more attractive to foreign buyers. The miners refused and the Government was forced to intervene again in the affairs of the coal industry. A new Royal Commission was set up to enquire into the running of the industry and meanwhile the Government paid a subsidy to the Coalowners to offset the losses they claimed they were making. In 1926 the Royal Commission reported that the coal industry was badly in need of re-organisation and once this was carried out it believed the miners should accept some wage cuts. The Coalowners, however, insisted on large and immediate wage cuts as shown in Source 289 below, whilst the Miners Federation of Great Britain under the leadership of the Welsh miner A. J. Cook (shown in Source 290) *(See page 122)* fought these proposals on the slogan 'Not an hour on the day. Not a penny off the pay':

Source 289

	Present Wages.	Owners' Terms.	Reduction per day.
	s. d.	s. d.	s. d.
Scotland–			
Coal hewers	9 4 ...	7 6 ...	1 10
Labourers	6 8¼ ...	6 0 ...	8¼
... South Wales and Monmouthshire			
Hewers	9 9¼ ...	7 2½ ...	2 6¾
Labourers (day)	8 0¼ ...	*6 8 ...	*1 4¼
... North Wales			
Hewers	9 4½ ...	7 8 ...	1 8½
Labourers	6 5 ...	5 0 ...	1 5

*If married. For single men the rate would be 5s. 9d. a day, a reduction of 2s. 3¼d. a day."

Source: Records of the South Wales Miners Federation, University College of Swansea Library.

On 30th April 1926, miners who refused to accept the Coalowners' terms were locked-out of work and the British coalfields came to a stop. The miners were not left to fight alone for the Trade Union Congress had promised to call all trade-unionists out on strike if the miners were forced to accept these terms. On 3 May 1926, therefore, a *General Strike* began in Britain. The supporters of the Government now believed that the country was being faced by almost a revolution and the sense of alarm they felt can be seen in this South Wales newspaper of the period (Source 291). Supporters of the strike, however, often felt that for the first time they were taking control of their own

Source 290

Source: South Wales Miners' Library, University College of Swansea.

Source 291

South Wales Argus

Coal Crisis Emergency Issue.
OUR EXPLANATION.

Because of the General Strike we are unable to publish the "South Wales Argus" in the usual form, we therefore give the news in brief as best we can.

Source: South Wales Argus, 4 May, 1926.

communities. The diagram (Source 292) *(See page 123)* shows some of the activities of the Merthyr Tydfil Strike Committee.

After 9 days the T.U.C. called off the General Strike arguing that the Government now wanted to negotiate a settlement to the dispute. The miners, angry at what they considered to be a betrayal, were left to fight on alone, which they did until the end of the year when starvation drove them back to work defeated. The two sources which follow show how 1926 became a year that a whole generation in South Wales would never forget:

Source 293

Do you remember 1926? That summer of
   soups and speeches,
The sunlight on the idle wheels and the
   deserted crossings,
And the laughter and the cursing in the
   moonlit streets?
Do you remember 1926? The slogans and the
   penny concerts,

The jazz-bands and the moorland picnics,
And the slanderous tongues of famous cities?
Do you remember 1926? The great dream and
   the swift disaster,
The fanatic and the traitor, and more than all,
The bravery of the simple, faithful folk?
'Ay, ay, we remember 1926,' said Dai and
   Shinkin,
As they stood on the kerb in Charing Cross
   Road,
'And we shall remember 1926 until our blood
   is dry.'

Source: I. Davies, *Gwalia Deserta,* 1938.

Source 294

November 11th

30 Plymouth police escorting a miner from his house to *Aberaman Colliery* were attacked from front and rear by a crowd of several hundred, including women and children who threw stones. They called out "blackleg", "waster", "rotter". Several police hit badly. Police gave a charge in both directions. Only lasted 15 minutes.

DIAGRAM ILLUSTRATING ORGANISATION OF GENERAL STRIKE COMMITTEE.

Source 292

Souvenir Report of the Merthyr Tydfil Strike Committee, 1926.

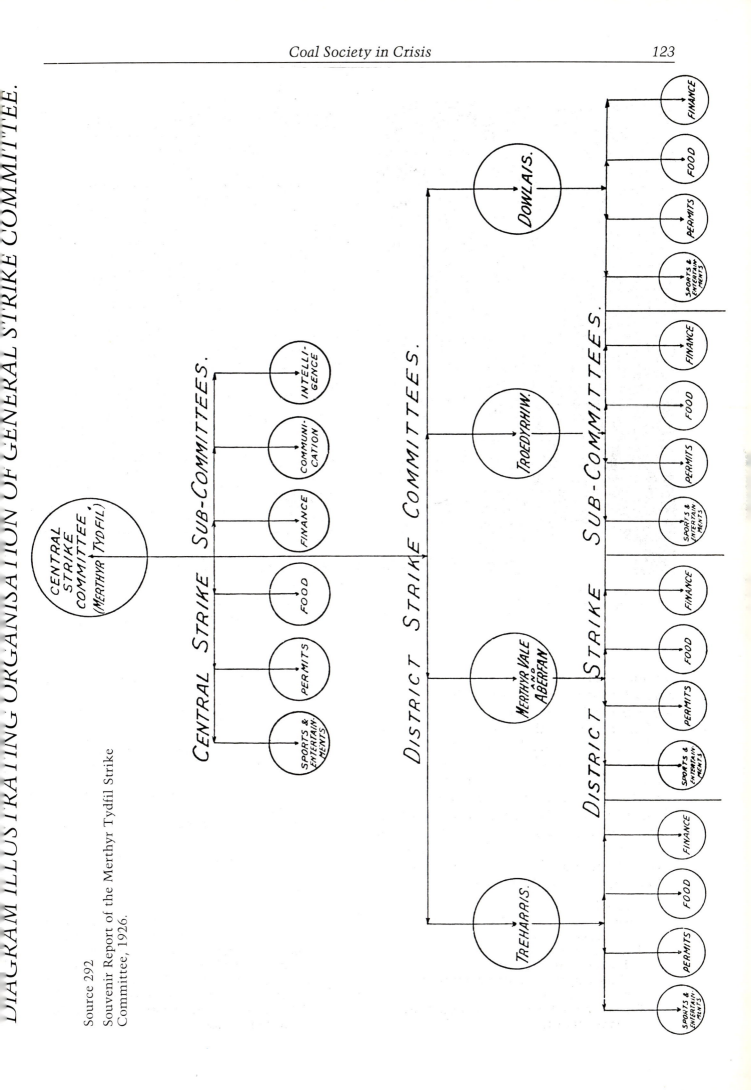

November 11th

 3 *Abercwmboi* miners given 2 months prison with hard labour. 3 others given £15 fine or 21 days.

November 12th

 96 summonses for 13 miners and 3 women for disturbance at *Gelli*.

November 12th

 34 defendants including Iorrie Thomas (Chairman of Park and Dare Lodge) tried for disturbance at *Cwmparc*.

November 17th

 Blaengarw miner dropped stone on railway line to prevent coal being shipped out.

November 19th

 A record of 395 persons to be tried at the Swansea Assizes. To be tried in groups of 2 to 45. Dock to be enlarged.

Source: Western Mail, November 1926.

Work and Working Conditions

Part of the miners case against the Coalowners was that the coal industry is South Wales could be made more productive only if the Owners were prepared to re-invest some of the profits they made out of the industry into new machinery and mining techniques. Some types of work in the pit did change during this period between the two World Wars. Conveyors, for example, were widely introduced for use in moving coal from the coalface to pit bottom. However, as the figures below show, the Coalowners were slow to introduce coal-cutting machinery and as is shown in the photograph which follows of Penallta Colliery in 1930, the work of colliers hardly changed at all. Compare this photograph with those in Sections 2 and 3 of this book:

Source 295

QUANTITY AND PERCENTAGE OF COAL CUT BY MACHINERY IN SOUTH WALES AND MONMOUTHSHIRE.

Year.	Quantity of coal cut by machinery.	Percentage of Total Output.
1913	639,719	... 1
1920	1,076,530	... 2
1921*	852,620	... 3
1922	1,818,172	... 4
1923	2,217,108	... 4
1924	2,619,948	... 5
1925	2,566,966	... 6
1926*	1,518,227	... 7
1927	3,212,184	... 7
1928	3,318,122	... 8
1929	4,178,341	... 9
1930	4,328,714	... 10
1931	4,355,741	... 12
1932	4,092,932	... 12
1933	4,402,169	... 13
1934	5,235,056	... 15

Source: The South Wales Miner, June 1936.

Source 296

Source: Big Pit Mining Museum, Blaenavon.

Progress was made in one aspect of the miner's work in 1937 when the S.W.M.F. persuaded the South Wales Coalowners to reduce the number of grades of miners from 150 to 6. This *National Day Wage Agreement* was a move towards the principle of equal pay for equal work by miners and it was achieved in South Wales almost twenty years before it was adopted in the other British coalfields.

As the following tables (for all the British coalfields) show the dangers of a miners life changed very little during this period:

Source 297

FATAL ACCIDENTS AT ALL MINES DISTINGUISHING THE PRINCIPAL CAUSES.
Number of Persons Killed per 100,000 employed.

Year	Explosions of firedamp or coal-dust	Falls of ground	Shaft accidents	Haulage accidents	Other accidents	Total below ground	Above ground	Below and above ground
1914	3·0	70·0	8·0	33·5	13·5	128·0	63·6	114·9
1915	5·4	88·8	8·2	34·6	17·5	154·5	64·8	135·4
1916	2·7	89·4	5·6	32·9	16·2	146·9	72·4	131·3
1917	2·4	89·0	8·0	37·5	13·1	150·0	73·0	133·9
1918	19·8	86·0	6·1	33·0	15·5	160·3	56·6	137·9
1919	2·8	63·4	8·1	24·9	11·7	110·9	47·1	97·5
1920	2·6	55·7	4·2	23·6	12·6	98·7	52·5	89·0
1921	3·0	55·0	3·1	24·8	12·3	98·2	42·6	87·1
1922	7·8	58·8	4·3	22·5	13·6	107·0	45·9	94·8
1923	6·1	59·6	6·1	31·7	16·7	120·2	48·1	105·8
1924	3·5	62·1	6·4	26·5	13·0	111·5	45·0	97·7
1925	3·2	62·1	4·1	28·9	18·3	116·6	47·1	102·3
1926	1·0	67·6	6·4	31·8	15·4	122·2	51·9	107·7
1927	8·6	68·6	6·6	27·8	13·8	125·4	43·3	108·3
1928	4·7	66·5	4·0	30·4	13·9	119·5	49·7	104·8
1929	4·3	74·7	5·4	28·3	16·6	129·3	41·3	111·1
1930	9·2	68·9	4·5	31·9	11·1	125·6	37·4	107·1
1931	15·3	60·5	2·9	25·2	10·4	114·3	37·2	98·0
1932	11·7	67·8	6·1	26·5	12·5	124·6	41·2	106·7
1933	5·6	72·3	4·4	25·2	13·8	121·3	37·4	103·0
1934	46·9	71·2	2·5	25·2	14·9	160·7	42·0	134·5
1935	6·0	76·9	3·1	30·4	13·0	129·4	51·1	111·9
1936	11·6	63·0	3·3	26·9	16·6	121·4	32·7	101·5
1937	9·9	70·3	4·9	28·3	14·1	127·5	38·3	107·5
1938*	14·3	65·8	2·5	30·8	12·2	125·6	43·4	107·0
1939	8·3	67·3	4·4	28·1	12·1	120·2	34·1	100·3

Source: The Colliery Year Book, 1960.

Major disasters were not as frequent in South Wales as they had been, although in 1927, at the

Marine Colliery, Ebbw Vale, twenty-seven men lost their lives in an explosion. The problem of lung diseases caused by dust increased, however, with the spread of machinery in South Wales mines. The dustiness of South Wales mines was well known and between 1931 and 1948 of the 22,999 men who left British mines suffering from pneumoconiosis, 85% came from South Wales. The S.W.M.F. worked actively to build up medical knowledge of dust diseases among miners and to win compensation for those who suffered from them. The Coalowners resisted all attempts to reach agreement on this, but in 1943 Parliament passed laws making compensation compulsory. In some of the anthracite pits of West Wales more than half the miners (many of them in their 30s and 40s) now had to be laid off work because they were found to be suffering from 'pneumo'. Compensation ('compo') was paid to them but most found they were far worse off financially.

The Anthracite Coalfield

The anthracite area of the coalfield fared much better than the rest of South Wales in these years of depression up to the Second World War. Demand for anthracite coal for use in central heating systems was still growing during this period and South Wales had some of the best reserves of it in the world. Production of South Wales anthracite rose from 3,199,330 tons in 1921 to a peak of 6,133,934 tons in 1934. As the anthracite industry grew so did the tendency for the small mines, sometimes still controlled by a single Coalowner, to be swallowed up by giant combine companies— by 1928 the Amalgamated Anthracite Combine controlled 80% of anthracite production in South Wales. This one area of the coalfield

which was still growing offered a haven for at least some of the army of unemployed miners in the rest of South Wales. Some families moved permanently to the anthracite coalfield, others travelled long distances each day by train from the depressed areas of the coalfield into the anthracite valleys as an investigation in 1937 found:

> Source 298
>
> Thus, 542 workers from Merthyr, and 420 from the Aberdare Exchange area travel to Glynneath, 12 miles each way in the case of the Merthyr men, and 10 miles a day in the case of the Aberdare workers; 89 workers from Dowlais, Merthyr, and Aberdare travel even further afield to Onllwyn and Banwen in the Dulais Valley (17 miles from Merthyr). In addition, 120 Dowlais and Merthyr men travel to Bedwas (22 miles from Dowlais), 50 to Cilfynydd (13 miles), and 115 to Abercynon (11 miles from Dowlais and 10 miles from Merthyr). Thus, from these three Exchange areas alone, over 1,300 workers are travelling distances over 10 miles each way.
>
> *Source:* The Second Industrial Survey of South Wales, 1937.

The Aftermath

The anthracite coalfield was very much an exception to the experience of the rest of the South Wales coalfield during the inter-war years. Although the decline of the coal industry did level off as the 1930s wore on, the loss of further markets for coal during the 1939-1945 World War, meant that by 1945, 142,000 less miners were employed and 34 million tons less coal was produced in South Wales than had been the case in 1923. This decline of the coal industry in the South Wales mining valleys was almost as spectacular as had been its rise in the 19th century.

The Depression: Effects

Just as the growth of the coal industry in South Wales up to 1914 created the mining valleys of the coalfield and a unique society grew up in the communities of the area, the collapse of the coal industry in the inter-war years was also to have a profound effect on that society and the way of life people lived within it.

Unemployment

The decline of the coal industry during the period 1919-1939 turned South Wales into an

area of mass unemployment. The graphs in Source 299 *(See page 126)* show the levels of unemployment in South Wales between 1923 and 1948 and relates these figures to the main cause of them—the decline in the coal industry.

In Wales as a whole, 13.4% of the working population was unemployed in 1925: by 1932 this percentage had risen to 36.5%. This was bad enough but in some areas of the South

Source 299

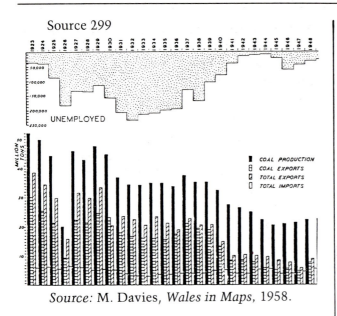

Source: M. Davies, *Wales in Maps*, 1958.

Wales coalfield it was even worse than this. Whereas in the Amman Valley in the anthracite coalfield only 13.8% were unemployed, in Dowlais 73.4% were without work. It was the Heads of the Valleys mining communities which suffered worst of all. Why was this the case? In fact even these figures do not show the full effect of unemployment because even those in work in the collieries that were still open, would often work 'a short week' of sometimes as little as two days.

Emigration

One of the main effects of widescale unemployment in the coal industry, in an area where there were hardly any other jobs, was that people left the valley communities in droves to try and find work elsewhere. Altogether something approaching 500,000 people left South Wales in the years between the Wars, thus completely reversing the trend of the previous half-century. The Rhondda, for example, lost 36.1% of its population between 1921 and 1951, a percentage which of its kind was probably the highest in Europe. Source 300 *(See opposite column)* gives some figures showing the loss of population in certain towns and districts of South Wales, through people leaving to go elsewhere between 1921 and 1931.

Where did all these people go and what did they do? Most went to towns in England where new manufacturing industries were developing —Wolverhampton, Slough, Oxford, for example. Source 301 is a photograph of one group of men from Blaina working in Brighton in 1930. What

Source 300

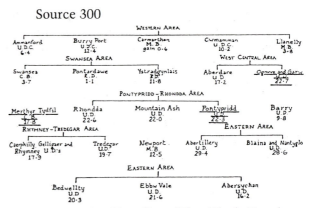

Source: A. Chandler, 'The Black Death on Wheels: Unemployment and Migration—The Experience of Inter-War South Wales' in T. Williams (Ed.), Papers In Modern Welsh History.

work do they appear to be doing? What identifies them as ex-miners?

Source 301

Source: National Museum of Wales.

In 1928 Arthur Exell from Beddau decided to leave for Oxford, where like many other Welsh emigrants he found work in the booming car industry of the town. Here he describes how the Welsh were not always welcomed and how his brother followed him:

Source 302

My only worry was my mother who cried her eyes out when I left . . . I saw that there was a job going as a milkboy for the Oxford Direct Milk Supply. The pay was 30 shillings a week for seven days and that seemed fabulous to me . . . I was about 18. I didn't know a soul in Oxford but I was lucky enough to get digs with a Mr. and Mrs. Sawyer up the Cowley Road. It wasn't easy to get digs . . . The Oxford people didn't want the Welsh . . . because when the Florence Park housing estate was being built in 1933-34 it was built by Welshmen brought here . . . These men worked for a shilling an hour. When I went to live on the estate the hatred there against the Welsh was terrible . . . My younger brother Ivor came up from Wales in 1932 . . . He came up in short trousers, he was just 14. His first job was riding a three-wheeler trike . . . He'd deliver clothes and collect others in for the cleaners . . .

Source: A. Exell, 'Morris Motors in the 1930s, in *History Workshop*, Spring 1979.

Some went even further afield as a Rhondda Minister shows in this account of an experience he had whilst in the United States of America in 1931:

Source 303

I preached at Nanticoke, a Pennsylvanian mining town, and three parts of the congregation were made up of Welsh men and women who had heard me preach in South Wales during the previous seven or eight years. I went to see one old miner, a native of the Rhondda. He had lost his sight as a result of working in the mine . . . I can still see that pathetic figure standing at his door as I went down the road after bidding him farewell. His last words to me were ''weep not for the dead! weep for the living, who will never see their native land again''.

Source: R. J. Barker, *Christ in the Valley of Unemployment*, 1936.

Survival

For those who decided to stay in South Wales in the 1920s and 30s the priority was *survival*, because wage levels fell during these years for those in work as well as those unemployed. In fact a survey of South Wales in the late 1930s showed that one-third of single men and nearly one-half of married men received more in unemployment benefit than they had in their previous jobs. The level of unemployment benefit in the early 1930s was about 20 shillings 3d. a week for a man, his wife and 3 children. This did increase to about 36 shillings a week in the late 1930s but the longer a man was unemployed the more likely it was that his benefit would be reduced because the insurance contributions he had paid when he was in work could run out. He then would have to apply for unemployment relief which meant submitting to the 'means test' where a complete inquiry into all his private affairs would be carried out to see if he had any savings or other money. What was the effect of this on living standards? Here are some details from a survey carried out in Blaina in 1937 of two households (one with an employed miner, the other with an unemployed one) showing their income and items they spent money on other than food. This is followed by a table issued by the Co-operative

Wholesale Society in Cardiff in the same year showing the price of certain foods. What food would each of these households be able to afford and what sort of diet might they have had?

Source 304

1. Unemployed Miner, Wife & 4 children. Income 39 shillings per week from unemployment Assistance Board.

Expenditure:

Rent	10s. 4d.
Doctor	1d.
Hospital	1d.
Light	1s. 0d.
Coal	6d.
Soap	9½d.
Starch	1½d.
Blue	1d.
Cleaning things	4½d.
Insurance	8d.
Clothes	1s. 6d.

2. Employed Miner, Wife and 2 children. Income 52 shillings per week.

Expenditure:

Fares	1s. 9d.
Carbon for Lamp	10d.
Rent & Rates	6s. 0d.
Clothes	3s. 0d.
Fuel	2s. 6d.
Nursing	1d.
Insurance	1s. 8d.
Newspapers	8d.
Trade Union	6d.
Cleaning things	2s. 6d.
Pocket Money	3s. 0d.
Furniture	2s. 6d.
Children	1s. 2d.
Amusements	1s. 4d.
Radio	3d.

Source: P. Massey. 'Portrait of a Mining Town', in *Fact*, November 1937.

Source 305

Co-operative Wholesale Society
Food Prices June 1937

Butter	1s. 4d. lb
Lard	7d. lb
Cheese	9d. lb
Bacon	1s. 4d. lb
Eggs	1s. 4d. Dozen
Margarine	6d. lb
Tea	2s. 2d. lb
Sugar	2½d. lb
Jam	7½d. pot
Potatoes	1½d. lb
Flour	3½d. lb
Currants	6d. lb
Sultanas	8d. lb

Biscuits	6d. lb
Cereals	5½d. lb
Green Peas	4d. lb
Salt	2½d. lb
Rice	3d. lb
Salmon	1s. 2d. tin
Milk	3½d. tin

Source: The South Wales Miner, June 1937.

This evidence is also a basis to make some comparisons between the employed and the unemployed. Poverty (of the employed and the unemployed) led to a great deal of malnutrition (semi-starvation), disease (especially tuberculosis) and general hardship in the valley communities during these years. Death rates in South Wales were much higher than other parts of the country: whilst the average death-rate in England and Wales in 1937 was 9.3 per 1,000, in Rhondda it was 13.4.

Despite real poverty and the threat of disease that it brought, many visitors to the South Wales valleys during these years noticed how much pride mining families had and a dislike of asking for charity. Here is a story told by a South Wales miner to a visiting journalist in the 1930s:

Source 306

Some of the worst cases of hardship I've known have been in homes where the father was trying to keep the six children on £2 5s. a week and was too proud to accept help from anyone . . . When you're on a shift you fall out for twenty minutes and eat bread and butter, or bread and cheese which the wife puts in your food tin . . . One day we were sitting like this talking when Bill didn't answer . . . He'd

fainted. So I lifted him and carried him to the pit bottom to send him home, but before I did this I gathered up his food tin. There wasn't a crumb in it! There hadn't been a crumb in it for days! He'd been sitting there in the dark pretending to eat, pretending to me—his pal— Now that's pride . . .

Source: H. V. Morton, *In Search of Wales*, 1932.

When pride was not enough the unemployed and the employed preferred self-help rather than charity. Keeping allotments, relying on the support of 'the Co-op' shop and, here at Brynmawr, picking coal from the mountainsides, were some of the ways of surviving.

Source 307

Source: National Museum of Wales.

Particularly at times of strikes and lock-outs, 'soup-kitchens' and special 'distress funds' were other means of trying to manage. Here are the staff of a soup-kitchen at Salem Chapel, Nantyffyllon, during the 1926 Lock-out and this is followed by part of the balance-sheet for a distress fund set up at Maerdy in the Rhondda.

Source 308

Source: R. G. Keen, *Old Maesteg and the Bridgend Valleys in Photographs*, 1979.

Source 309

Balance Sheet of the Mardy Distress Fund Accounts.

RECEIPTS.

	£ s. d.	£ s. d.
South Wales Miners' Federation, in conjunction with the Mardy Workmen's Institute	850 0 0	
S.W.M.F.—Rhondda District	338 0 0	
Tylorstown Lodge	20 0 0	
Ferndale Lodge	10 0 0	
S. Wales & Mon. Examiners' Association (Mardy Branch)	10 0 0	
Master Hauliers' and Foremen Association	8 15 0	1236 15 0
Mardy Brass Band on Tour	30 0 0	
Concerts, Dramas, &c.	17 9 5½	47 9 5½
Mardy Women's Knitting Guild, per Mrs. Alf. Evans	50 0 0	
Teachers, Tradesmen, Railwaymen, Colliery Officials, &c. (per Messrs. Alf. Evans and A. Martin)	229 14 2	279 14 2
Conservative Club, Mardy	16 10 0	
Mardy Athletic Club	5 2 0	
Mr. W. Blake, Royal Hotel	36 0 0	
Mr. E. W. Harries, Mardy Hotel	36 0 0	93 12 0
R.U.D.C. (Feeding of Children)		1016 12 0
Bethania Church	4 0 0	
Ebenezer Church	17 10 0	
Siloa Church	9 0 0	
Salvation Army	0 10 0	
All Saints' Church	6 0 0	
Carmel Church	3 0 0	
Seion Church	12 0 0	
Spiritual Church	5 0 0	57 0 0
Women's Labour Section	8 0 0	
Women's Labour Unionist Section	5 12 6	
Economic Class	6 0 0	19 12 6
Colliery Office Staff and Weighers (per Mr. R. D. Davies, Cashier)	24 7 0	
Colliery Weighers, in addition to the above (per Mr. W. Davies)	1 5 0	25 12 0
Mardy Cinema (per Mr. J. Jones)	50 0 0	
Mardy Institute Employees	8 9 0	58 9 0
Mardy Branch, Bristol, West of England (Mr. D. Jones)	3 3 0	
R.A.O.B., "Castell Nos" Lodge (per Mr. W. Pike)	0 10 6	
Mardy Cork Club (per Mr. T. R. Evans)	0 10 0	4 3 6
Collected by Messrs. Lewis Lloyd and Pryce Jones from Tradesmen, &c.		57 19 0
Rhondda Blind Institution (per Mr. H. E. Maltby)	5 0 0	
Cardigan Roadmen Association (per Sec. S.W.M.F.)	7 10 0	
N.U.R. Branch (per Mr. W. Bradfield)	3 0 0	15 10 0
Messrs. Thomas & Evans, Porth	5 0 0	
Mr. David Lewis, J.P., Rhondda Miners' Secretary	2 2 0	
Mr. and Mrs. Dickinson, London (per Mr. Jos. E. Jones)	1 10 0	
Councillor Abel Jacob, Ferndale	1 0 0	
Councillor A. J. Cook, Miners' Agent	1 0 0	
Inspector Reed, Ferndale	0 10 0	11 2 0
Rhondda Council Employees (per Councillor J. Bowen)	3 3 0	
Collected by Councillor John Bowen, Ferndale	6 15 0	
Porth Party (per Mr. D. Rees, 8 Richard Street)	3 0 0	12 18 0
Ferndale Juvenile Choir (per Mr. Rhys Jones)	4 4 0	
Mr. Davies, Port Talbot (Eisteddfod Adjudicator)	0 10 6	4 14 6
Mr. Ailey (per Mr. J. Addison)	1 10 0	
Messrs. Rigsley & Wakelin, Cardiff	1 14 6	
Messrs. Weaver & Co., Swansea (per Mr. J. Addison)	1 15 0	3 19 6
Mrs. D. Roberts	0 10 0	
Mr. Evan Davies, 30 Pentre Road	1 0 0	
,, T. Howells (Winder), 33 James Street	0 10 0	
,, David Thomas (Winder), 8 Station Terrace	1 0 0	
,, Bert Williams, Electrician	0 14 0	
,, John Addison, Baker	0 10 0	
,, William Butler, 17 Hill Street	0 10 0	
,, James Jones, Bookseller	0 10 0	
,, George Taylor, 38 Edward Street	0 10 0	
,, Rees Moore, 38 Edward Street	0 10 0	
Mrs. David Evans, 8 Mardy Road	0 5 0	
Mr. John Jenkins, 10 Blake Street	0 3 6	6 12 6
No. 3 Pit Checkweighers' Fund (per Mr. T. Jones)	0 4 6	
Anonymous	0 1 1	
Sale of Surplus Goods	0 13 2	0 18 9
Total Receipts		**£2952 13 10½**

EXPENDITURE.

	£ s. d.	£ s. d.
To Provisions, and Utensils for Kitchens		2766 17 9½
,, Leather, &c., for Repairing Boots		77 13 1
,, Crier, for announcing Meetings	3 5 0	
,, Boys, announcing Meetings	0 6 0	3 11 0
,, Barclays Bank, for Cheque Books		1 13 4
,, Repairs to Siloa Boiler, and Coal used	5 9 0	
,, Repairs to Ebenezer Boiler and Clock	1 15 0	
,, Mr. William Lane, for old Boots	1 15 0	
,, Mr. James Jones, Bookseller, for Stationery	0 9 0	9 8 0
,, Printing of Balance Sheet		2 10 0
Refunded to Mardy Lodge, S.W.M.F., and Mardy Institute		91 0 8
Total Expenditure		**£2952 13 10½**

In addition to the above, the Committee have received the following Goods free of charge.

Co-operative Butchery Dept.—Meat, value 16/-

Messrs. Corbett & Turner, Bakers—790 Cakes.

Mr. Bennett, Chemist—80lbs. of Peas ; 150lbs. of Beans ; 12 Pots of Beef Tea ; 12 Pots of Marmite.

Mr. William Jones, Grocer—One case of Boiled Beans.

Mr. Samuel Hall, Bungalow—Two Loaves of Bread.

Miners' Office, Porth (per Mr. D. Lewis, District Sec.)—One case of Neave's Food , one case of Margarine ; one bag of Beans ; one case of Jam ; 100lbs. Tapioca.

Mr. W. T. Maddock—500 Perforated Credit Slips

Meals served out, 195,808.

Source: Maerdy Lodge, South Wales Miners Federation Records, University College of Swansea Library.

As can be seen in these two Sources women were particularly active in such ventures and in general in the 1920s and 30s, women became much more involved in community life. Here Elizabeth Andrews of Pentre, the Women's Organizer of the Labour Party in South Wales, describes the relief work carried out by miners' wives during the 1926 Lock-Out:

Source 310
Parcels of food, medical supplies and clothing were given to those in need . . . We made maternity outfits, baby garments, and children's clothes as well as adult clothing. We cut up old clothing from parcels sent to us . . . Boot repairing centres were established . . . Besides hundreds of parcels and sacks of clothing, we received boxes of condensed milk, cocoa and baby food, and also large cases of footwear . . . Parcels came from Denmark, Norway, Sweden, Germany, Canada, Australia and other countries.

Source: E. Andrews, *A Woman's Work is Never Done*, 1948.

Charitable organisations such as the Carnegie Endowment and religious groups such as the Quakers were also active in the coalfield in setting up Unemployed Clubs and Educational Settlements to provide re-training and support for the unemployed.

The Depression: Resistance, Protest and Despair

South Wales by 1920 was an area with a reputation for trade-union and political militancy and these traditions were also to the fore in the years of the Depression in resisting and protesting against its effects.

Unemployed Movements

The spread of mass unemployment in Britain led to an organisation called the *National*

ever seen in South Wales when throughout the coalfield something like 300,000 people protested against cuts in unemployment benefits proposed by the Government. A little over a month later a similar demonstration at Blaina turned into a pitched battle with the police and as this newspaper report, Source 312, shows, eighteen of the leaders were to be charged with causing a riot.

Source 311

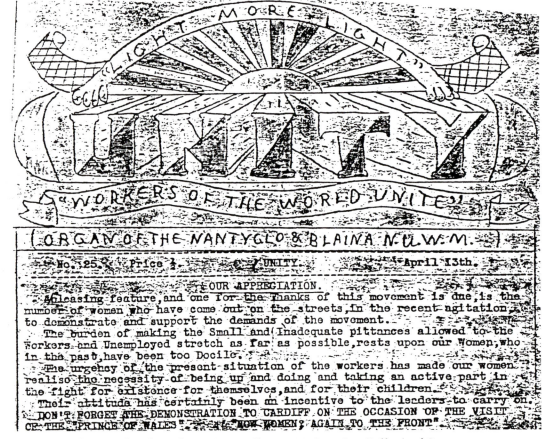

Source: South Wales Miners Library, University College of Swansea.

Unemployed Workers Movement being formed to represent the interests of the unemployed. The N.U.W.M. had a strong presence in South Wales and as the newspaper extract (Source 311) shows it encouraged women as well as men to be active in the struggle against unemployment.

On Sunday, 3 February 1935, the N.U.W.M. and many other organisations joined together in one of the largest political demonstrations

Five of the leaders were to be imprisoned for 9 months, but the strength of these demonstrations did persuade the Government to put off making the cuts. The N.U.W.M. along with the S.W.M.F. (which allowed unemployed miners to continue to belong to the union) helped to organise the Hunger Marches which left South Wales in the late 1920s and 30s. The purpose of these marches is made clear in this extract from a poster calling the first march in

Judge Threatens Demonstrators

Here are 17 of the 18 accused in the Blaina Trial.

Back Row : L. Hill, W. Sheargold, C. Reed, H. Thomas, F. Landon, W. Madden.

Middle Row : C. Brown, County Councillor P. Abraham, Councillor J. Jones, J. Doyle, H. Lloyd, C. Lloyd.

Front Row : B. Jenkins, B. John, J. Penny, C. Luffman, S. Corp. (Absent : R. Lexxe.)

Source 312

Source: The Daily Workers, 6 March 1935.

As Blaina Trial Opens

500 CHEER ACCUSED: POLICE STORY

"IF there is any repetition of the demonstration which took place outside the court this morning I will take immediate steps to prevent its recurrence, even if it means estreating the bail of the defendants."

This threat was made by Mr. Justice McNaghten when the trial began at Monmouth Assizes yesterday of 18 Monmouthshire workers who are charged with Great Riot in connection with a demonstration against the Unemployment Act at Blaina on March 21.

Five hundred workers in and around the Assize Square had come from all over the county of Monmouthshire, and in addition their ranks were supplemented by a large number of sympathetic Monmouth town workers and trades people.

When the judge arrived, the crowd made fun of what they called the "circus."

At the dinner-hour the Assize Square was full of enthusiastic workers, who were clapping and cheering the accused.

Police Superintendent Admits Waiting For Marchers

1927 (Source 313). Two photographs then follow. Source 314 shows part of the 1931 March in Bristol and Source 315 a section of the Garw Valley contingent in that march, supported by the Pontycymmer Women's Section of the Labour Party.

The Struggle against Company Unionism

The South Wales Miners Federation also campaigned vigorously against unemployment and because it allowed unemployed miners to remain members of the union, at one time it had more unemployed than employed members. For much of the inter-war period, however, the S.W.M.F. faced a situation where its membership was dwindling. By 1934 only 76,000 of the 140,000 employed miners in South Wales belonged to 'the Fed'. Some of those who did not join the union had lost faith in it after the defeat in 1926, many more simply could not afford to pay their dues. To combat this non-unionism the S.W.M.F. began a

campaign to re-build its membership. Source 316 *(See page 133)* shows the kind of tactics used by the union.

The S.W.M.F. also faced the challenge of a rival in the coalfield. In 1926 the *South Wales Miners Industrial Union* was set up by men who returned to work during the lock-out. The S.W.M.I.U. accused 'the Fed' of being a politically motivated union which did not look after the proper interests of the miners. It said it was non-political and existed only to offer its members benefits in times of illness or upon death and to negotiate improved wages and conditions but never to take strike action. The S.W.M.F. rejected it as a 'scab' and 'company' union—accusing it of being made up of men who had blacklegged in 1926 and of having being set up and financed by the Coalowners. In many places where the S.W.M.I.U. was set up it was quickly driven out and it never had more than 6,000 members in the coalfield. However its membership was concentrated in a small number of pits and here the S.W.M.F. found it very difficult to shift. Walter Haydn Davies

South Wales Marchers' Organising Council.

SOUTH WALES MINERS' MARCH to LONDON

CALL TO ACTION! VOLUNTEERS WANTED!

Arising out of the pronouncement by A. J. COOK, 18/9/27, a Miners' March to London from S. Wales is being organised. The March will commence on the day Parliament opens--Nov. 8th, and the Marchers will arrive in London on Nov. 20th, where they will be received by an <u>All London</u> Working Class Demonstration.

The object of the March shall be two-fold, to arouse a Nation-wide feeling concerning the Appalling Conditions in the Minefields created by the policy of the Government and the Coal-owners, and to seek an interview with the Prime Minister, the Minister of Mines, the Minister of Labour, and the Minister of Health.

Source 313   *Source:* South Wales Miners Library, University College of Swansea.

Source 314   *Source:* South Wales Miners Library, University College of Swansea.

Source 315   *Source:* R. G. Keen, *Old Maesteg and the Bridgend Valleys in Photographs,* 1979.

Source 316
SOUTH WALES MINERS' FEDERATION.

P.D. Combine Committee
SHOW CARDS

FELLOW WORKMEN,

The above Committee has decided that a SHOW CARDS will be held during THE WEEK ENDING FEBRUARY 11th, when it is expected that every Man and Boy will have joined by then.

There is no need 'to point out the advantages gained by a 100% Organisation—both to Surface and Underground Workers. We all realise the substantial increases made in the last Wages Agreement—Day-wage and Surface Craftsmen in particular. Holidays with Pay are now an established fact; whilst even during unemployment and intermittent working you are protected at the Labour Exchange, besides Compensation, Hours, Customs, and protection in work.

Ask yourselves is it not worth ONE PENNY A DAY to protect these necessities?

To Trade Unionists! Assist your Lodge Committee by standing with them at the Pit Gates, and see that every man shows his Card. Also, we urge that every member wears his Badge during this week. THIS IS URGENT!

To Non-Unionists! The responsibility lies with you if strike action is forced upon us. Therefore, join whilst there is yet time, as this Combine is adamant that the ranks shall be finally closed. THIS IS THE FINAL APPEAL.

THE NEXT MOVE IS ACTION!

By Order of the Combine Committee.

C.J.P., CARDIFF.

Source: South Wales Miners Federation Records, University College of Swansea Library.

from Bedlinog describes here the bitterness that this 'civil war' between the two organisations could cause. The hostility shown towards members of the S.W.M.I.U. can be imagined from Source 318, *(page 134)*, a photograph showing police protection given to them as they went to work in Blaengarw in 1929:

Source 317

There was enough bitterness engendered to split the village asunder, socially, culturally, and even religiously. People who had been friends and neighbours for years now became bitter enemies. Women refused to sing in choirs with those whose husbands were members of the "scab" union and not of the S.W.M.F. Such enmity was even carried into chapel services. There, if a family had an attachment to the new "Industrial Union" and stood to sing the hymn the minister had announced, those who favoured the official miners' union promptly sat down in protest. Vindictiveness even went to such lengths as daubing paint on "enemy" houses, damaging rival property, and even (so it was rumoured) throwing snails from one garden into the other as an expression of animosity and disgust with those who could not agree as to union membership.

Source: W. H. Davies, *The Right Time, The Right Place . . .* 1972.

From 1934 onwards the S.W.M.F. began to concentrate its efforts on trying to remove the S.W.M.I.U. from its strongholds such as Taff Merthyr Colliery, Trelewis; Nine Mile Point,

Source 318

Source: R. Page-Arnot, *The Miners: Years of Struggle*, 1953.

Cwmfelinfach; Parc and Dare Collieries, Treorchy and Bedwas, near Caerphilly. The propaganda war that went on can be seen in these leaflets, Source 319 *(See page 135)* and Source 320 *(See opposite column)*, issued by the two organisations at Taff Merthyr.

Propaganda was not enough to win victory for 'The Fed', however, for in these collieries the Owners would only recognise the S.W.M.I.U. and would refuse work to miners who were members of the S.W.M.F. A new tactic was needed and it was found through the weapon of the 'stay-down' strike. Secret members of the S.W.M.F. at these collieries would refuse to come up the pit at the end of their shift until the Owners granted the men a secret ballot to decide which union they wished to represent them. This was obviously a dangerous tactic and the S.W.M.F. did not officially approve of it as can be seen from this newspaper report of 1935.

Source 321 *(See page 136)*

It was successful, however, and by 1938 the S.W.M.I.U. was defeated and although the S.W.M.F. had not achieved 100% membership, it was stronger than at any time since 1926.

Source 320

The South Wales Miners' Industrial Union.

To the Taff Merthyr Workmen.

Bedwas is now going through a period identical with that which you have gone through. The tyranny of the South Wales Miners' Federation did not break you in 1934 and it will not break Bedwas in 1936, whatever lying literature might say. The Federation's claim of its increase of membership is on a par with all the lying statements they have made at Taff Merthyr.

At Taff Merthyr, the ranks of the Miners' Industrial Union are whole and steady, in spite of the mass intimidation and physical violence which you have endured.

During the next few weeks the South Wales Miners' Federation will try your patience in many ways, hoping to cause trouble and strife at the Colliery. They will try to break through our ranks with unscrupulous propaganda, but together we can hold back this Red tide of Communism.

TAFF MERTHYR COMMITTEE,

The South Wales Miners' Industrial Union.

Source: South Wales Miners Library, University College of Swansea.

Source 319

Taff Merthyr Lodge, S.W.M.F.

INDUSTRIAL UNION RECORD.

Extracts from Balance Sheets of M.I.U.

IS THIS WHERE THE FOURPENCES GO ?

1934	One Motor Car	-	-	£325		
1935	One Motor Car	-	-	£468		
1936	The Price of a Hearse ?					
1934	Legal Charges – Compensation			Nil		
1935	Legal Charges – Compensation			£4	7	0
1934	Pit Examinations	-	-	£12	0	0
1935	Pit Examinations	-	-	£5	10	0
1934	Vacuum Cleaner	-	-	£20	0	0
1935	Vacuum Cleaner, Balance			£8	0	0

More spent on a Vacuum Cleaner than on Pit Examinations.

200 times more spent on Motor Cars than on Compensation Cases.

What was spent on Negotiations for Wages Increases ? NOTHING !

What was spent on Conferences for Members? NOTHING !

Source: South Wales Miners Library, University College of Swansea.

Source 321

South Wales Echo

SIXTH
EDITION

& Evening Express

No. 16,175   Estab. 50 Years. ONE PENNY.   THURSDAY, OCTOBER 17, 1935.

STAY-IN STRIKERS DEFY FED

NINE MILE POINT,
CWMPARC & GARW
MEN STILL IN PITS

*"Will Not Leave Until Rival
Union Workers Clear Out"*

OFFICIALS' VAIN PLEA

*Risca and Rhondda Miners
Up: Some Resume
Work To-day*

" Stay-in" miners at the Nine Mile Point,
Dare, Cwmparc, Parc No. 2 and the Ocean
Garw Valley collieries have refused to leave the
pits, despite the advice of the Federation Executive Committee to do so.

Federation officials spent an hour in the three pits com-
prising the Nine Mile Point Colliery, but the men remained
adamant.

It is stated that they are determined to remain below
until the owners' verbal agreement to employ only Federation men is translated to black and white, while the men in
the Cwmparc and Garw pits declare their determination to

Source: South Wales Echo.

Political Movements

By 1918 the Labour Party had replaced the
Liberals in popular political support in most
parts of the South Wales coalfield. In the 1920s
and 30s the South Wales valleys consistently
returned Labour candidates as Members of
Parliament for the coalfield constituencies.
The strength of the Labour Party in Parliamentary seats can be judged by the results
for coalfield constituencies in the 1945 General
Election in Source 322 *(See page 137).*

These Labour M.P.s were active in
Parliament in making the Government and the
nation aware of the plight of people in the South
Wales coalfield. They fought for fairer
treatment for the unemployed and for South
Wales and other depressed areas of Britain to be
given special assistance by the Government.
From 1934 onwards South Wales was one of the
depressed areas of Britain declared 'Special

Areas' by the Government and some success
was achieved in bringing new industries to
South Wales to provide employment, with the
Trefforest Trading Estate, set up in 1938, and
the re-opening of the Ebbw Vale Steel Works in
the same year being two of the most important
developments. Local authorities in South
Wales were also firmly under the control of the
Labour Party and many of these authorities
brought some relief to the depressed mining
communities by means of free education, milk
and school meals for children, the opening of
local parks and swimming pools and other such
schemes.

As can be seen in the Rhondda East result in
Source 322 the main challenge to the Labour
Party in a coalfield seat in the General Election
of 1945 came from the Communist Party. In
fact one of the strongest areas of support for the
Communist Party in Britain existed in parts of

Source 322

Neath

Williams, D. J.	(Lab)	37,957
Bowen, D. J.	(Nat)	8,466
Samuel, W.	(Welsh Nat)	3,659
	Lab Maj.	29,491

Ogmore

Williams, E. J.	(Lab)	32,715
Davies, Maj. O. G.	(Nat)	7,712
Morgan, T.	(Welsh Nat)	2,379
	Lab Maj.	25,003

Pontypridd

Pearson, A.	(Lab)	27,823
Treherne, Capt. C. G.	(Con)	7,260
Williams, J. E.	(Lib)	5,464
	Lab Maj.	20,563

Rhondda East

Mainwaring, W. H.	(Lab)	16,733
Pollitt, H.	(Comm)	15,761
Davies, J.K.	(Welsh Nat)	2,123
	Lab Maj.	972

Rhondda West

John, W.	Unopposed Lab.	

Carmarthen

Morris, R. H.	(Lib)	19,783
Hughes, R. M.	(Lab)	18,504
	Lib Maj.	1.279
	Lib Gain.	

Llanelly

Griffiths, J.	(Lab)	44,514
George, Maj. G. O.	(Con)	10,397
	Lab Maj.	34,117

Source: Western Mail.

Abertillery

Dagger, G.	(Lab)	28,615
Hayward, Surg. Cmdr. J. J.	(Nat)	4,422
	Lab Maj.	24,193

Bedwellty

Edwards, Sir C.	(Lab)	30,480
Tett, Lt. H. I.	(Con)	6,641
	Lab Maj.	23,839

Ebbw Vale

Bevan, A.	(Lab)	27,209
Parker, Flt. Lt. S. C.	(Con)	6,758
	Lab Maj.	20.451

Merthyr Tydfil

Davies, S. O.	(Lab)	24,879
Jennings, S.	(Ind)	5,693
	Lab Maj.	19,186

Aberdare

Hall, George.	(Lab)	34,398
Clover, Capt. C. G.	(Con)	6,429
	Lab Maj.	27,969

Aberavon

Cove, W. G.	(Lab)	31,286
Llewellyn, Capt. D. T.	(Con)	11,860
	Lab Maj.	19.426

Caerphilly

Edwards, Ness.	(Lab)	29,158
de Courcy, Capt. J.	(Con)	7,189
	Lab Maj.	21,969

Gower

Grenfell, D. R.	(Lab)	30,676
Aeron-Thomas, J.	(Lib Nat)	14,115
	Lab Maj.	16,561

Pontypool

Jenkins, A.	(Lab)	27,455
Weeple, J. G.	(Con)	8,072
	Lab Maj.	19,383

South Wales. The C.P. was active in most of the organisations which campaigned against unemployment and its effects and, particularly in the Rhondda, it was successful in County Council and local elections. Source 323 *(See page 138)* is an extract from the newspaper it published in the Rhondda and it is followed, Source 324 *(See page 138)* by a photograph from Maerdy (known as 'Little Moscow') showing the Young Comrades League lining up in front of a banner presented by Russian miners.

The struggles of members of the Labour and Communist parties in South Wales did not mean that they closed their eyes to wider political issues. There was a strong 'internationalism' (interest in international issues affecting working people) in the coalfield which perhaps had something to do with the fact that there were Italians, Spaniards, Frenchmen and other national groups living in the valleys. This interest and commitment was shown between 1936 and 1939 when 122 miners from South Wales fought with the International Brigade on the Republican side during the Spanish Civil War. Thirty-three of them died including these three men from the Rhondda, who in Source 325 *(See page 139)* are remembered in a leaflet published for their memorial meeting.

Despair

Faced by the Depression there were people in the mining communities who protested and resisted. There were also those who gave up and left for a new life elsewhere and there were those who stayed and struggled simply to survive. In many ways the rich culture and social life of valley communities was put severely to the test in the years of the Depression. The Workmen's Institutes which depended on deductions from the wages of miners at the local collieries, were faced by a crisis of survival when these collieries closed. Many survived and offered in their Newspaper Rooms and Billiard Halls, somewhere for the unemployed to spend their time. However,

RHONDDA VANGUARD

THE OFFICIAL ORGAN OF THE RHONDDA COMMUNIST PARTY.

No. 6.   February, 1936.   Price—O

They Die to Give Their Children War

What's Wrong with Llwynypia Hospital

The treatment of certain children of unemployed parents is really outrageous. Certified, times out of num-

Death on the Tips

Every day, fresh reports of death and accidents in the search for coal. Tips and outcrop levels are reaping an increasingly heavier toll of life and limb. The whole valley was horrified when

Source 323   *Source:* South Wales Miners Library, University College of Swansea.

YOUNG COMRADES' LEAGUE

Source 324   *Source:* South Wales Miners Library, University College of Swansea.

Source 325

Source: South Wales Miners
Library, University College
of Swansea.

IN PROUD MEMORY
of

David Jones   *Frank Owen*   *W. Davies*
(PENYGRAIG)   (MARDY)   (BLAENCLYDACH)

who died fighting in the

BRITISH BATTALION
of the

International Brigade in Spain

★ *In Memoriam* ★

WILLIE DAVIES

OF Court Street, Blaenclydach, joined the International Brigade in November, 1936. One of the first to volunteer he was on active service until his death. Leaving London, where he was then staying, with Ralph Fox, noted writer and Political Commissar of the International Brigade, Willie was in the first big battles; he was one of those heroes that saved Madrid when the hour was darkest for the people of Spain, when everyone thought that all was lost.

Although wounded, his spirit was unquenchable. All the terrors of Fascism could not break his heroic spirit, and on recovering he was again in the front line, cheering his comrades and playing a magnificent role. Again he was wounded and the Medical Commission offered him his discharge, even providing him with facilities for returning home. He refused, and from his last letter to his mother and father we quote, with grief and pride, his reason:

" I was willing to pay the supreme sacrifice for my ideals and I knew to what I was coming—war, the most loathsome thing ever known. Although I have been wounded I still hold to my views.

" I am not going to pretend to be any kind of a hero by saying that I don't want to come home, because I do wish to return, but as long as the workers of Spain need my services I shall stay."

Comrade Paynter, Political Commissar of the International Brigade, said of Willie Davies: " He was one of our best comrades and his comrades fight on, inspired by his example."

DAVID JONES

OF George Street, Penygraig, was an ex-Grenadier Guardsman and joined anti-Fascist forces in London, where he was then living, in November, 1936. Proceeding to Spain, he joined the International Brigade on its formation and took part in all of its activities until he was killed in action in February last.

Comrade Springhall, leader of the London Communist Party, who was Political Commissar in the International Brigade during this period, said of our late comrade: " He was a splendid comrade, capable and reliable. His previous military training was utilised to the full in helping to train his comrades and sustaining their morale under fire. He carried his political convictions to the uttermost by making the supreme sacrifice."

★

Unconquerable

Spirit!

FRANK OWEN

OF Pentre Road, Mardy, had been a member of the Communist Party since 1936 and a member of the committee of the Mardy Lodge, S.W.M.F., since 1935.

He was imprisoned three times for his working-class activities. At the time of joining the International Brigade he was the " Daily-Worker " agent for Mardy.

Answering the call for the defence of Spanish Democracy, he joined the Brigade in April of this year, and was killed in the recent big Government offensive on the Madrid front.

Writing to his wife in June, Frank said: " I'll come home sometime. I have no fear that anything will happen to me, but I must leave it to you to impress on the kids that I'll be home sometime. While I'm on this point, I must say that I came here to do a job which I must go through with and am more determined now than ever I was when I started from home. The line which I took and which you, fortunately, were a party to, has been proved correct a dozen times over since I came here. It's an ideal worth fighting for. I fought Fascism back home and read quite a lot concerning it, but you cannot visualise the brutalities of German, Italian and Spanish Fascism until you come here, see it in its most horrible nakedness and hear what the poor people tell you of conditions before and during the civil war. I do not wonder why these people are fighting with a determination previously unknown. Further, it is only a matter of time, as the legal Spanish Government has at its command an army second to none."

Of Comrade Frank Owen, Will Paynter, Political Commissar of the Brigade, said: " He proved himself worthy of the revolutionary traditions of ' Red Mardy.' A disciplined soldier, ready at all times to respond when a job had to be done."

THEY WHO LIVE IN THIS UNCONQUERABLE SPIRIT CAN NEVER DIE, AND FOR ALL TIME
WILL THEIR MEMORY SERVE TO INSPIRE HUMANITY TO LIBERTY AND FREEDOM

many more went into rapid decline and with no income to maintain the buildings, the great workmen's libraries and many other activities came to an end. The adult education movement which had been so closely connected with the Institutes also faced a crisis, particularly because the South Wales Miners' Federation could no longer afford to support it financially in the way it once had. Through the work of the National Council of Labour Colleges and the W.E.A. it too survived, however. The Chapels to some extent were also casualties of the Depression. There was a loss of membership and more and more people were turning away from religion, some to the new attractions of the Cinema and Jazz and Band Music, which the Chapels frowned upon. Shortage of money also meant that it was difficult to pay for the upkeep of the Chapels and their Ministers. The gradual decline of the chapels and the attractions of a new 'Americanised' culture also played some part in the continuing decline of the Welsh language and the Eisteddfodic culture in many parts of the coalfield. The new 'culture' was often much less serious than the 'old', although perhaps the type of 'escapism' represented by the popularity of Jazz Bands (the Pentre Alexandra Deaths Head Orphans are shown in Source 326) and Carnivals (one at Wattstown, Rhondda in 1928 is shown in Source 327) in the coalfield during these years is understandable in the light of continuing unemployment and hardship:

Sources 326/327 *(See page 141)*

It would be wrong to suggest that everything in the South Wales mining valleys during the inter-war years was depressed or depressing. There was still plenty of vitality and fight in the people and communities of the coalfield. But this was a reaction to mass unemployment, poverty, streets of boarded-up shops and empty houses where people had left. This was a time of depression even in sport. Cardiff City who had won the F.A. Cup in 1927 were bottom of the 3rd Division by 1932, and Aberdare Athletic and Merthyr Town lost their places in the Football League. The loss of many talented players who turned professional because it provided them with money was one reason why this was an unsuccessful period for Welsh rugby. It is easy to understand how one unemployed South Wales miner could describe the valleys in the following way:

Source 328

The majority of mining towns are drab and dreary in nearly every detail . . . One sees the same long straggling rows of houses . . . The same type of Pits. Some huge sidings, black with coal, with coal dust flying everywhere. The same hills, covered with great stocks of slag and rubbish. The same film advertisements. The same girls with painted faces . . . With their slang phrases hot from the cinemas, Oh-yea, Baby, its O.K. with me, I'll be right there etc . . . The same rows of men aimlessly rotting their lives out, waiting. The same children looking ill nourished, ill clad. The same petty housing schemes . . . One feels one would like to blot it all out and start afresh.

Source: H. Watkins, *Unusual Students*, 1947.

The South Wales Coalfield Since 1945

Nationalisation

During the 2nd World War the coal industry in Britain was once more taken over by the Government. At the end of the War in 1945 an Inquiry set up by the Government recommended that the industry should be permanently taken over by the state. The miners (now members of the National Union of Mineworkers which had been set up in 1944) must have feared that 1921 would be repeated and that the coal industry would again be handed back to the Coalowners. However, the newly elected Labour Government (of which former South Wales miners' leaders such as Aneurin

Bevan and James Griffiths were important members) accepted the Report and on 1 January, 1947, the industry was taken over by the nation and the *National Coal Board* came into existence to manage it on their behalf. The Coalowners received generous compensation and very few regrets were felt at their passing. The enthusiasm with which nationalisation was greeted in South Wales can be seen in the photograph below, Source 329 *(See page 142)*, of the scene at the Lewis Merthyr Colliery, Porth, on 'vesting day', 1 January, 1947, and the poster, Source 330 *(See page 142)*, advertising some of the celebrations held in the Rhondda to mark nationalisation.

Source 326

Source: C. Batstone, *Old Rhondda in Photographs*, 1974.

Source 327

Source: C. Batstone, *Old Rhondda in Photographs*, 1974.

Source 329
Source: National Museum of Wales.

Source 330

COAL NATIONALISATION CELEBRATIONS

PROGRAMME OF EVENTS

Tonypandy, Sunday, February 23, 1947

A SACRED CONCERT

The Williamstown Gleemen
The Tonypandy Ladies' Choir

WORKMEN'S HALL, FERNDALE

Sunday, February 23rd

A SACRED CONCERT

Given by The Pendyrus Male Choir

SUPPORTED BY LOCAL ARTISTES

Chairman: Ald. Alfred Evans, J.P.

At THE DRILL HALL, PENTRE

Monday, February 24th, at 6 p.m.

The Official Opening of the Ministry of Fuel and Power

MINING AND FUEL EFFICIENCY EXHIBITION

By Mr. AERON G. THOMAS, *Vice-Chairman of the South Western Divisional Coal Board*

WORKMEN'S HALL, TON PENTRE
SUNDAY, FEBRUARY 23rd

A SACRED CONCERT

MADAME DANFORD GEORGE'S LADIES' CHOIR
AND THE MORGANNWG GLEE PARTY

SUPPORTED BY THE CORY WORKMEN'S BAND

Polikoff's Ltd., Factory Canteen

A MANNEQUIN PARADE

Tuesday, Feb. 25th, at 6 and 7.30 p.m.   *Admission 6d.*

Park and Dare Hall   Wednesday, February 26th

A GRAND CONCERT BY THE PARK AND DARE BAND

Source: National Museum of Wales.

Changes in the Industry

Under the management of the National Coal Board the mining industry in South Wales has changed tremendously during the last 40 years. One of the most welcome developments has been that the industry is a much safer place to work in and although in 1960 at Six Bells Colliery, Abertillery, 45 men lost their lives and five years later at the Cambrian Colliery, Tonypandy, 31 men died in an explosion, the Coal Board and the South Wales Area of the N.U.M. have worked together to improve safety standards. The system of wage payment for miners has also changed—national wages agreements in 1956 and 1966 introduced a daily wage for all miners, doing away with the piecework system which the miners' union had

long attacked as a factor which contributed to accidents in the mines by pushing miners to produce as much coal as possible and neglect safety conditions. Despite the opposition of the South Wales Area of the N.U.M. in 1978, however, an element of piecework was re-introduced in a national productivity scheme which introduced 'bonuses' for high production of coal. The work of miners also changed dramatically with the widescale introduction of coal-cutting and other machinery into the pits, particularly in the new 'super-pits' opened since 1947 such as at Cynheidre and Bettws in the anthracite coalfield. These two photographs of another of these pits Abernant Colliery near Pontardawe—show how different modern collieries look above and below ground to the old mines:

Source 331

Source: National Museum of Wales.

Source 332

Source: National Museum of Wales.

Pit Closures

These changes in the coal industry in South Wales have not, however, prevented the continuing decline of the industry. Until the mid 1950s the coal industry maintained a steady level of production and employment, but since that time there has been a continuing decline in the number of pits and the number of miners employed. Most of the pits which have been closed still had coal left in them to mine but with oil and even coal available more cheaply from abroad, successive Governments and the National Coal Board have been unwilling to keep open what they have regarded as 'uneconomic' pits where coal was mined at a loss. Although some new pits have been opened in South Wales, nowhere has the decline of the British coal industry been more dramatic than in the South Wales Coalfield. Much of the

market for its high quality steam-coal had been lost and with its difficult geological conditions underground, South Wales was particularly vulnerable to closure on grounds of the 'economic cost' of production. The greatest number of pit closures in South Wales was in the 1960s when 74 mines were closed across the coalfield. Below, Source 333 *(See page 144)*, is a list of collieries which were closed in each year of the 1960s. Compare the number of pits in your area which were closed to the number left in your area today.

In the 1970s and 80s the pace of closures slowed down but there has been a steady trickle of pit closures each year as the coalfield goes on contracting. By July 1985 only 31 collieries remained in South Wales and of these six are either due for closure or under the threat of closure. The map below shows the collieries

Source 333

COLLIERY CLOSURES IN SOUTH WALES 1960-70

1960	1964	1967
Brittanic	Cwmgorse	Elliot
Cannop	Daren	Abergorki
Hendy Merthyr	Garth Tonmawr	Crumlin
North Rhondda	Nine Mile Point	Wyllie
Tylorstown No. 9	Norchard	Pentreclwyder
Carway	Onllwyn No. 1	International
Rock	Pochin	Newlands
	Rhigos	Ynysycedwyn
1961	Varteg	
Clydach Merthyr	Wern Tarw	1968
Graig Fawr		Cwmcarn
Maritime	1965	Groesfaen
Llanbradach	Glyncastle	Llanhileth
	Fforchaman	
1962	Felinfran	New Rock
Aberaman	Wernos	Cefn Coed
Blaenhirwaun	Aberbeeg South	National
East	Northern United	Pantyffynon
Gelli	Garngoch No. 3	Penllwyngwent
Great Mountain	Parc	
Llanharan	Pwllbach	1969
New Cross Hands	Norton Hill	Tirpentwys
Onllwyn No. 3		Waterloo
Princess Royal	1966	Avon
	Dillwyn	Mountain
1963	Old Mills	
Cwmgwrach	Cambrian	
Bryn	Cwmrhondda	
Ffaldydre	Albion	
Harry Stoke	Risca	
New Rockwood	Duffryn Rhondda	
Seven Sisters	Abercrave	

Source: H. Francis and D. Smith, *'The Fed': A History of the Miners in the Twentieth Century,* 1980.

which still exist—compare it to Source 23 in Section 2 of this book (which shows the number of collieries at the peak of the coalfield's development) to get a vivid picture of the overall decline of the coal industry in South Wales. The figures in Source 335 give a statistical picture of that change.

Source 334 *See bottom of page)*

Source 335

South Wales Coalfield:
Manpower and Production

Year	Manpower	Tons of Coal Produced
1913	232,800	56,830,000
1947	108,000	22,712,000
1957	101,000	24,269,000
1983	22,071	6,562,000

Source: H. Francis and D. Smith, *'The Fed': A History of the South Wales Miner in the Twentieth Century,* 1980.

The Effect of Pit Closures

The continuing closure of collieries since 1955 obviously threatened that the mass unemployment of the inter-war years would return to the South Wales mining valleys, which were almost totally dependent on the

Source 334

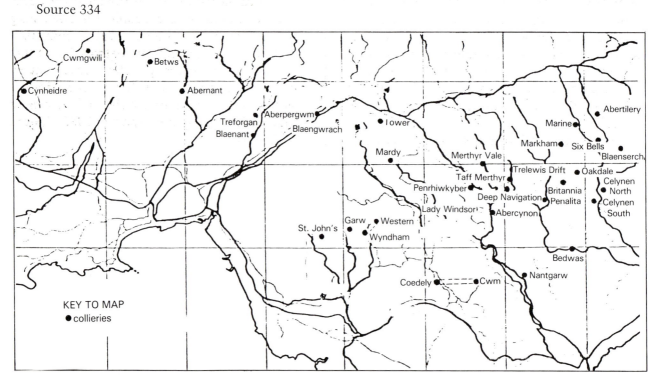

Source: H. Francis and D. Smith, *'The Fed': A History of the South Wales Miner in the Twentieth Century,* 1980.

coal industry. However, in the 1950s and 60s, Government policy encouraged many new industries (such as engineering, manufacturing and car assembly) to establish themselves in South Wales. Along with the employment still provided in the traditional industries of South Wales—coal, steel and tinplate—something approaching full employment actually returned to South Wales. This probably helps to explain why so many colliery closures were accepted by the miners employed in these pits. Often there was a fight against closure and the National Union of Mineworkers (under the leadership of former South Wales miners leaders Arthur Horner and Will Paynter) continuously challenged the energy policies of Conservative and Labour Governments. The South Wales Area of the N.U.M. continued to play an important part in the life of the coalfield despite the constant decline in its membership as the industry contracted. Through the South Wales Miners Eisteddfod (which started in 1948) and the annual Miners' Gala (begun in 1953) along with its traditional trade-union activities, the union has retained its influence and strength. In the national miners' strikes of 1972 and 1974 (the first since 1926) the South Wales miners were to the fore in the new confidence which seemed to sweep the coalfields after decades of depression. Not only did these strikes result in a raising of wage levels of miners, they also showed the strength of the miners union in a situation where coal was seen to still play a crucial part in the nation's energy needs. With massive increases in the price of oil in the mid-1970s the future for the coal industry looked more secure. However, by the late 70s a new wave of colliery closures began in South Wales. By this time due to a new industrial depression many of the jobs which

had been brought to South Wales in the previous years disappeared as factories and firms closed down and unemployment returned to the area. Therefore, there was a greater desire to fight for existing jobs in the coal industry in South Wales. The N.U.M. waged resistance to closure such as that threatening Deep Duffryn Colliery in 1979 and Tymawr-Lewis Merthyr Collieries in 1983, but in the long run these were to prove unsuccessful. In 1984-85 in one of the longest and most bitter disputes ever seen in the coal industry, the South Wales miners were again to the fore in a national strike by the N.U.M. against pit closures.

The 1984-85 strike brought together in South Wales large numbers of people who were concerned not only about the loss of jobs in the mining industry in South Wales but also the effect colliery closures had on the whole of the mining communities. The continuing decline of the coal industry in the valleys has often seemed to threaten the very existence of communities which were only brought into existence because coal was to be found below the valley floors. As pits closed from the mid 1950s whole communities, their institutions (miners institutes, chapels, schools and so forth) and the way of life faced a crisis for survival. Of the new employment that was brought to South Wales much was to be found away from the valleys in the towns on the edges of the coalfield. Many people travelled long distances each day from their valley communities to work in these new industries, but others (particularly younger people) moved away permanently from the valleys. The kind of crisis which seemed to face the valleys can be seen here in a newspaper report in 1985. Source 336 *(See page 146).*

Source 336

Boarded up and closing down: A Valley town on the ropes

The boarded windows of shops in Maesteg's Commercial Street (above and below) symbolise the decay that has cracked this once flourishing town. The community has suffered from the decline of the mining industry and has recently lost its development area status. MARIO BASINI reports on attempts to reverse the decline.

AT LUNCHTIME on a Tuesday in January, Maesteg's main shopping area is as deserted as the streets of a Wild West town waiting with bated breath for a shoot-out between the sheriff and the bad guys.

The cafes and public houses cater for a handful of customers between them. Boarded up shop fronts and for sale notices line Commercial Street with the frequency of parking meters in more affluent London.

An air of decay envelops the town, as tangible as the masonry which occasionally comes crashing down off some of the empty buildings in the street.

"Maesteg is more depressed now than I have

- **Masonry falls from its empty buildings**
- **Its last pit is threatened with closure**
- **900 miners remain where 10,000 once worked**
- **Lotteries try to save its dwindling trade**

Source: The Western Mail, 14 February, 1985.

Conclusion

The South Wales mining valleys have had a fascinating and exciting history and whatever future is in store for them, they have made a unique contribution to the life and history of modern Wales and Britain. It is also important to note that whilst the problems which the decline of the coal industry has presented to the communities of the South Wales coalfield are real and pressing ones, all is not 'gloom and doom'. The closure of collieries has been followed by the removal of many of the ugly slag heaps and the coal tips which once despoiled the valleys, for example. The terrible disaster at Aberfan in 1966, when 111 schoolchildren were killed in their classrooms by the collapse of a tip, brought home to everyone the scale of this problem. Now as in this photograph of Pentre in the Rhondda today, Source 377 *(See bottom of page)* many valleys are returning to the natural beauty which they enjoyed before the coal industry changed them.

It was in the Rhondda Valley that this book began. By 1900 the once beautiful Rhondda had been transformed by the coal industry into perhaps the most famous coalmining area in the world. Then it had over one hundred large collieries producing coal which was sent all over the world. Today the valley has but one mine—Maerdy Colliery—and that is now faced with possible closure. Although many of the scars of the coal industry have been removed and a new generation is growing up which knows little of the coal industry and the way of life that grew up around it in mining communities such as the Rhondda Fawr and Rhondda Fach, these like all the other valleys of the South Wales coalfield, are still the special places which their history has made them. As the valleys face up to a difficult future, perhaps the spirit which helped them to survive an earlier period of depression will be their strength again. In 1935 an author, Felix Green, visited the Rhondda to collect material for a book he was preparing on the effect of mass unemployment on people. This is what one Rhondda miner, John Evans aged 47, told him:

Source 338

I'm glad I haven't a son . . . It must be a heartbreaking business to watch your boy

Source 337

Source: C. Batstone, Photographer, Pentre, Rhondda.

grow into manhood and then see him deteriorate because there is no work for him to do . . . I've been out of work now for eight years, and I've only managed to get eleven days work in all that time. Work used to shape the whole of my life and now I've got to face the fact that this won't be so any more. I am really glad I live in the Rhondda. There's real kindness and comradeship here, and that *just* about makes

life worth living. The spirit here in this valley helps to soften many of the hardships of unemployment.

Source: F. Green, *Time to Spare*, 1935.

This last Source tells us a great deal about the society whose history has been considered in this book.

Further Work on the Evidence

1. Look at Sources 280, 281 and 282 and then answer the questions below:
   a. Describe the argument in favour of nationalisation of the mines which James Winstone puts forward in Source 280. What other arguments in favour of nationalisation do you think miners might have put forward?
   b. Describe the argument against nationalisation put forward by Hugh Bramwell in Source 281. What other reasons do you think Coalowners would have had to oppose nationalisation?
   c. Explain what is meant in Source 282 by the phrase 'legislation acquiring the Coal Royalties for the State'.
   d. Which of these Sources do you think is biased on the question of whether the coal industry should have been nationalised in 1919? Do you think one Source is less biased than the others? Explain your answers.

2. Using Sources 283 and 289 answer the following:
   a. Draw up a table showing the wages of colliers and labourers in the mines of South Wales:
      (i) In 1921 (as shown in Source 283)
      (ii) In 1926 (as shown in Source 289)
      (iii) After 1926 (the Owners Terms in Source 289)
   b. Having done this try to work out:
      (i) the reduction in the amount of wages which colliers and labourers were forced to accept
      (ii) the percentage reduction in their wages.
   c. Having noted who produced these two Sources, why do you think you would need to look at other evidence on this question of miners' wages in South Wales

between 1920 and 1922? What other evidence would you look for?

3. Look at Source 300 and then try to answer the following questions:
   a. Which area of South Wales has the highest percentage of people who have left in the period 1921 to 1931? Why do you think this was so?
   b. Which area has the lowest percentage? Why do you think this was so?
   c. Why do you think that places like Swansea, Llanelli, Barry and Newport had quite low percentages compared to other areas of South Wales?
   d. How do you think this evidence on emigration from South Wales was collected (the years 1921 and 1931 should give you a strong clue)? How might you collect evidence on where the people who left South Wales went?

4. Look at Source 319 and 320 and then consider these questions:
   a. What organisation produced Source 319? What do you think is meant in this source by the 'fourpences' which are mentioned?
   b. Describe the argument which Source 319 makes against the South Wales Miners Industrial Union. What evidence does it use to make its claims about how the M.I.U. spends it's money?
   c. What organisation produced Source 320? Describe the argument it makes against the tactics used by the South Wales Miners Federation at Taff Merthyr Colliery?
   d. Do you think either or both of these Sources put forward a fair view of the struggle which was taking place at Taff Merthyr Colliery? Explain your answer. What other evidence might you need to look at to get a fuller and more reliable picture of what was happening there?

Appendices

APPENDIX I: GLOSSARY OF TERMS

Many words and terms are explained where they occur in the text of the book. Therefore, only terms which have not already been explained or which appear a number of times in the text are explained here.

B

Balance Sheet: a financial statement which shows the assets (property, money in the bank etc.) and liabilities (debts etc.) of a Company.

Barriers: areas of coal on the boundaries of land owned by different persons, which were left unworked.

Birth-Rate: the percentage of people born in a particular year compared to the existing size of population.

Blacklegs: the name given by workers on strike to people who worked during the strike.

Board Schools: primary schools set up by the Education Act of 1870 and run by local School Boards which could pay for them out of the rates.

British Schools: day-schools set up by the British and Foreign School Society an organisation set up by the Nonconformist chapels.

Bunkers: coal stations set up around the world on steam-shipping routes where coal could be taken on board.

C

Charabanc: an open-topped and single-decked motor bus.

Combines: a number of different companies and businesses joined together into one 'combine' which had overall control.

Company Unionism: 'trade unions' set up and controlled by the Owners or their agents, rather than the workers.

County Schools: also known as 'Intermediate Schools'. Schools providing a secondary education up to the age of eighteen, which could be set up by County Councils in Wales as a result of the Welsh Intermediate Education Act of 1889.

Curling Boxes: flat-bottomed and three-sided scoops used by the collier or his assistant to load coal into trams.

D

Deacons: the elders of a Chapel, chosen to decide upon the policies and activities of the Chapel.

Death-Rate: the percentage of people who died in a particular year compared to the existing size of the population.

Deputies: a management official in a mine.

Dividends: a share of the profits in a business paid to the shareholders on the basis of the number of shares held.

Domestic Service: working as a maid, butler etc.

Duck Trousers: trousers worn by miners and made out of a heavy and hard wearing cloth called 'duck'.

E

Engineman: men who worked the various steam engines used in the mines.

F

Firemen: a management official in the mines employed to carry out safety inspections, especially to detect the presence of gas.

Friendly Societies: organisations which collected weekly contributions from members, which could be claimed back in times of illness, old-age and death, by them or their families.

H

Haulage: the movement of coal (in trams or on conveyors) from where it is cut by the collier to the bottom of the pit shaft ready to be wound up; a job done by hauliers.

Heading: a passageway driven at right-angles from the main roadways of a mine to the coalface, along which miners and trams could pass.

Hewers: another name for colliers—the men who 'hewed' or won the coal.

Higher Grade Schools: the name given to some of the first secondary schools set up by local authorities.

Hitchers: miners who were in charge of the cage once it reached the bottom of a pit.

Hunger marchers: unemployed men who marched (usually to London) in the 1920s and 30s to protest against unemployment.

I

Indenture: an agreement made between two or more persons.

Independent Working-Class Education: the movement whereby working people tried to provide their own adult education, believing that the education offered by others was to keep them in their place.

Iron Ore: rock containing iron which has to be smelted to separate the iron from the rock.

L

'Lib-Lab': the name given to trade-union leaders and working men who were members of the Liberal Party.

Limestone: solid deposit of lime which was used along with coal to produce iron.

Limited Liability Company: where the liability (or responsibility) of a shareholder in a company for its operations is limited to the number of shares held.

Lock-Out: where employers refuse work to those who are not prepared to accept the terms of employment offered.

Lodge: the name given to branches of the miners union at a particular pit.

M

Mandril: a special type of pick-axe used by colliers.

N

National Schools: day-schools set up by the National Society an organisation founded by the Church of England.

Nonconformists: members of chapels i.e. of groups which had broken away from the Church of England and set up their own religious denominations.

O

Ostlers: miners whose job was to look after the horses used underground.

Overmen: a management official responsible for overseeing the work of miners.

P

Poor Relief: assistance (in money or goods) given to poor people under the Poor Law in the nineteenth century.

Price-List: a list agreed between the owners of a colliery and the miners showing the prices to be paid for different jobs done in the mine.

R

Radicals: members of the Liberal Party who wished to see widescale social reforms being made.

Rippers: miners who 'ripped away' the roof and the floor of a seam in a coalmine so that there was sufficient height to bring horses up to the coalface.

Roadmen: miners who maintained the condition of the main roadways in a mine, which connected the working places to the pit bottom.

S

'Scotch Cattle': secret organisations of miners who in the early nineteenth century, when trade-unions did not exist among the miners, carried out raids and attacks on strike-breakers and others. They disguised themselves by wearing cattle-hides.

Screens: where on the colliery surface, coal was sorted into different sizes and any rubbish in the coal was picked out.

Sea-Coal: coal mined to be sent for export.

Sinking: driving a shaft down from the surface of a colliery to the underground coal seams.

Sliding-Scale: the system where miners' wages would move up and down as the average selling price of coal changed.

Smelting: applying heat to a mineral rock in a furnace to separate the mineral from the rock.

Sprags: short lengths of timber used in the mine to support coal when it was being undercut.

Stalls: the working place of the collier at the coalface.

Subsidy: an amount of money paid to help offset losses being made by a company.

Suffragettes: women who campaigned for their sex to have the right to vote in elections.

syndicalism: the idea that by organising themselves into one single trade-union, workers might be able to take over their industries, leading to workers' control of society.

T

Temperance: abstaining from drinking alcohol.

'The Fed': the popular name for the South Wales Miners' Federation.

Tithes: a proportion of everyone's wealth which had to be paid each year to the Church of England.

Tommy-box: the metal box in which miners would keep their food for the pit.

Tonic Solfa: the system whereby people could learn to read music by sight.

Tram: the wagon in which colliers loaded the coal they cut and which was then taken up to the colliery surface.

Tramroads: a type of railway, below and above ground, along which horses pulled trams.

U

Undercut: the method used by colliers to free coal, by undercutting it with a mandril and then bringing it down in large lumps.

W

Washeries: where on the colliery surface coal was washed.

Water-jack: a metal can in which miners took water or tea to the pit.

APPENDIX II: CONVERSION TABLES

Old Money to Decimals

It was in 1971 that the decimal coinage which we use today was introduced in Britain. Until then the value of our money was expressed in pounds, shillings and old pence (£.s.d.). Therefore most of the amounts of money mentioned in the Sources in this book are expressed in these old money values. To convert them into the decimal values of today you should use the figures below:

Old Pence/shillings/Pounds		New Pence
1 old pence	=	0.41 new pence
12 old pence or 1 shilling	=	5 new pence
240 old pence or 20 shillings or £1	=	100 new pence or £1

Price Equivalence

As we know all too well what our money is worth *today* (that is how much it can buy) will not be what it will be worth in a year's time. This is because of *inflation* which simply means that over a period of time the value of £1 will decrease as prices rise. Over a long period of time, such as the period of about 150 years which we have looked at in this book, there will be a terrific change therefore, in the value of money. Throughout this book the Sources include references to money, such as how much a miner earned and how much things cost to buy. To get some idea of what these figures mean we need to try and relate them to the value of our money today. This is not at all an easy thing to do and we have to be very careful with such calculations, therefore. However, one of our major Banks has tried to do these calculations for the period 1883-1983 and its figures are set out below. They should give you some help in making sense of what the various prices mentioned in the Sources actually mean in terms of our money today.

1883

£1 then	=	3½p today
1 shilling then	=	0.17p today
1 old pence then	=	0.014p today

1913

£1 then	=	3½p today
1 shilling then	=	0.17p today
1 old pence then	=	0.014p today

1923

£1 then	=	6p today
1 shilling then	=	0.3p today
1 old pence then	=	0.025p today

APPENDIX III: PLACES TO VISIT

There are a number of museums and historical sites in South Wales which tell the story of the history of the South Wales coalfield. Hopefully you will be able to visit some of these places on trips organised by your school during the period you are using this book. You may also be able to visit these places in your own free time and therefore brief details of some of these places are given below. You should always contact these places before you plan to make your visit to check on opening times, admission prices and how to get to them.

Big Pit Mining Museum, Blaenavon, Gwent. This Museum was opened on the site of the Big Pit Colliery (one of the oldest shaft mines in South Wales) when it closed in 1980. On the colliery surface you can visit the various workshops and see colliery craftsmen at work. There are also exhibitions which tell the story of the pit's history and the development of the mining community of Blaenavon and a typical miner's cottage has been recreated. The underground tour is led by ex-miners at the colliery and you can experience at first-hand the work and working conditions of the miner.

Cefn Coed Coal and Steam Centre, Crynant, Neath, West Glamorgan. This centre has been opened at the site of the Cefn Coed Colliery which, when it was opened in 1926, was the deepest anthracite mine in the world. There is a display of mining equipment and machinery and an exhibition traces the history of coalmining in the Dulais Valley.

Cyfarthfa Castle Museum, Cyfarthfa Park, Merthyr Tydfil, Mid-Glamorgan. Cyfarthfa Castle was built in 1825 as the home of the Ironmaster, William Crawshay. The Museum contains various exhibits dealing with the development of the iron industry in Merthyr Tydfil and the early history of the coal industry.

Elliot Colliery, New Tredegar, Gwent. The Winding House and the Steam Winding Engine of this colliery have been preserved by the National Museum of Wales.

Welsh Industrial and Maritime Museum, West Bute Dock, Cardiff, South Glamorgan. At the basin of the Bute West Dock, which grew in importance due to the development of the coal industry, the National Museum of Wales have opened a museum dealing with the history of various industries in Wales. There is a display of industrial machinery and the development of transport and regular exhibitions tell the story of the history of industries in Wales.

Nantgarw Colliery, Nantgarw, Mid-Glamorgan. At this working colliery the National Coal Board organizes tours of the surface of the mine which explain how a modern coal mine works. There is also an exhibition area showing the underground workings of the mine and tracing various aspects of the history of coalmining.

National Museum of Wales, Cathays Park, South Glamorgan. In the Industrial Gallery of the National Museum of Wales, there are various exhibits dealing with the history of coalmining in Wales, including a 'make-believe' underground mining gallery. Outside the Museum building a Water-Balance Winding machine can also be seen.

South Wales Miners' Library, University College of Swansea, Hendrefoilan, Swansea, West Glamorgan. This Library is one of the major centres where historians carry out research into the history of the South Wales coalfield—particularly into the history of the miners. Among the various holdings of the Library are books from Miners Institute Libraries, Trade-Union Banners and a large collection of documents, photographs and other historical evidence.

Valley Inheritance Centre, Pontypool Park, Pontypool, Gwent. This centre contains various exhibits which tell the industrial and social history of the Torfaen District of Gwent.

Welsh Miners Museum, Afan Argoed, Cynonville, West Glamorgan. This museum concentrates on the work of coalminers and the history of mining communities. There are displays of mining equipment, old photographs and documents and there is a special feature on the work of children in the mines.

Industrial Trails. It is also worth visiting different valleys in South Wales, as every valley has developed in a slightly different way and tells a different story. A good way of doing this is to follow one of the many 'industrial trails' which have been prepared to show the history of particular areas. Among areas which have such trails are the Rhondda, Merthyr Tydfil, the Cynon Valley, Gilfach Goch and Abertillery. Further details on these trails and other places worth visiting can be found in a book published by the Wales Tourist Board. It is called 'A Glimpse of the Past' and it costs 80p. It can be obtained from the Wales Tourist Board, Bruner House, 2 Fitzalan Road, Cardiff, CF2 1IY.

Index